THE GOO

THE GOOD GOVERNOR

Robert Ray
and the Indochinese Refugees of Iowa

Matthew R. Walsh

Dear Diane,

You are a junior delegate
Ray would be proud of!

Best,
Matthew Walsh

McFarland & Company, Inc., Publishers
Jefferson, North Carolina

LIBRARY OF CONGRESS CATALOGUING-IN-PUBLICATION DATA

Names: Walsh, Matthew R., 1982– author.
Title: The good governor : Robert Ray and the Indochinese refugees of
   Iowa / Matthew R. Walsh.
Other titles: Robert Ray and the Indochinese refugees of Iowa
Description: Jefferson, North Carolina : McFarland & Company, Inc.,
   Publishers, 2017 | Includes bibliographical references and index.
Identifiers: LCCN 2017016867 | ISBN 9781476669472 (softcover : acid free
   paper) ∞
Subjects: LCSH: Indochinese Americans—Iowa—History—20th century. |
   Ray, Robert D., 1928– | Governors—Iowa—Biography. | Iowa.
   Governor's Task Force for Indochinese Resettlement. | Lao (Tai
   people)—Iowa—History—20th century. | Boat people—Vietnam. |
   Vietnam War, 1961–1975—Refugees. | Refugees—Indochina. |
   Refugees—Iowa—History—20th century. | Iowa—Politics and
   government—20th century.
Classification: LCC F630.I43 W35 2017 | DDC 977.7004959191—dc23
LC record available at https://lccn.loc.gov/2017016867

BRITISH LIBRARY CATALOGUING DATA ARE AVAILABLE

ISBN (print) 978-1-4766-6947-2
ISBN (ebook) 978-1-4766-2888-2

Front cover: Governor Robert Ray, circa 1969, Des Moines, Iowa
(State Historical Society of Iowa, Des Moines); background
images © 2017 iStock

Printed in the United States of America

McFarland & Company, Inc., Publishers
   Box 611, Jefferson, North Carolina 28640
   www.mcfarlandpub.com

For my son Nolan

Acknowledgments

First and foremost, I must thank those who shared their experiences with me, especially Iowa's Indochinese refugee community. In particular, Houng Baccam, Som Baccam, Siang Bachti, Matsalyn Brown, Wing Cam, and Dinh VanLo's contributions to this project must be recognized.

I am also indebted to David Gavin and Pamela Riney-Kehrberg for reviewing the manuscript and offering suggestions for improvement.

Most of my archival work was conducted at the State Historical Society of Iowa in Des Moines, and the entire staff there provided an ideal research environment.

Finally, I would like to thank the Ray family and the families of all public servants. Though it is an individual who is elected or appointed to a position, his or her entire family serves too.

Table of Contents

Preface

In December of 2008, I accepted a teaching position at Des Moines Area Community College's Urban Campus. To my longtime girlfriend's horror, I would be moving from the Pittsburgh area to Iowa. In dismay, my girlfriend (and future wife Dana) quipped, "Have fun sitting on wicker furniture and flirting with farm girls in Iowa." Worse yet, some of my acquaintances began asking if I liked potatoes. Had they just realized my Irish surname? No, they had just confused Iowa with the state of Idaho. I, too, had false expectations about the Hawkeye state; I anticipated teaching students of mostly German and northern European ancestry. To my surprise, names like Baccam, Chau, Dzaferagic, Nguyen, and Yousif dotted my class roster. I soon learned that much of the state's diversity stemmed from its long history of resettling refugees. It is hoped that this book combats the stereotype of Iowa as a land of all white farmers.

My coworker Laura Douglas first suggested Indochinese refugee resettlement as a research topic. After watching the compelling Iowa Public Television documentary *A Promise Called Iowa*, I wanted to learn more about resettlement during Governor Ray's term in office. Soon thereafter, I obtained permission to use the Robert D. Ray Papers at the State Historical Society of Iowa. Ray's refugee program papers are unique in that only the state of Iowa operated as a resettlement agency throughout the post–Vietnam War years; private organizations carried out this work in all other states. These papers allowed a detailed look into the state's refugee program from 1975 through 1982.

The richest sources in the archives were the hundreds of letters sent to the Governor's Office. Iowans wrote with such candor and in detail about why they approved or disapproved of Ray's refugee policy; this has resulted in a more nuanced look at American attitudes on Indochinese refugee resettlement than the basic numbers from opinion polls used by other scholars. People corresponded from outside of Iowa too. One annoyed Texan cynically asked Ray to take all of the "wetback Mexicans" from his state. Other Americans compared their governor's inaction to Ray's humanitarianism. From Asia, refugees like Dr. Tam Khac Nguyen wrote because they had heard Iowa had a good governor who might be willing to help. After reading all the documents, I have concluded that Ray is one of the most overlooked humanitarians of the twentieth century. Though his name appears in the title and his position on refugee matters is detailed, this book is not a biography of Robert Ray. Hopefully, this book about Ray's refugee program will spark someone's interest, and a full biography he is so deserving of will be written in the near future.

In addition to the Ray Papers, oral history interviews with public officials and refugees informed my arguments. I would describe myself as having a polite yet reserved personality. Looking back, I am surprised by the lengths to which I went to contact potential interviewees, but I was so fascinated that I needed to learn more. At a citizenship ceremony, I approached Ray, a former governor, and told him about my project. Later, I walked into the World Food Prize headquarters and asked to interview Kenneth Quinn, a former U.S. ambassador. I cold-called numbers from phonebooks and internet searches. I asked a church employee about one of its parishioners. One individual was tracked down through the county assessor's property listing webpage, and then I wrote him a letter explaining my project. Connections were made with Tai Dam by attending their New Year celebration and emailing officers listed on the Tai Village's webpage. After these initial contacts, snowball sampling led to even more interviews. All participants signed an informed consent document detailing the voluntary nature of the project, and my desire to share their insights via publication.

Interviews were conducted at local libraries, private homes, the Tai Village, Des Moines Area Community College, and the workplaces of some of the participants. A list of questions guided interviews, but they were generic and intended to get the interviewee to open up. Sessions ranged from about forty-five minutes to over two hours in length. Light editing occurred during transcription. Literal translation was avoided because I did not want to perpetuate stereotypes about Asian Americans speaking "broken" English. Pauses such as um, ah, and repetitions were removed. This was also done for native English speakers to help the narrative flow. Family members served as translators in less than a handful of interviews.

For some of the refugees, speaking about their traumatic past was cathartic. I can admit that for others, old wounds had been reopened. Initially, I began to ask myself why on Earth any of these people would speak to me, a complete stranger, about these intimate wartime experiences. Then, I realized that the Iowa Tai Dam has never been covered, and participants wanted that to change. Since so few people know anything about this ethnic minority from northwest Vietnam, a major goal of this book was to provide the Tai Dam's perspective. Any resettlement history that focuses on Robert Ray and the state's viewpoint is not complete. The Tai Dam's cultural background and experiences in war torn Southeast Asia directly influenced their successful resettlement, and their voice must be heard.

In the pages that follow, readers will be walked through some of the darkest chapters in human history. Rape in Southeast Asia, starvation in Pol Pot's killing fields, torture in communist prison camps, death in the Indochina Wars, and racism in America are detailed. Nevertheless, the chronicle of refugee resettlement in Iowa is ultimately a positive one. That is because of the humanitarianism of a governor, the compassion of many Iowans, and most importantly, the resiliency of the refugees.

Introduction

On the Northside of Des Moines, Iowa, a Tai Dam priest has just returned home from tending the sick one afternoon in March of 2014. Khouang Luong learned the craft from his uncle, a longtime priest who healed many Tai Dam in Iowa. In the *Tai Chronicle*, which tells the sacred origins of the Tai Dam, the Luong family is designated as the priestly class. According to their traditional beliefs, each human body is comprised of thirty-two spirits that represent major organs of the body. Khouang heals the afflicted by recalling wayward spirits, which have fled the body and caused the illness. He reads from a holy text and invites the spirits to take part in a feast prepared to appease them. Luong is one of the few Tai Dam priests healing the sick in the Western Hemisphere. How did Iowa become home to the largest Tai Dam population outside of Asia?

Answers to this question begin to emerge when reading through the list of voluntary agencies (VOLAGS) responsible for resettling refugees in the United States following the Vietnam War. Separate from that group of eight, the State Department listed an odd ninth in a footnote: the state of Iowa. From the close of the Vietnam War to 2010, Iowa alone continually resettled refugees as a state-run voluntary agency. Iowa's unique role began when Governor Robert D. Ray created the Governor's Task Force for Indochinese Resettlement in 1975; he charged it with bringing the Tai Dam to the Hawkeye State. Iowa's peculiar role must be removed from the footnote of history, especially since one of the main arguments of this book is that Robert Ray wielded more influence over Indochinese refugee resettlement and relief than any other governor.

As of today, this peculiarity of Iowa history has yet to be told in detail. Average Iowans may know that Ray helped bring the Tai Dam to Iowa, but these same folks may mistakenly think Ray brought all Indochinese refugees to the state. Little more than surface level knowledge of Iowa's relationship with this population is understandable because no scholar has fully explored Iowa's refugee program. Dorothy Schwieder, "the Dean of Iowa History," wrote the definitive work on the state's past: *Iowa: the Middle Land*. However, Schwieder devotes only two pages to the Southeast Asians in Iowa. Jon Bowermaster compiled the testimonials of roughly two hundred-fifty persons in route to publishing *Governor: an Oral Biography of Robert D. Ray*. Though useful for addressing the political climate and background information of the Ray years, "The Refugees," at a mere five pages, is one of the shortest chapters in the book. Mary Hutchinson Tone's "On the Road to Ioway" is an excellent article on how the Tai Dam evacuated Laos and came to Iowa, but it does not address refugee resettlement and policy in detail. To date, the sixty-minute Iowa Public Television production, "A Promise Called Iowa," remains the best introduction to this topic.

The gap in the history of Southeast Asians in Iowa can largely be applied to the Midwest as well. Initially, immigration histories focused on the uprooted Europeans who flocked to America. Professional historians only began to study Asian Americans in the latter half of the twentieth century, but these authors mostly analyzed Chinese and Japanese American communities. Tragically, the upsurge in attention to Southeast Asians came about in part due to America's waging its longest war in Vietnam, and a natural interest in studying the horrors committed in Pol Pot's Cambodia. Most histories of Indochinese refugees focus on their transition to life in places like California. The largest body of literature on refugees in the Midwest has discussed the Hmong, an ethnic minority used by the CIA in a secret war on communism.

Governor Robert Ray, circa 1969, Des Moines, Iowa. Ray was elected governor in 1968. During the divisive Vietnam War and Watergate years, Ray maintained high approval ratings and was reelected four times, a testament to his popularity in Iowa. He chaired the Midwestern, Republican, and National Governors Associations during his state-record 14 consecutive years in office (State Historical Society of Iowa, Des Moines).

Aside from fine works by linguistic scholars, the Tai Dam are among the least studied of all Southeast Asian ethnic groups. Unfortunately, next to nothing has been written about the faction of Tai Dam who relocated to Iowa beginning in 1975. When asked by fellow Iowans about their ethnicity, some present-day Tai Dam have resorted to telling others they are Lao; this is easier than trying to explain their cultural background to the vast majority who know nothing about the Tai Dam. Because of this dearth of information and their intimate relationship with the state's resettlement program, this book focuses on the Tai Dam experience while also addressing other Indochinese refugee communities in the state. A Tai Dam creation narrative closes with the phrase, "Then our fame echoed over the world."[1] It is hoped that this study will help that phrase ring truer by promoting future works on this population.

Chapter 1 provides a much needed historical overview of the Tai Dam from their creation narrative until North Vietnam's fall to communism forced them to seek asylum in Laos. The Tai Dam were not a backwards or pure culture living in isolation as has been argued by Vietnamese, Thai, French, and American scholars. They were shrewd negotiators who managed centuries of survival among more powerful neighbors. This interpretation has been built from the study of underutilized or neglected Tai Dam sources, especially folklore, oral history interviews, and an unpublished history written by their political leader Wing Cam.

The Iowa Tai Dam, a minority people originally from northwest Vietnam, are culturally and linguistically related to the Thai and Lao. Their rejection of Buddhism and unique script differentiate the Tai Dam from their ethnic cousins. According to the *Tai Chronicle*, the history of its people began with a deluge that wiped out nearly all living creatures. After the flood, mythical lords fell from the heavens in gourds and began conquering lands in what is now northwest Vietnam. As the descendants of these lords, the Lo Cam family held a divine right to leadership over the Tai Dam. By the medieval era, the Twelve Tai Principalities had been established with the Lo Cam playing a major role in governance. One of these medieval rulers, King Cobra, holds a prominent place in Iowa Tai Dam folklore. King Cobra had dealings with Kublai Khan, warred with the ruler of Annam, faced exile in Laos, and triumphantly returned to his homeland in the year 1300. His exploits were not indicative of a people isolated in the mountainous region of Vietnam, but of a culture heavily involved in the political landscape of Southeast Asia.

By the time the French arrived in their homeland during the late nineteenth century, the Tai Dam had ample experience playing off more powerful neighbors. After World War II, they found themselves in the middle of an intense conflict between French imperialists and Vietnamese communists; the Tai Dam who ultimately came to Iowa sided with the French. In their oral history interviews, they retold how the Indochina Wars uprooted their lives. An officer who narrowly escaped capture at the Battle of Dien Bien Phu, a young mother who slept under a rock shelter during bombing raids, a girl forced to marry a Tai Dam soldier against her will to save her father's life, and a twelve-year-old boy separated from his parents during the bombardment of an airfield are among those profiled. By 1952, warfare pushed the anticommunist Tai Dam leadership to Hanoi where they remained until the French defeat at Dien Bien Phu.

In 1954, the Iowa Tai Dam split into two factions. One group, mostly soldiers and their families, went to South Vietnam to continue fighting the communists; the other group found asylum in Laos. Eventually, most of the Tai Dam in Laos moved to the capital of Vientiane where they rebuilt their lives. They attended Lao schools, served in the Royal Lao military, and worked as domestics. Unfortunately, the United States lost the Vietnam War, and the communists made political gains in Laos. Fearing reprisals for their anticommunism, the Tai Dam fled to Thailand in May of 1975. At the Nong Khai Refugee Camp, Wing Cam wrote his *Thai-Dam History* in the hopes of promoting a greater understanding of his people. At the camp, Cam and other political leaders diligently campaigned for asylum abroad.

As explained in Chapter 2, the process by which the Tai Dam found sanctuary in Iowa complicates traditional refugee policy histories. Instead of focusing on the national level debates between presidents, congressmen, State Department officials, and private organizations, this book demonstrates how an American governor and the Tai Dam influenced refugee policy. During the summer of 1975, Ray received correspondence from American educator Arthur Crisfield on behalf of the Tai Dam in Thailand. The refugees informed Ray that their anticommunist past meant certain imprisonment and or execution at the hands of the Pathet Lao. Though the Tai Dam wrote to thirty U.S. governors, only Ray answered their plea. To resettle them in Iowa, Ray had to navigate the turbulent waters of U.S. refugee policy. The Tai Dam escaped Laos before the Royal Lao Government collapsed to communism in December of 1975, and they wished to be relocated to Iowa as a group. This complicated matters for Ray because Congress had only appropriated funds for Vietnamese and Cambodians fleeing communist-controlled nations, and the State Department officially practiced a dispersal policy that would have scattered the Tai Dam across the United States. Meeting with President Gerald Ford and Secretary of State Henry Kissinger, Ray asked for and received an exemption to bring the Tai Dam to Iowa as a cluster, with the state of Iowa serving as the resettlement agency.

Humanitarianism alone does not fully explain why an Iowa governor decided to create his own resettlement program to aid the Tai Dam. Christian ethics, greater power to state and local government, and welfare reduction have been traditionally associated with the Republican Party's platform, and all three informed Ray's decision. As a Christian, Ray believed he had a moral responsibility to help others in need. In addition to aiding U.S. allies, Ray's state-run voluntary agency also permitted him greater control over a federally-dominated process. Without consulting governors, the federal government decided which individuals to admit as

Black Tai Girl of Thuan-Chau by Jean Despujols, Vietnam, circa 1937 © Meadows Museum of Art, Centenary College of Louisiana. The headscarf is called a *piav*, the black blouse *seua koom,* the butterfly buttons *maa paem,* the belt *saay ayev,* and the skirt *sin.* The name Tai Dam or Black Tai originates from the distinctive clothing worn by females. Jean Despujols' Indochina artwork and examples of Tai Dam textiles are housed at the Meadows Museum of Art in Shreveport.

refugees and how many. Private VOLAGS oversaw the refugee resettlement process, and they had little accountability as they went about their work. Ray, a fiscal conservative, abhorred the number of refugees who went on welfare. To remedy this problem, he designed his refugee program with a work-first philosophy. Colleen Shearer, the director of Job Service of Iowa, also served as the head of the Governor's Task Force. Ray planned to help the Tai Dam not just by bringing them to America, but also by finding them jobs. Refugees could best assimilate to hardworking Iowa culture by becoming productive members of the state's labor force.

Though Ray's patronage proved crucial, the Tai Dam played an active role throughout their long journey to America. Before the Tai Dam had ever heard of Iowa and Robert Ray, they negotiated with a Laotian governor to obtain safe passage from Hanoi to Xiang Khoang Province in 1954. Less than two years later, the refugees earned approval from the prime minister of Laos to relocate to the capital. These moves occurred before USAID first started assisting Laotian refugees in 1960. That same year, political revolt in Vientiane caused Wing Cam, the National Director of Rural Public Works, to build a Tai Dam village near the border with Thailand. When the Tai Dam decided to evacuate to Thailand, the village of Nong Pen served its intended purpose as an escape route.

As had happened so many times before, Tai Dam political leaders engaged in shrewd diplomacy to ensure safe entry abroad. After discussing their common ethnic heritage and historic ties of friendship, a governor of Thailand agreed to let the Tai Dam reside at Nong Khai. From the grounds of a Buddhist temple complex, the newcomers campaigned for sanctuary in the West. The Tai Dam sent a delegation to France, and they asked Arthur Crisfield to write to American governors. Because the United States restricted refugee status to Vietnamese and Cambodians, Wing Cam argued that the Tai Dam were Vietnamese refugees, only they had evacuated Vietnam in 1954, twenty-one years prior to the fall of Saigon. A State Department official learned of a Tai Dam military officer with Vietnamese ancestry, and this loophole permitted the Tai Dam U.S. entry under the designation of their ethnic rivals. During their two plus decades of exile, the Tai Dam stressed the importance of staying together because their survival had depended on it. Their journey to the American Midwest represented the fourth time the Tai Dam had left as a group. Their successful transition to Iowa resulted in Ray's continuance of the refugee program beyond its first two year contract.

Chapter 3 examines the state of Iowa's resettlement methods during Robert Ray's tenure as governor. Three main and interrelated characteristics underpinned the state's early refugee program: work-first, cluster resettlement, and individual sponsorship. Colleen Shearer used Job Service of Iowa offices to coordinate employment efforts. Resettling the Tai Dam as a cluster eased the job placement process because the state had only one cultural and linguistic group to employ. If just one Tai Dam spoke English, they could serve as interpreters for their refugee coworkers. During hard times, the Tai Dam might rely on each other for financial assistance instead of turning to welfare. The Governor's Task Force assigned all Tai Dam an individual sponsor, and good sponsorship entailed job placement and keeping their charges off cash assistance. Several Task

Force members provided interviews for this project, and their personal experiences resettling the Tai Dam appear throughout this chapter.

Initially, the state's refugee initiative clashed with the Department of Health, Education, and Welfare (HEW), private voluntary agencies, and Iowa's new Vietnamese community. In a controversial 1976 review, HEW representatives charged the Governor's Task Force with denying hundreds of eligible refugees' access to welfare benefits. According to HEW, state officials and sponsors pressured the Tai Dam to refuse welfare, and the refugees feared accepting cash assistance might hinder the future resettlement of their loved ones still in Southeast Asia. The very existence and work-first philosophy of the Governor's Task Force alienated private VOLAGS operating in the state. All resettlement agencies competed for State Department funding which they received on a per capita basis. Additionally, Colleen Shearer publicly complained of the Catholic Church's resettlement of the Vietnamese in Iowa. She compared the high number of Vietnamese on welfare with the hardworking Tai Dam resettled by the state. Her comments intensified an already strained relationship between the Kinh, the ethnic majority of Vietnam, and the Tai Dam. Coming from Vietnam's dominant socioeconomic class, some of the state's Kinh population considered the Tai Dam to be their inferiors. In Iowa, this relationship had been inverted. Worse yet, the Vietnamese accused the state's refugee program of favoring the Tai Dam; the Governor's Task Force initially turned away needy Vietnamese who came to its resettlement office seeking aid.

Over time, the state repaired its relationship with other VOLAGS, and it started working with all refugees in Iowa instead of just the Tai Dam. To emphasize this shift, The Governor's Task Force was renamed the Iowa Refugee Service Center in 1977. Headquartered in Des Moines, the IRSC coordinated the resettlement efforts of all VOLAGS in the state. The IRSC's work-first philosophy, emphasis on sponsorship, volunteer tutor program, and cooperation with other VOLAGS earned praise from other states. Michigan and Idaho established short-lived state resettlement programs after consulting with IRSC representatives. Australian officials modeled their own tutoring program after Iowa's, and Germany sent a delegation to learn more about the IRSC's efficient policies.

Though the state's resettlement methods cannot be ignored, an analysis of the Iowa experience reveals that refugees must not be seen as voiceless, or blank slates being molded by the Governor's Office, federal officials, and sponsors. Chapter 4 demonstrates how the Tai Dam's cultural, historical, and political background influenced the resettlement process. The

Tai Dam had false expectations about what life in America would be like. Some of the refugees did not know of the existence of African Americans; they assumed all Americans were white. One Tai Dam leader initially disliked African Americans because he associated them with the African soldiers who fought on behalf of French imperialism in Southeast Asia. The newcomers had to confront their racial ignorance and prejudice immediately because Gateway Opportunity Center, an African American community organization, sponsored over seventy of the first Tai Dam. The refugees envisioned being resettled in bigger and newer "American" homes. When Gateway officials housed the group in a lower-class Des Moines neighborhood, the Tai Dam complained. This offended Gateway personnel who charged the Tai Dam with being ungrateful racists.

Aside from racial issues, patriarchy also hindered the Tai Dam's adjustment to Iowa. In the old country, men were the unquestioned political and religious leaders. Female stories of sexual assault and forced marriage in northwest Vietnam provide a glimpse into this patriarchal culture. Once in Iowa, the Tai Dam encountered different gender norms. To the dismay of some Tai Dam males, Colleen Shearer directed the Governor's Task Force. Tai Dam men also argued that childrearing had become more difficult in Iowa. As opposed to Southeast Asia where females oversaw childcare, fathers in America were expected to be actively involved. One Tai Dam father found it difficult to discipline his children without resorting to corporal punishment; a parenting method that had less approval in Iowa.

Though false expectations and patriarchy proved problematic, the Tai Dam possessed a lot of human capital which facilitated their resettlement. Initially, the Task Force believed the newcomers would become farmers, but few of the first 1,228 Tai Dam who migrated to Iowa had been farmers. Those who fled communism came from the political and religious elite. Because of their leadership experience, the state asked Wing Cam, Houng Baccam, and Faluang Baccam to join the Task Force, and they played important roles in resettling their fellows. In addition to these three, many Tai Dam were literate in multiple languages, and this helped them learn English in Iowa. While residing in Vientiane, the Tai Dam had access to education and experienced urban living more so than later Indochinese arrivals. The Tai Dam's turbulent history also prepared them for life in Iowa. Through many upheavals, these professional refugees understood the importance of communal living. In Iowa, the Tai Dam worked mostly menial jobs, but community members pooled their resources to purchase cars and homes for one another. As the state continued resettling Tai Dam, other refugee disasters developed, and Iowa's governor responded.

Chapter 5 describes the origins of the boat people crisis, Ray's advocacy for greater refugee intake, and the reaction of Iowans to their Governor's controversial decision. The United States withdrew from Vietnam in chaotic fashion, and this resulted in the abandonment of hundreds of thousands of Vietnamese allies. Former soldiers, government officials, and businessmen of the toppled Republic of Vietnam endured indoctrination, starvation, and torture in communist "reeducation camps." By the late 1970s, communists established firmer control over the South, and this resulted in the closure of businesses. At the same time, Vietnam found itself at war with neighbors China and Cambodia. Fear of political reprisal, communist economic policy, and military escalation caused hundreds of thousands of people to flee Vietnam by sea. In their attempt to reach asylum, the boat people suffered many hardships in small and often unseaworthy vessels. As explained by Iowans Kiet Tran and Vinh Nguyen, boat people faced robbery, rape, and murder at the hands of pirates. Ed Bradley's *60 Minutes* special report brought the boat people's suffering to a wider audience. One of those watching was the Governor of Iowa.

Moved by Bradley's broadcast, Ray became the first elected official to publicly support increased admissions for the boat people. In January of 1979, Ray announced that Iowa would admit 1,500 additional refugees. As explained by a *Des Moines Register* poll and the hundreds of letters that poured into the Governor's Office, a majority of Iowans disagreed with his decision. For many, the Vietnam War seemed to be an old wound that would not heal. Critics reasoned America had lost the war because the Vietnamese were poor allies, so how could their governor award asylum to cowards or secret communists. Many Iowans argued that Ray must alleviate problems at home before he tried to help refugees. Iowa's rural poor and elderly community were more deserving of assistance than foreigners, they contended. Opponents also noted how refugees stole jobs from Iowans. Some members of Iowa's African American community resented the state's perceived favoritism of refugees. To prospective employers and the general public, IRSC members and Ray promoted Asian refugees as model minorities, but they did nothing to counter the high unemployment and poverty rates of Iowa's black population. Racism underpinned the arguments of some naysayers of resettlement. They loathed the idea of a mostly Caucasian state being overrun by a Yellow Peril. Countering the above arguments, sponsors and others who interacted with refugees were the staunchest supporters of resettlement. Ray proved to be no exception. He had come to adore the Tai Dam, a grateful and hardworking community that showered him with praise.

Ray's continued support of the Tai Dam also brought him face to face with the greatest humanitarian disaster of the post–World War II era. In October of 1979, Ray led a small delegation of governors on a trip to Asia. After touring China, the party visited Tai Dam and Cambodian refugee camps in Thailand. Cambodia had been devastated by civil war, U.S. bombardment, and worst of all, the murderous rule of the communist Khmer Rouge. Nearly two million Cambodians perished in Pol Pot's killing fields. After Vietnam invaded Cambodia in December of 1978, large numbers of Cambodians fled to Thailand. At the Sa Kaeo camp, Ray and company watched as emaciated refugees died; on one day of their visit, over fifty Cambodians perished. The experience moved Ray and company. Immediately, the Governor and Kenneth Quinn, an aide on loan from the State Department, began to devise a plan to help Cambodian refugees.

Chapter 6 analyzes the Iowa SHARES[2] Cambodian relief program coordinated from the Governor's Office. Launched during the 1979 Thanksgiving holiday, the program eventually generated over $540,000. Iowans bought a share in humanity, which was the equivalent of an Iowa bushel of corn. Proceeds were used to send food and medicine to Cambodian refugees. SHARES also funded teams of Iowa doctors and nurses who worked at the Khao I Dang refugee camp in Thailand. Iowans supported and opposed the relief effort for a myriad of reasons. Inspired by Pope John Paul II's recent visit to Living History Farms, Christian piety compelled many Iowans to donate. Recalling the international community's failed response to the Holocaust, Iowa's Jewish leaders backed the initiative as well. However, some supported SHARES for secular reasons. Funds aided America's anticommunist ally Thailand, and helped depopulate a country recently invaded by communist Vietnam. Some community members disapproved of SHARES because they saw it as a continuation of the Cold War; they wanted relief directed to Cambodia instead of Thailand. As explained in angry letters to Governor Ray, many opposed SHARES because it diverted resources from needy Iowans. To this argument, Ray countered, "If we don't have the heart, or the spirit to save human lives, then how can we be expected to help those whose lives are already assured."[3] Personally witnessing the Cambodians' suffering, especially the children, made Ray resolute in his decision.

Aside from Ray and others who went to Southeast Asia, very few Iowans understood how Indochinese children suffered. Chapter 7 devotes attention to the homeland experiences of Iowa's child refugees. In autobiographical accounts, Des Moines' Indochinese schoolchildren remembered life in their birthplaces being disrupted once communist governments seized power. They spoke of fathers disappearing in the night, being wrenched from family and friends, and harrowing escapes to nations of first asylum. Though their suffering cannot be denied, Indochinese children were not merely the quintessential victims of war. Rather, they were the most resilient group of refugees. Insulated by youthful naiveté and protective caretakers, Indochinese children often failed to grasp the full realities of life as refugees. While parents worried in refugee camps, children played and made powerful friendships. Child refugees also demonstrated their resiliency upon arrival in America.

Chapter 8 focuses on the experiences of Indochinese refugee children in the United States. Youths constantly referenced their homelands while trying to make sense of Iowa. Many Indochinese children missed the physical beauty of their birthplaces. They contrasted the wide open plains of the Midwest with the mountain ranges of their native lands. In Iowa, child refugees confronted American life in a different arena than their parents. Whereas adults adjusted to the workforce, their children adjusted to the schoolyard. Overall, the newcomers agreed that Iowa teachers seemed nicer because they did not spank students as had instructors in Southeast Asia. Unfortunately, these nice American teachers could not stop numerous Indochinese students from being taunted by their classmates. Surrounded by Caucasian peers, some refugee students developed poor self-images. They wanted to be white "Americans." At the same time, parents and grandparents wanted their young to retain the cultural norms of their homelands. As a result, refugee youths felt trapped between two worlds. However, the idea of freedom brought all generations together. Indochinese children came to appreciate the struggles their parents had borne to guide their family to a land of opportunity. As these Indochinese youths have come of age, their many success stories have brought vindication and joy to the governor who played such a prominent role in bringing them to Iowa.

Chapter 9 further explores Governor Ray's leadership on refugee matters and the continuing legacy of his refugee program. Ray's stature and changes in Iowa politics enabled him to accept refugees associated with America's most controversial war. The same year he admitted the Tai Dam, Ray became the first Iowa governor elected to a fourth term. In all of America, his percentage of victory was greater than any other statewide Republican candidate for senator or governor. In 1975, Ray held an amazing 81 percent approval rating, over thirty points higher than the national average. The year 1975 also marked the first time an Iowa governor would serve a four-year term. If the Tai Dam resettlement went poorly,

Ray was still guaranteed four years in office, and he would have had time to recover from any political damage associated with his refugee initiative. Ray also served as governor during an era when the executive became stronger than the state legislature. Because governors had been granted greater powers of appointment, many department heads had to answer to Ray. His longevity in office only enhanced his position. Since federal funding sustained his refugee program, Ray did not have to involve the state legislature in his initial decision to resettle refugees.

Even with these favorable political circumstances, Ray's advocacy on behalf of Vietnam War era refugees was a truly bold decision. Today, his humanitarianism seems all the more remarkable as a growing number of governors have sought to block Syrian refugees from entering the United States. Citing security concerns in the aftermath of the Paris terrorist attack, thirty American governors tried to halt the resettlement of Syrians in their respective states. On November 16, 2015, Governor Terry Branstad announced, "Until a thorough and thoughtful review is conducted by the intelligence community and the safety of Iowans can be assured, the federal government should not resettle any Syrian refugees in Iowa." The day after Branstad's statement, the Tai Dam celebrated their fortieth anniversary in Iowa at the state capitol building. Beginning with the Tai Dam forty years ago, many Iowans developed a strong sense of pride in their state's rich legacy of helping refugees, and they viewed Branstad's stance as a betrayal of this legacy.

Security concerns alone do not explain governors' opposition to Syrian resettlement. A poorly funded refugee program and a lack of governors' involvement in policy are also to blame. Ray played an integral role in the passage of the Refugee Act of 1980. Using his influence within the National Governors Association, Ray successfully lobbied for a three year period of federal reimbursement to states for refugees drawing cash and medical assistance. During the Reagan presidency, federal reimbursement dropped to a period of just eighteen months, and even Ray grew disillusioned over refugee resettlement. By 2010, the rising expense of resettlement and lack of federal funding resulted in the closure of Iowa's refugee program. In 2015, the federal government reimbursed states for only eight months of cash and medical assistance used by eligible childless couples or single adults. Currently, the State Department provides voluntary agencies less than $2,000 per refugee resettled. VOLAGS use these meager funds to purchase basic necessities for refugees' first three months in America.

Iowa's refugee program should be resurrected as a model for resettlement. Having governors actively involved would only reinforce their commitment to the nation's refugee program and reduce tensions between state executives and the federal government. For this to work, the federal government would have to be willing to provide greater funding to the states. If the federal government supported this endeavor, state governments could do their part in alleviating refugee crises as Ray and Iowans once did. Perhaps it is naïve to think that these changes in policy can occur. If that is the case, it is hoped that present-day governors and average Americans can be inspired to help others after learning about the Iowa program. As the recent events in Syria so poignantly demonstrate, there is no shortage of those in need.

1

Beginnings and Endings at Dien Bien Phu

The Tai Dam of Iowa trace their roots back to three provinces in northwest Vietnam: Lai Chau, Son La, and Yen Bai. Presently, the Socialist Republic of Vietnam officially recognizes over fifty ethnic groups, and the Tai are the second largest minority population. The over one million Tai of Vietnam are subdivided into three main groupings: White, Red, and Black. Tai Dam means "Black Tai" after the distinctive black clothing worn by their people. The Tai Dam speak the Southwestern Tai branch of the Tai-Kadai language family. Linguistically and ethnically, the Tai Dam are closely related to the Lao and Thai majorities in Laos and Thailand, but the Tai Dam use a unique script and reject Buddhism. Unfortunately, Thai, French, American, and Vietnamese scholars have all characterized the Tai Dam as being chronically isolated. Supposedly, this isolation makes the Tai Dam backwards and or culturally pure. In reality, the Tai Dam have always been enmeshed in the political tumult of Southeast Asia as is evident in their chronicles and folklore. The warfare that ultimately pushed the Tai Dam to Iowa must be seen as just one example of the many disruptions the group has historically endured.

Long before the Vietnamese defeated the French there, Dien Bien Phu was the ancestral homeland of the Tai Dam. Each of the Tai Dam's *Kwam to Muang*, or history of the principality, begins with a creation story. In the beginning, the sky and the earth pressed against one another: "There was no room to raise up the arm of the rice pounder. There was no room to draw out thread in spinning. The ox had his hump caught against the low sky. The wild boar caught his tusks against the low sky."[1] To remedy the situation, Grandmother Earth and Grandfather Sky cut the cord that held the land and the sky together, permitting the sky to rise. However, chaos reigned over the barren landscape. Lacking rulers, hill peoples massacred one another, and all life wilted in a terrible drought. Once more, Grandmother Earth and Grandfather Sky intervened by performing rituals to bring rains. The Grandparents wrapped a toad in a shroud. Across Southeast Asia, ethnic groups have associated toads, who cry out before downpours, with the ability of communing with the heavens. The Grandparents' rainmaking pleas worked, but a catastrophic flood ensued. Three months passed before the water abated. All creatures perished save for a lone duck and a chicken that rode on the duck's back.

After the flood, humans descended from the sky, and Tai rulers established law and order throughout the land: "The Sky placed everything in eight gourds. There were thirty clans of hill people. There were fifty clans of Tai people. There were three hundred thirty kinds of rice for the fields.... There were sacred manuscripts of priests and shaman and of astrologers and prophets. There were the old traditions, the twelve village customs, and the twenty-four kingdom laws."[2] In addition to humans and their sacred texts, the creatures of the world also descended in gourds. Separate from the ordinary people, Lord Cuang and Lord Silver fell from the heavens. These two figures possessed brass pillars, which symbolized the power of the ruling class. The lords and their descendants became divine sovereigns across Southeast Asia. The most important descendent, Lan Cheuang, explored and conquered many lands while marching east to west in what became Tai Dam country. Eventually, he established a kingdom in the west called Muang Theng: the Tai name for Dien Bien Phu.

Unlike the biblical flood described in Genesis, the flood in the Tai Dam chronicles does not occur as a punishment for sin. The rains simply happened in several versions, but in one chronicle, talking animals asked the god Ten to kill all humans with a deluge. Like nearly all others, the Tai Dam's creation story seeks to explain how a new and more advanced order emerged from a more primitive one. Gourds play an integral role in many Southeast Asian creation narratives. During a time when humans mostly practiced hunting and gathering, the planting of gourds provided a crucial food source that resulted in the formation of larger societies. Tai Dam political leader Wing Cam has a more ominous interpretation of the gourds and brass pillars associated with his ancestors. His ancestors came to northwest Vietnam as invaders who conquered Mon-Khmer speakers who already inhabited the land. The sacred gourds represented large ships and the brass pillars their masts.[3]

The actual origins of the Tai people are anything but clear. Wing Cam

Map of the Tai in Vietnam. The Twelve Tai Principalities were Lai, So, Chian, Than, Theng, Muay, La, Mua, Lo, Wat, Sang, and Toek. List taken from Yukti Mukdawijitra, "Ethnicity and Multilingualism." © OpenStreetMap contributors (map creator James Harken).

claims his ancestors emerged from Mount Altai just south of Mongolia circa 4,000 BCE. Using Chinese sources, anthropologist Dang Nghiem Van placed the Tai in southern China, and the group began migrating into northwest Indochina by 1,000 BCE. Iowa Tai Dam trace their ancestry to the Kingdom of Nan Chao. In 862, Nan Chao lost in battle to Chinese forces, causing the Tai to flee southward. Led by the two mythical lords mentioned in the flood narrative, the Tai peoples began conquering territories in modern-day Vietnam in the late ninth century. Undeniably, the Tai Dam established political entities in northwest Vietnam by the medieval period.[4]

After their conquests, the Tai peoples created a political structure called the Sip Song Chau Tai, or Twelve Tai Principalities. A hereditary prince descended from the Lo Cam family governed each of these twelve territories called a *muang*. Traditionally, the White Tai held power in the northern Tai states while the Black Tai controlled the middle principalities of Theng, Muay, La, Mua, Lo, and Wat. The Red Tai held sway in the southeast. In theory, one lord who had distinguished himself from the others governed all Twelve Tai Principalities. In reality, no single ruler could control the powerful princes. Fighting among the Tai was constant as one prince tried to increase his power at the expense of another. However, this lack of centralization made conquering the Tai difficult for invading powers.

The Tai Dam inhabited lowland river valleys in the mountainous region of northern Vietnam. In these valleys, they established villages based on wet rice cultivation. As rulers, the Lo Cam distributed the rice fields and demanded labor and tribute from others. Limits on the amount of land suitable for rice cultivation also required some Tai Dam to engage in slash and burn agriculture. Tai Dam families included the Cam, Lo, Vi, Lu, Leo, Luong, Ka, Tong, and Quang. The Me and Nguyen also lived among the Black Tai, but they were not considered "pure Tai" because of their mixing with the Vietnamese and Chinese.[5] The Tai Dam used the derisive term *Sa* to refer to the original inhabitants of the land, and this group lived on the mountainsides. The Hmong, latecomers to the region, lived on the mountaintops and engaged in slash and burn agriculture. Additionally, the Hmong produced opium and sold their product to Tai Dam middlemen.

Black Tai religious belief reinforced their hierarchical society. In the *Tai Chronicle*, the god Ten Luong designated the Lo Cam as the rulers and the Luong as the priests. These political and religious elites supervised ceremonies dedicated to the spirits of the sky and spirits of the land. The

Ten were the most powerful spirits, and they resided in heaven. Ten Luong sat atop the Black Tai pantheon of gods. Beneath the Ten were lesser spirits. Each village and principality had protector spirits that needed to be appeased by performing at least annual ceremonies. The spirit of the village resided in a house while the spirit of the principality resided within a tree or sacred pillar. The Lo Cam and Luong performed religious rites to ensure good harvests and peaceful times.[6]

The Tai Dam believed every human body to be comprised of thirty-two souls. When an individual became ill or frightened, this meant that one or more of their souls had fled their body, causing illness. During healing ceremonies, religious figures made food and drink offerings to coax these wayward souls to return to the sick person's body. When an individual passed away, some of their souls remained and roamed the earth. In each Tai Dam home, the male head of household oversaw an altar dedicated to the remembrance and worship of his ancestors. Females maintained their own altars to relatives, but these altars resided outside of the home. If individuals did not venerate their ancestors' souls with offerings of food and drink, misfortune befell the living.

When a Tai Dam dies, some of their souls travel to a Muang Fa or the village in the sky. The village to which one belonged depended on that person's status in life. The souls of commoners and children who passed away before the age of five live in Lam Loi. At this village, commoners must work as they did while living. Unfortunately, after a certain period of time, their souls must depart heaven and return to the living world where they cause harm to others. The petty nobles of the Lo Cam family live at Gien Pan Noi. There, food and drink are plentiful and the climate ideal. Sadly, the souls of the petty nobles must also leave heaven and return to the living world. Only the souls of the prominent Lo Cam family enjoy a permanent afterlife in the village in the sky. They live in a paradise called Gien Pan Luong.[7]

The living Tai Dam ushered their deceased loved ones to the village in the sky with the all-important *San Song* funerary ceremony. After a notable individual passed, relatives washed and laid out the corpse on a mat. The sons and daughter-in-laws made boiled chicken, liquor, and other offerings to their deceased loved one. The mourners' wails awakened the dead. On day two, a son-in-law oversaw funerary rites. By the time the son-in-law arrived, the son of the dead, dressed in white, had prepared another offering tray of chicken and pig brought by relatives. The son-in-law, dressed in black, then kneeled before the dead and asked its spirit to take the offering. During the night of day two, the son-in-law read to the deceased. The reader began with a plea for the dead to listen. Next, the Tai Dam flood narrative was recounted. Afterwards, the history of the principality and its glorious chiefs, usually relatives of the dead, was read. Reciting the text might have taken as long as three hours.

Just before dawn, the son-in-law sang the *San Song*. In preparation for their own funerals, the living, especially the Lo Cam, maintained detailed genealogies and a list of all of their travels. The son-in-law then recited in reverse chronological order all of the places the individual had traveled. All Tai Dam spirits are eventually guided back to the same place on Earth: the Tat Pi Fai Waterfall. Purportedly in Son La, this waterfall represents the place where Grandmother Earth and Grandfather Sky had cut the cord that once held the land and sky together. From the waterfall, the son-in-law ushered the dead to the village in the sky according to their rank. After the son-in-law saw the dead to their destination, he had to hurriedly guide himself back to the living world. Once the *San Song* had been performed, the son-in-law oversaw the cremation of the corpse on day

Nhot Luong oversees funerary rites for Don Baccam, Des Moines, Iowa, 1994. Luong calls the spirits of the departed to return to the ancestral altar. There, the spirits of the deceased will have food and drink offerings and be honored by loved ones. Today, Khouang Luong continues his family's tradition as religious leaders of the Tai Dam by performing these ceremonies in Iowa (Houng Baccam).

three. Eventually, the dead's ashes were placed at their tomb. The son-in-law sacrificed a white buffalo, and then he performed the *San Song* once more to ask the deceased to take the sacrificed animal to the commoners who farmed in the village in the sky. In the near future, the relatives of the departed held a ceremony whereby priests invited some of the dead's souls to remain on an ancestral altar. They made offerings to the recently deceased and other ancestors in their genealogical list.[8]

In the late twentieth century, Sumitr Pitiphat of Thammasat University in Thailand wrote about Tai Dam spiritual beliefs. The anthropologist argued that the Thai and Lao have long had cultural contacts with Buddhism and Hinduism. In contrast, the Black Tai in northwest Vietnam have not been influenced by Indian and Chinese cultures. Pitiphat concluded that the Thai and Lao people can learn about their ancient ancestors by studying present-day Tai Dam. Pitiphat's argument presupposes the Tai Dam to be a static and isolated culture, pure of foreign influence, but Tai Dam accounts challenge such a notion. In Wing Cam's history, the Tai Dam constantly faced invasion from outside forces. He wrote, "The Twelve Tai Principalities was subjected without end to the invasion of neighboring countries: China, Annam, and the traffic of pirates. What we see now as temples, stone bridges, and certain words were proof of it. Most often, to respect the good neighbors, the leader of the Twelve Tai Principalities had to send courteous missions with substantial gifts. In return, the leader received honorable titles which frightened neighboring lords and pirates. If anytime the leader missed this rule, war began."[9] At differing times in their history, the Tai Dam had been vassals to many external powers; they constantly found themselves embroiled in the political rivalries between the Lao Kingdom of Luang Prabang, China, Vietnam, and Siam. By the late nineteenth century, the French became just the latest foreigners to compete for power in Tai Dam country. When they encountered the Black Tai, the French did not find an isolated culture naïve to power politics, but a politically astute group who managed to maintain some form of independence among more powerful and quarrelsome neighbors.

The motivating forces behind French imperialism in Indochina were manifold. Conrad Malte-Brun, a geographer working for the Napoleonic regime, first coined the term Indochina in 1804. The word "Indochina" demonstrated the marginal position Europeans ascribed to the vast territory between British India and the Chinese empire. French desire to access trade in China had always underpinned their interest in Southeast Asia. Since the English dominated markets in eastern China, the French hoped to obtain a foothold in western China by controlling the Mekong and Red Rivers. For centuries, China had been the dominant power in the region. Rulers throughout Southeast Asia, including those of the Twelve Tai Principalities, had paid tribute to their more powerful neighbor to the north. In order for French power to take root in Southeast Asia, China had to be subjugated.

French activities in Indochina unfolded during a period of intense competition between rival Western powers. In 1857, the Special Commission for Cochinchina described how this imperialist competition required France to increase its involvement in the Far East: "Are we to be the only ones who possess nothing in this area, while the English, the Dutch, the Spanish, and even the Russians establish themselves here?"[10] To be a world power, France needed trade and military outposts in Southeast Asia. Envious of the English, France hoped to turn Saigon into a French Singapore. From 1858 through 1867, France seized control over territories in southern Vietnam and the kingdom of Cambodia. In the midst of the Taiping Rebellion (1850–1864), China could not prevent this extension of French influence. After suffering military defeat in the Franco-Prussian War of 1871, France looked to expand in the Far East to regain great power status. Between 1882 and 1897, France established protectorates over Laos and the northern portion of Vietnam. Territories in northern Vietnam provided French ships access to coal fields and trade links via the South China Sea.

Aside from purely economic considerations, a civilizing mission motivated French imperialism in Indochina. French missionary efforts in Vietnam began in the seventeenth century; the Jesuit Alexandre de Rhodes helped develop the Vietnamese alphabet *quoc ngu* to facilitate Christianization. French Catholics' desire to spread the faith in the East only increased when the French revolutionaries dismantled religion. In 1799, Bishop Pigneau de Behaine declared, "Precious Cross, the French have knocked you down and removed you from their temples. Since they no longer respect you, come to Cochinchina."[11] The Nguyen dynasty of Vietnam viewed French missionizing with disdain; the Catholic faith challenged the Confucian-based authority of the emperor. In 1832, ruler Minh Mang authorized violent attacks against Christians. In response, clergymen and their converts demanded the French take measures to protect them in Vietnam. Throughout the nineteenth century, anticlericalism in France increased, but the nation still developed a secular version of the civilizing mission. France would bring modernity and republican values to the backward Southeast Asians, including the Tai peoples French ethnographers classified as primitives.

In the 1880s, the French became just the latest foreigners seeking influence over the Twelve Tai Principalities. At first, White Tai leader Deo Van Tri resisted the French, but the Deo family switched sides in 1890. This marked the beginning of a long partnership between the French who used the White Tai as allies against Vietnamese nationalism, and the Deo who used the French to bolster their family's influence in Tai country. While trying to establish authority in the region, the French attempted to weaken the power of the Tai ruling class. They wanted leadership positions in Tai country to be elective rather than hereditary. However, Tai Dam religious belief required rulers to be a Lo Cam as specified in their creation narrative. This royal family also supervised important religious rites that maintained the well-being of their principality. Though leadership positions became elective under French rule, the Lo Cam still dominated politics. The name "Cam" means gold in the Tai Dam language. A proverb describes that family's monopoly on power, "If gold should disappear, it must be replaced by other gold."[12] From the late 1880s until the end of World War II, the Tai Dam experienced relative peace as compared to earlier periods of invasion. Unfortunately, this peace did not last.

Only the eldest living Tai Dam experienced a serene childhood in Tai Dam country. Born in Son La in 1925, Neth Rasavanh described how her playing helped others in her village of Thong: "I remember loving to climb trees…. I was known as the expert tree climber. I could climb well like a monkey; my body felt so light. When people wanted [fruits] from the trees, they would call on me to pick the fruits for them." Tai Dam homes consisted of one big room separated by curtains. Since her father held a leadership position, Neth's family lived in a larger home with ten rooms. Though peace existed in those times, Neth remembered life in Tai Dam country being difficult. Neth's father had three wives, and her mother was of humble status compared to the other two. The high-ranking wives wanted Neth's father to leave her mother. Being female, Neth never went to school in Son La. She explained, "Girls were only encouraged to work the fields and create textiles. Parents told girls that they cannot make a living or support a family if they took time for education and do not learn how to work the fields and create textiles." Parents often pressured children to marry a certain partner, but Neth fell in love on her own. She married her husband La, an educated official who worked for the French.[13]

In contrast to Neth, warfare interrupted Nga Baccam's childhood. Born in Muang Sai around 1942, Nga remembered a mountain dividing her homeland. On one side, the Tai Dam built their homes. A large river flowed along the other side of the mountain. Her childhood routine consisted of working the fields then swimming in the river. Only Tai Dam lived in Nga's village. She believed that Vietnamese and other foreigners could not drink the water without falling ill. Nga's father held a leadership position, and this required him to oversee important rituals. She explained, "We held an annual ceremony every year. If it was not held, the fields would not be productive and the livestock may not survive…. My father would sacrifice a water buffalo from our own farm for the entire village. All the residents of the village would join in and help out with the ceremony, which was held at the river. At least one family member from each household would attend." Nga grew up on a farm surrounded by many different animals: cows, chickens, ducks, water buffalos, and dogs. Nga left her village around the age of ten. She lamented, "We had to throw everything away because of the war."[14]

After World War II, the Tai Dam lived in the middle of an escalating conflict between the French and the Vietnamese communists. French forces in the area had been forced to flee to China during World War II, but they attempted to regain control over Vietnam after the Allied victory. To win Tai support and weaken Vietnamese nationalism, the French created the semi-autonomous Tai Federation in 1948. Deo Van Long of the White Tai served as its president, and Quy Baccam of the Black Tai held the position of Vice President. The French also created three battalions of Tai soldiers who served under French officers. In 1952, teenager Bao Lo Cam of Son La joined a Tai battalion. He explained, "We did not accept the communist regime. We had to fight them." Bao served as an officer alongside the French, and later in South Vietnam, the Americans. He compared the two allies: "The Americans were better because the French were colonizers. They commanded us, unlike the Americans who were our friends. We were colonies. They did not treat us too well."[15] By the time Bao joined the service, the Vietminh had experienced victories in Tai Dam country using the *pourrissement* or rotting away strategy. In the mountainous terrain, the Vietminh fought small scale skirmishes against the French, who could not deploy their larger forces.

By the early 1950s, Tai Dam who supported the French feared being captured by the enemy. Elders reflected on how the fighting disrupted their lives. The communists forced Neth Rasavanh to leave her home at gunpoint: "The Vietnamese relocated us to an area where there was no food to eat for days. We had no choice but to take the children and babies with us. The men were forced to go with them to another place to do hard labor. They were not allowed to go with the women and children. The women had to carry the children and whatever they could handle carrying from home on their backs." Being relocated did not remove Neth from the warzone. French and Vietnamese planes fought one another. She described living in constant fear: "We had to sleep under rocks to keep secure from the ammunition. We also had to forage for food in the forest to cook whatever we found. However, if they saw smoke from our cooking, or if they saw anyone on the ground, they would also shoot at us. It was very difficult. I remember this going on for days. Many people were killed during this time." After about one year, the French regained ground and Neth returned to her village, but her homecoming proved short-lived.[16]

By 1952, the French position in Tai Dam country had deteriorated, and they decided to evacuate their Tai allies to the relative safety of Hanoi. Nga Baccam and Houng Baccam recalled their last days in Tai Dam country. Nga fled Muang Sai with her father, two older sisters and their four children. She described her long journey, mostly by foot, to an airfield in Phuan San: "The French led our way. I remember holding a French soldier's hand as we were walking. We took a water buffalo with us on our journey. It was a long ways, and we had to stop and sleep on the way there. I remember my feet aching. The French and the Vietnamese were there in Phuan San fighting as well. I remember the French being on one side and on another side were the Vietnamese. We had to run to the French side as quickly as possible before someone from the Vietnamese side captured us. If they captured women and children, they would return us to our village to live under the communist rule if we were not shot first." Houng Baccam, a twelve-year-old from the village of Pieng in Son La, remembered his harrowing evacuation to Hanoi in November of 1952: "Suddenly, the Vietminh attacked the airport and everyone rushed to the airplanes. There were about fifteen airplanes.... Once the refugees rushed the airplanes, they filled up and shutoff [the doors]. My sister and I missed my parents. They went off to the airplane and it shutoff. We did not know where to go. We thought that if we went to the first airplane, there would be more people. We went to about the fourth airplane. An official there took us into the airplane. Luckily, we met our parents at the airport in Hanoi."[17] The Tai Dam hoped their stay in Hanoi would be temporary. Once the communists had been defeated, they would return home.

In Hanoi, most of the Tai Dam lived in a place called Chai Lor Ngok, which had been a school for the Vietnamese. The group built their own shelters along a nearby river. The adults could not find work, and the young could not attend school. Nga Baccam's family struggled to survive in the capital, "My family and I had to sell everything we had, including some of our clothes and even some jewelry that we had on us, for food.

Ngan VanLo in the Son La region of Vietnam, circa 1952. Overall, most Black Tai allied with the communists. However, those who ultimately came to Iowa had a long history of anticommunism. VanLo served as a sergeant in the French Foreign Legion. He died in Laos in 1960 (Dinh VanLo).

My father was able to sell the water buffalo that we had brought with us on our journey to Phuan San...."[18] The refugees had no land to cultivate and no wood for cooking. As a result, the Tai Dam had to scavenge for resources. Vietnamese locals accused the refugees of stealing their crops, and they threatened to kill Tai Dam.

In 1954, the French succeeded in drawing the Vietminh into a traditional-style battle at Dien Bien Phu. After fifty-six days of fierce combat, the Vietminh defeated seventeen French-commanded battalions. Out of 16,544 soldiers, three thousand died on or near the battlefield, and another three thousand survived the siege. Nearly ten thousand soldiers died during death marches and from torturous treatment in communist prison camps. Bao Lo Cam, then a second lieutenant in a Tai battalion, narrowly escaped becoming one of those prisoners of war. Bao reflected, "I was over there, but I was not captured. The French had information that the communists had a division moving towards Laos. We came from Dien Bien Phu to Muang Sai by plane to bomb the communists.... We stopped them. We tried to go back to Dien Bien Phu, but the anti-aircraft was too heavy. We could not land. After that, we had an operation close to Hanoi."[19]

Thuong Lo, a translator in the Third Tai Battalion, blamed French naiveté and Chinese intervention for the loss at Dien Bien Phu. The gullible French believed they could make treaties with the Vietminh, and the Chinese provided troops and material that turned the tide in favor of their fellow communists. The American press also blamed Chinese assistance for the disaster. Others attributed the defeat to the effective guerrilla style of warfare waged by the Vietminh. In reality, the French failed at Dien Bien Phu because they did not comprehend northern Vietnam's complex ethno-political situation.[20]

In contrast to the Vietminh, the French miscalculated in their dealings with the area's minorities. With French support, the White Tai Deo family involved themselves in Black Tai politics. The Black Tai who had been removed from power or passed over for key appointments offered important support to the communists. Many Black Tai also resented French favoritism toward the White Tai. Furthermore, France's recognition of the Tai Federation threatened the Hmong. An inherent tension existed between the upland Hmong and the lowland Tai. The Hmong cultivated opium and sold their crop to the Tai, but they believed Tai middlemen offered unfair prices. The Vietminh exploited this rivalry. Access to the Hmong's opium trade helped the Vietminh finance their war effort, and Hmong served as guides and porters to the victorious forces at Dien Bien Phu.

Neth Rasavanh has a difficult time comprehending the politics of a complicated war. She reflected, "The Vietnamese communists were very cruel. They executed my father at the age of ninety because he was an official and had worked with the French." Neth does not harbor positive feelings towards the French either. She explained, "They would hurt the people and sometimes held the Tai Dam people hostage if they did not have any money for them. They were so cruel. I believe that is why they had led us to lose our country. I do not understand why they did the things they did.... We were so poor and had a tough life."[21]

Throughout this struggle, Tai Dam also suffered at the hands of their fellows. Em Quang of Son La remembered Black Tai soldiers raiding her hometown of Kute. While the invaders razed her village, the twelve-year-old girl fled to the fields. Troops eventually caught up with her and others. Soldiers looked over the Tai Dam girls and forced their favorites into marriage. As Em's father held a leadership position, her refusal to marry the soldier would have jeopardized her father's life. To protect her father and prove her family's loyalty, Em had to marry the soldier. It would be the beginning of an eleven-year marriage she never wanted. After Em and fellow villagers rebuilt Kute, the soldier returned for his bride and took her to Hanoi. When Dien Bien Phu fell, Em realized she would not be able to return to Tai Dam country; she never saw her parents again.[22]

For the Iowa Tai Dam, Dien Bien Phu represented the beginning of a permanent dislocation from their ancestral homeland in northwest Vietnam. The roughly two thousand exiles in Hanoi split into two groups. Bao Lo Cam joined a small contingent of soldiers who moved to South Vietnam. Another faction obtained permission to relocate to northeastern Laos. On July 20, 1954, the majority of the Tai Dam evacuated Hanoi for Xiang Khoang, Laos. In their new land, the Tai Dam built the village of Na Ngam. By this time Quy Baccam, the highest ranking Black Tai official, had fled to France. His relative Suc Baccam assumed leadership of the Tai Dam in exile during their stay in Xiang Khoang. At Na Ngam, the Tai Dam divided the land into four parts based on the four different regions the group came from in Tai Dam country. Those with political titles in the old country retained them in this recreation of the Tai Dam homeland.[23]

The Tai Dam remembered life in Xiang Khoang as a time of hardship. The exiles attempted to cultivate rice, but the land was of poor quality. The uncooperative soil had a distinctive red color, and trees covered much of the landscape. In the higher elevation, the Tai Dam experienced colder temperatures. Nga Baccam explained, "I remember it being cold and there was frost in the mornings. We did not have adequate clothes either. We had to wait until the sun came out at about noon until we could take our baths. I remember having to curl up to keep warm." With minimal success raising crops, the Tai Dam endured the indignity of begging locals for food. Nga's family received uncooked rice and made it into soup. Tai Dam elders have mixed feelings about their early treatment by the Lao. Some Black Tai appreciated the assistance they received from their new neighbors. Others believed the Lao initially looked down upon them because the Tai Dam had lost their homeland and needed handouts. In this precarious position, Suc Baccam flirted with the idea of relocating the group to South Vietnam. However, Souvanna Phouma, the former prime minister of Laos, learned of their plight and arranged for the Tai Dam to be moved to the capital. After just under a year and a half, the Tai Dam migrated to Vientiane.[24]

In Vientiane, the Tai Dam rebuilt their lives. They lived in villages on the outskirts of the capital. Like the experiment at Na Ngam in Xiang Khoang, the Tai Dam recreated their old villages in their new homeland. In the capital, they held diverse jobs. Many men worked for the Royal Lao Government as soldiers and officials while the women worked as domestics. Children also had greater access to schooling in Laos. Over time, many Black Tai obtained Lao citizenship, but they still enjoyed their local self-government. By 1956, Quy Baccam, the former Vice President of the Tai Federation, rejoined his people, and he resumed leadership of the Tai Dam community in Laos.

The Tai Dam experienced tension over whether or not to assimilate with the Lao or preserve their culture. As a young student, Mike Rasavanh felt ashamed to be a Tai Dam, and he attempted to blend in with his Lao peers by hiding his accent and Tai Dam ancestry. In contrast, his mother Neth continued to wear the distinctive Tai Dam attire. Because of the similarities between the two cultures, some Tai Dam parents did not mind their children marrying Lao. However, life in Vientiane disrupted traditional marriage patterns. In the past, a woman's sewing ability made her a desirable spouse in northwest Vietnam. As a rite of marriage, a bride had to offer her new relatives handmade gifts of clothing. Of particular importance were the quality and quantity of black cotton scarves a bride sewed for her mother-in-law. Black Tai women used a scarf as a shawl, baby sling, and shield from the sun. In contrast to the older generation who married in northwest Vietnam, the Tai Dam living in Vientiane could purchase readymade clothing, which deemphasized the importance of sewing ability. Instead of weaving skills, some men desired ethnically "pure Tai Dam" women as brides while living in Vientiane.[25]

Nga Baccam in Vientiane, Laos, circa 1965. Nga was part of the elder Tai Dam generation who endured hardship during the First Indochina War. After the communists defeated the French, Nga fled northern Vietnam for Laos. In 1981, Nga arrived in Iowa with her sister Sinh Baccam serving as sponsor (Nga Baccam).

The Tai Dam's dealing with these cultural tensions paled in comparison to what the group would have dealt with had they remained in Xiang Khoang. Shortly after they left, the area became a hotly contested warzone between communist and anticommunist forces. In 1990, author Timothy Castle flew over the bombed out landscape. He described the water-filled craters below as resembling thousands of shiny coins. American B-52 bombers had created many of those craters.[26] The French defeat at Dien Bien Phu permitted the Vietminh to spread into Laos, and it also intensified American involvement in stopping the spread of communism in what had been French Indochina. As U.S. military interests in the region increased, so too did American desires to learn about the peoples of Vietnam.

American researchers first began to study the Tai Dam in the late 1950s, but they too classified the Tai Dam as being isolated. Gerald Hickey, a doctoral student from the University of Chicago, described the Tai Dam as an "aloof and untouched" culture in the late 1950s. Similarly, a 1972 U.S. Army study categorized the Tai Dam as being "comparatively isolated from outside influences. Their beliefs and customs have thus been identified as similar to those of the early Thai peoples…."[27] American opinions of the Tai Dam have been informed by the political situation in North Vietnam. By the time U.S. scholars had an interest in studying the Black Tai, North Vietnam had fallen to communism, and this complicated any chance of conducting fieldwork in the northwest. Hickey had to rely on French and Thai sources housed in Paris or on Tai Dam refugees who had fled to South Vietnam.

In contrast to American scholars, ethnographer Dang Nghiem Van portrayed the Tai Dam as a people long involved in the economic and political history of Vietnam. For centuries, Dien Bien Phu served as a cultural crossroads and trade center. Merchants sold many products and caravans sometimes reached several hundred animals in size. People traded in Lao, Chinese, Vietnamese, and Burmese currencies in the Tai homeland. The Tai Dam also had political dealings with rulers from Laos, China, Vietnam, and Siam.[28] To survive among their more powerful neighbors, the Tai rulers frequently shifted their allegiances; warfare was constant.

Unfortunately, Dang Nghiem Van's research on the Tai Dam has been compromised by communist ideology. He presented the northwest as a dysfunctional region "shaken by troubles" until its liberation by the communist Democratic Republic of Vietnam. Under the leadership of the Kinh, oppressive French imperialists had been defeated at Dien Bien Phu, and the Tai had finally been joined to the nation as equals. Though all peoples in communist Vietnam were equals, backwards groups such as the Tai Dam needed communism to push them into the modern era. "Primitive" Tai Dam farming techniques had been modernized with the use of hydro-electric dams, chemical fertilizers, and metal tools. Armed with the tools of modernity, Tai farmers annually harvested two or three rice crops instead of only one as in previous years. Similarly, Tai Dam went from living under exploitation to living in a land of plenty. Inside their formerly barren homes, one now found writing desks, bookshelves, mantle lamps, radios, and other "signs of modernity." According to Dang, the modern science of the communists had also nearly eradicated malaria in the north-west, and modern medicine led to a decline in the superstitious religious beliefs of the Tai Dam.[29]

In his study of the Black Tai, Dang has constructed a communist cre-ation myth whereby the Kinh imposed order and brought progress to the chaotic northwest and its backwards peoples. Together, all minorities joined in uprisings against their French and American oppressors. Accord-ing to Dang, "The common struggle against French imperialism and then American imperialism has solidly welded together the various national-ities of Vietnam…. Economic progress, social reforms, transportation facilities, eradication of malaria—all these factors have contributed to a closer and closer national integration."[30] In this communist creation myth, the Tai Dam who fought against communism and ultimately relocated to Iowa have been removed from history.

Tai Dam folklore mentions a legendary figure named King Cobra. In the thirteenth century, King Taav Kwak governed the principality of Muoi. While visiting his people, the King overheard a *Sa* woman mock the Queen for being rude. This woman, named Nang Sor, believed she would be a better queen. Angered, the King called the *Sa* woman in for questioning, but Nang Sor stood firmly behind her derogatory statements about the Queen. Impressed by her boldness, the King took Nang Sor as a concubine, and she bore him the son who went on to become King Cobra.

As the offspring of a Tai king and a *Sa* woman, King Cobra possessed the perfect lineage. The noble blood that ran through his veins made him fit to be a great ruler whereas the wild *Sa* blood gave him the ruggedness that struck fear into his enemies. As a child, Cobra continuously confronted the slighted Queen who sought revenge. She plotted his death on at least two occasions. First, she had two soldiers lure the seven-year-old Cobra to the bottom of a hill. From the top of that hill, the soldiers hurled sharp-ened bamboo poles at the child. To their amazement, the young Cobra caught the poles out of midair. Second, rumors swirled that a golden bird rested inside of a tree of the realm. The Queen asked her husband to order the young Cobra to collect the golden bird for the glory of the kingdom. However, hidden inside that tree sat not a golden bird but a poisonous snake. Cobra's mother knew of the Queen's treachery, but her son had to follow the order of the King. Anticipating a trap, she wrapped her son's head in cloth for protection. When harvesting the so-called bird, a huge golden cobra attacked, but its fangs sank harmlessly into the boy's clothing. In the event that earned him his name, Cobra ripped out the serpent's tongue and ignorantly presented the snake to the King and his terrified officials.

About three years later, Cobra and his father traveled for diplomacy with a Vietnamese ruler just west of modern-day Hanoi. While his father met with the ruler, Cobra strolled through the town. Soon, he came upon some Vietnamese soldiers guarding their king's golden boat, which rested on the waters of the Black River. Annoyed by the child's interest, the Vietnamese troops mockingly told Cobra to leave because "you do not even have enough strength to even hold the golden paddle." Infuriated, Cobra boldly declared, "Why don't you let me try ... and you will see how the Tai people, even children, can paddle upstream in the rushing river." Amused, the soldiers humored the child by telling him he might keep the boat if he paddled it upstream. Cobra backed up his boast by feverishly paddling the boat 125 miles to his homeland of Muoi. Cobra knew the Vietnamese troops would soon find him, so he decided to hide the golden boat by anchoring it underwater at the confluence of the Nam Muoi Creek and Black River. When the soldiers located Cobra at the palace, the youngster told them that the boat had sunk. During times of sadness, Cobra raised the golden boat and paddled the Nam Muoi Creek to cheer himself up before returning it underwater. Tai Dam lore states that during times of trouble, the golden boat lifts out of the water for a brief moment; some Tai Dam swear to have seen it rise out of the water just a short time before the disastrous defeat at Dien Bien Phu.[31]

The Tai Dam are not an untouched culture. Centuries before the French and Vietnamese communists arrived, King Cobra had to engage in shrewd diplomacy with foreign powers. He allied with the Mongols to expand his kingdom of Muoi. Soon after, Vietnamese King Tran Nhan Tong feared this expansion and attacked Cobra in 1290. The Vietnamese overpowered Cobra's forces and took his father and second son hostage. King Cobra sought haven in Laos under King Kam Fong's protection, and the Lao King set aside the territory of Chiang Toong for Cobra to govern. Cobra's relatives and friends followed him there, and all dutifully served the Lao

King for many years. As thanks for their loyalty, Cobra's sons received lands and titles from King Kam Fong. During his time in Laos, Cobra did not make war on the Vietnamese on account of his father being held hostage. In 1300, King Cobra returned with great ceremony to his homeland of Muang Muoi.[32]

The Tai Dam who came to Iowa identify with King Cobra because his life so closely paralleled their experiences after the French defeat at Dien Bien Phu. They found purpose and meaning in their own hardships by referring back to their past. Like the legendary figure, the Tai Dam had faced exile at the hands of the Vietnamese, and a Lao king had granted the Tai Dam safe haven once more. Similar to their ancestor, the twentieth-century Tai Dam dutifully served the Lao monarch as soldiers and officials, and they enjoyed self-government over their refugee villages. Wing Cam envisioned himself as a modern-day King Cobra. He noted, "I could set up Chiang Toong to defend the kingdom, but we were not as successful as Prince Cobra. Once again we had to leave this lovely country considered by [us] foreigners as haven."[33] King Cobra triumphantly returned to his homeland, but the Tai Dam ended up resettling a world away in Iowa. It is from this unlikely place that some present-day Tai Dam still perform the *San Song*. The oldest son-in-law guides the spirits of those whose lives have come to an end back to the lands near Dien Bien Phu. From there, the Tai Dam journey onward to a new beginning in the village in the sky.

2

Bending the Rules
of Federal Refugee Policy

The rapidity with which the South fell to the communist North in late April of 1975 took Americans and their Vietnamese allies by surprise. The image of dozens of Vietnamese frantically swarming towards an Air America helicopter perched on a Saigon building top is etched into the collective memory of a generation. Over thirty-five years later, current Davenport resident Dau Truong, a former interpreter for the CIA's Provincial Reconnaissance Unit, emotionally recalled the impact on his life: "To me, and I think to most Vietnamese, we lost all when Saigon fell you know. And until now we still thinking about that day you know.... I have not enough vocabulary to tell you...."[1] Many Vietnamese who had cooperated with the U.S. government, including interpreters such as Truong, feared the worst. Thousands panicked, fearing a repeat of previous violence, such as the 1968 massacre by communist forces at Hue. Rumors circulated that even the multiracial children of U.S. serviceman and Vietnamese women would not be spared in the impending bloodbath. President Gerald Ford passed a controversial "Baby Lift" to spirit the youngsters out of Vietnam. The United States sought to evacuate the Vietnamese who had helped the U.S. fight the communists or worked for U.S. businesses, as well as the wives and relatives of Americans. Collectively, this group became known as the "first wave" of refugees from Indochina.

During this tumultuous summer of 1975, Governor Ray received important letters from Arthur Crisfield of USAID, President Ford, and the former Vice President of the Tai Federation Quy Baccam. Though the humanitarian impulse to assist the Tai Dam cannot be denied, other factors need explained to understand why a Midwestern governor agreed to help the Tai Dam relocate to Iowa. Ray wanted to support his friend, to gain control over a federally-dominated refugee program, and to showcase his fiscal conservative ideals. Additionally, the important role of the Tai Dam, especially Wing Cam, and their cultural background cannot be overlooked when understanding how they arrived in Iowa as a group; the process in which the Tai Dam ended up in Iowa best illustrates how a governor and refugees influenced Indochinese refugee resettlement policy in the United States.

Humanitarianism has been offered as the sole reason why Ray brought the Tai Dam to Iowa, but the story proves far more complex. The script goes something like this; after the fall of Saigon, Ray received a letter from Arthur Crisfield. Crisfield, who had worked extensively with the Tai Dam as a language instructor in Laos, outlined the plight of his friends in a touching letter. Moved by the humanitarian concern to keep

Arthur Crisfield visits Black Tai friends in Des Moines, Iowa, 1976. To help the refugees find asylum, the educator and former USAID employee wrote English language letters to American governors. Once Ray agreed to resettle the group, Crisfield provided the Governor's Task Force with cultural information on the Black Tai. After the Vietnam War, he returned to Laos and created an instructional program to help reduce accidents from unexploded ordinance, called "bombies" by the locals (Houng Baccam).

a people and a culture together, the Governor traveled to the U.S. Capitol to obtain the blessings of President Ford and the State Department to allow the Tai Dam to resettle in Iowa as a cluster. Ray created the Governor's Task Force for Indochinese Resettlement, and the first several hundred Tai Dam arrived in Iowa in November of 1975.

There is truth to this humanitarian argument. While visiting his sister in France, Crisfield learned that the Tai Dam had become refugees in Thailand. He traveled to Thailand and immediately began to contact the English language newspapers to publicize the Tai Dam's plight. Ultimately, Crisfield wrote to thirty different U.S. governors in an attempt to resettle the group in America; only Ray took the time to answer their plea for help. In this succinct yet powerful letter, Crisfield described how communism had doggedly pursued the Tai Dam from the Tai Federation to Hanoi (1952), from Hanoi to Laos (1954), and from Laos to Thailand (1975). He sent his letter on the behalf of the Tai Dam languishing on the grounds of a Buddhist religious complex which served as their refugee camp in Nong Khai, Thailand:

> For the fourth time in twenty years, they left everything behind including homes and gardens and most of their possessions to seek refuge in a free country.... Twenty years of fighting the communists has left its toll of dead fathers, uncles, brothers, and sons. Though the Tai Dam have suffered and lost everything several times over, they have not given up the hope of finding peace and freedom somewhere in the world.... On their behalf, I am appealing to your good offices to make their plea known to the people of the state of Iowa that they seek in their hearts the charity to answer this plea and sponsor a place for the Tai Dam in their communities and their businesses.[2]

Crisfield stated that the Tai Dam had working professionals among the 250 families residing at the camp; they had already put their talents to good use by aiding anticommunist objectives as soldiers in the French and Royal Lao militaries. They would contribute to Iowa's society if given the opportunity.

Crisfield also notified the Governor that the preservation of a culture was at stake. On the whole, the Black Tai had aided the communists in Vietnam, but the victors of Dien Bien Phu still sought to transform the backwards Tai Dam into "socialist men." In order to uplift them, the communists desired to strip the Tai Dam of their traditional practices. Karl Marx once called religion the opiate of the masses. Unsurprisingly, the communists looked upon Tai Dam religion with disdain. Authorities cracked down on the traditional funerary practices that had allegedly venerated nobles over the masses. New laws required the dead to be buried within two days, which conflicted with traditional Tai Dam three-day burials. In the past, mourners sometimes decorated and raised large poles to mark the burial spots of the elite, but the communists demanded the Tai Dam use simple tombstones. Sacrifices of large animals at ritual events like funerals had been labeled as wasteful. Communists spoke out against superstitious ceremonies for rainmaking, fortunetelling, and healing. Throughout the 1960s and 1970s, communist officials burned Tai texts as did some Black Tai who feared possessing them under the new government. In this environment, the numbers of Tai Dam capable of performing the *San Song* ceremony to guide the spirits of the deceased to the Village in the Sky dwindled. Government policy promoted the migration of ethnic Kinh into the traditional Tai lands of the northwest.[3] Through their exile, the Tai Dam at Nong Khai had escaped the clutches of communism and represented a bastion of traditional Tai Dam culture.

To keep a people together and preserve their culture, Ray had to bend U.S. refugee policy. Throughout the Cold War era, the U.S. government operated under a system of "calculated kindness" whereby America warmly received refugees fleeing communist regimes; individuals persecuted at the hands of those who supported U.S. foreign policy objectives were largely ignored. The Tai Dam had the anticommunist credentials to come to the United States. Unfortunately for the Tai Dam, they had fled Laos in May, but the Royal Lao Government did not fall to the Pathet Lao communists until December of 1975. Therefore, the Indochinese Migration and Assistance Act of 1975 only made provisions to support refugees from communist-controlled Vietnam and Cambodia. Ray also faced another barrier to bringing the Tai Dam to Iowa. By 1975, the State Department and Congress desired to disperse refugees across the United States to prevent locales from being overwhelmed by one ethnic group. The director of the Interagency Task Force on Indochina Refugees stated that "every effort will be made to ensure that resettlement, to the extent possible, will not be concentrated in a few enclaves and will not result in economic or social service hardship."[4] The growing tensions between natives and Cuban newcomers in Dade County, Florida, guided their decision against the cluster resettlement that Ray sought for the Tai Dam.

That summer, Ray traveled to Washington, D.C., to discuss the dispersal policy with Secretary of State Henry Kissinger and President Ford: "I thought there was a good reason for the exception and so I worked with the State Department and the White House. And I remember making the trip to talk to Henry Kissinger and then to Jerry Ford. And in the final analysis they agreed and they made the exception; and so we were able to invite the Tai Dam to come to Iowa."[5] Since the Governor had agreed to resettle this group, the State Department found a loophole that allowed the Tai Dam to obtain refugee status by taking on the classification of their ethnic rivals. A U.S. official learned that a former South Vietnamese Defense Minister also served as a Captain in the Tai Federation; in a great irony, the Tai Dam came to Iowa as Vietnamese refugees. The state of Iowa, under the leadership of Robert Ray, contracted with the State Department in September of 1975 and began to resettle the Tai Dam. It was the beginning of an odd partnership that would last thirty-five years.

President Ford and the State Department allowed Ray to bend the rules in his implementation of a state refugee resettlement program because they desperately needed the support of anyone interested in alleviating the humanitarian nightmare following America's longest war. In the weeks prior to the fall of Saigon, the State Department had refused to formulate a detailed exit strategy for their Vietnamese allies. They feared these plans would be leaked to the public, which might have caused a panic and led to a quicker collapse of South Vietnam. Only on April 22 did the Senate Judiciary Committee approve President Ford's recommendation for 150,000 refugees to be resettled in the United States. Three days later, the U.S. government began to set up four processing camps for Vietnamese refugees: Camp Pendleton in California, Eglin Air Force Base in Florida, Fort Chaffee in Arkansas, and Fort Indian Town Gap in Pennsylvania. The camps soon swelled with tens of thousands of refugees. As July approached, only 41,000 out of the 130,258 evacuees had been resettled.[6]

On July 14, 1975, Ray received a letter from his friend President Ford. The President informed Ray that a federal Interagency Task Force on Refugees had been established to aid bringing Indochinese to the United States. In addition to the voluntary agencies who traditionally relocated refugees, Ford appealed to state and local governments to expedite the process for the tens of thousands waiting in the four military camps. He outlined how states could contract with the State Department to resettle refugees. As an incentive for state and local governments, Ford notified Ray that the federal government would compensate states for the costs of resettlement. In addition to paying for Medicaid, cash assistance, and other social services, the federal government planned to pay resettlement agencies $500 per refugee resettled. Despite these incentives, very few governors offered to help. Ray was one of the few who did.

In comparison to Richard Nixon, Ray developed a much closer relationship with Ford. The two men shared Midwestern roots, moderate

President Ford and Governor Ray in the Oval Office, Washington, D.C., 1976. Through the State Department, Ford granted Ray an exemption to resettle the Tai Dam as a group in 1975. In addition to humanitarianism, Ray was doing his friend a political favor as thousands of Indochinese awaited resettlement that summer. Pictured center is the wheel of the SS *Mayaguez*, a merchant vessel that had been seized in international waters off the Cambodian coast. The ship and crew were safely recovered in May 1975. Responding to crises in Indochina marked the tenure of both men (Gerald R. Ford Presidential Library).

Republican ideals, and a love of sports. Ray once said of Ford, "He's the kind of guy you can trust your wallet with." As state chairman of the Republican Party of Iowa in the 1960s, Ray had driven Ford around the state for speeches and meetings. Ray declined the President's offer of a position as Secretary of the Interior in 1975, and one year later, Ford strongly considered Ray as a Vice Presidential running mate. Ray viewed Ford as receptive to the problems facing governors, "Jerry Ford … would sit down with me, almost like a brother, and try and help."[7] So when the President asked for assistance after the fall of Vietnam, the Governor wanted to support his friend and fellow Republican.

As Ford's letter arrived in 1975, Ray found himself on solid enough political ground to help his friend with the Indochinese crisis, but it had not been an easy climb to that political stability. While campaigning for his first bid as governor in 1968, Ray narrowly escaped death in a plane crash before his long tenure in the capitol building ever began. He explained his harrowing experience to author Jon Bowermaster: "We hit so hard the fuselage right behind where I was sitting completely broke off, and then we slid in a mud field about a half mile. The wings came off, the gas tanks came off. Talk about God wanting something to happen, we didn't hit any buildings, we didn't hit any fences, we didn't catch fire. I was knocked unconscious. The next thing I remember was waking up in the hospital."[8] Ray recorded messages for the public while hospitalized, and his devoted wife Billie played them to eager audiences of Iowans. A powerful photograph of Ray leaving the hospital on crutches with his wife by his side caught the eyes of many potential voters. Bolstered by this publicity and a great campaign theme song "Step to the Rear" by Marilyn Maye, Ray won election to his first of five consecutive terms as governor. Had he not escaped that plane crash, the Tai Dam would not be in Iowa today.

By his own admission, Ray did not feel comfortable with all of the nuances of being governor until his third term in office. At the height of the Vietnam War, Ray's first two years as governor proved the hardest. Student protests had erupted on campuses across the state. On April 30, 1970, a water fight and failed panty raid led to a standoff between University of Iowa students and the police. Days later, University President William Boyd decided to cancel the 89th annual Governor's Day ROTC Awards, fearing a repeat of the Kent State violence that had occurred just days prior. As the campus unrest continued, Ray ordered protestors to be removed from the grounds of the Old Capitol Building, and a National Guard helicopter hovered over a crowd of annoyed protestors. Though the semester did not end until May 26, President Boyd offered students the option of taking a pass/fail or their current letter grade earned in their courses as of May 3 to entice rowdy students to leave campus.[9]

Later that same year, Ray also had to deal with the Woodstock of the Midwest. In the summer of 1970, the sleepy northeast Iowa town of Wadena swelled with over 40,000 concert goers. Scheduled headliners included the Chambers Brothers, Joan Baez, Little Richard, and Mason Profit. Anxious state officials feared the drugs, sex, and violence associated with such concerts. The concert had been intended to take place in Galena, Illinois, but local officials cancelled the event, and planners moved the concert west to a farm in Wadena. Fearing the backlash another cancellation might bring, Ray decided to let the concert take place. On July 31, he appeared on stage and told the rockers to have a good but law-abiding time. Though a drug stand operated out of a U-Haul truck and "some of the elderly women in town locked their husbands up" to keep their eyes off the thousands of skinny dippers in the Volga River, the concert took place peacefully.[10] Still, Ray faced criticism from conservative Iowans for his onstage appearance and permitting the show to go on.

In those turbulent days, it is no surprise that with the exception of Ray, all Republican governors in the Midwest lost their bids for reelection in 1970. Throughout the tumultuous Vietnam War and Watergate era, Ray in the executive office remained a constant. By the time Ford reached out to the nation's governors, Ray had already served as the state's executive chief for nearly eight years and had just begun his fourth term in office. As governor in 1975, his approval rating stood at an astounding 81 percent as compared to the national average of 49. Whereas other governors may have been preoccupied with political survival, Ray found himself in a comfortable enough political position to risk bringing in refugees associated with America's most controversial war. The United States had lost the war, and Ray wanted Iowa to do its part to help out the nation, but on his own terms.

Governors enjoy being in control, yet they wielded next to no influence over U.S. refugee policy. Part of the reason why Ray formed a state resettlement agency was his desire to gain control over a federally-dominated process. Without input from governors, the federal government made the initial decision on which refugees to bring to the United States and how many. Afterwards, voluntary agencies went about the task of divvying up these refugees and resettling them. However, refugees do not resettle in the federal government, but in the states and local communities overseen by the nation's governors.

Refugees are a type of immigrant and are therefore linked to the history of immigration. From the colonial era into the nineteenth century, America had an open door immigration policy epitomized by Emma Lazarus' famous poem on the Statue of Liberty:

> Give me your tired, your poor,
> Your huddled masses yearning to breathe free,
> The wretched refuse of your teeming shore.
> Send these, the homeless, tempest-tost to me,
> I lift my lamp beside the golden door!

Yet there have always been factions interested in guarding the golden door of the nation. Nineteenth-century nativists attached the stigma of cheap labor, political radicalism, and racial inferiority onto newcomers.

U.S. immigration law matured in the nineteenth century alongside these nativist calls for restriction. On the West Coast, economic competition and racist hostility towards the Chinese emerged. In 1870s California, white workers expressed their fears through a folk song:

O workingmen dear, and did you hear
The news that's goin' around?
Another China steamer
Has been landed here in town.
Today I read the papers,
And grieved my heart full sore
To see upon the title page,
O, just "Twelve Hundred More!"

O, California's coming down,
As you can plainly see.
They are hiring all the Chinamen
And discharging you and me;
But strife will be in every town
Throughout the Pacific shore,
And the cry of old and young shall be,
"O, damn, Twelve Hundred More."[11]

Two months before congressmen passed the nation's first general immigration law, they passed the Chinese Exclusion Act of 1882. In his *Harper's Weekly* cartoon "E Pluburis Unum, Except the Chinese," Thomas Nast satirized this discriminatory legislation that banned Chinese immigration and naturalization. This ethos of restriction dominated immigration law for decades to come. From the 1920s into World War II, U.S. immigration law operated under a racist quota system that privileged Western Europeans with more admissions. While enduring a Great Depression and a World War, the preoccupied Greatest Generation had little interest in admitting foreigners. Yet World War II had witnessed the United States vanquish the virulently racist Nazi regime, and it catapulted the nation into a position of world leadership.

Sensitive to this new burden, U.S. immigration law began to loosen for the foreign policy objectives of a nation that had emerged from the ashes of World War II as a dominant power. After the catastrophic conflict, world leaders faced the daunting task of finding new homes for millions of refugees. One group presented a unique challenge. Hundreds of thousands of Holocaust survivors had no place to go; many refused to venture back to the lands from which they had been forcibly removed. Fearing the return of Jews to Poland, civilians and police launched a pogrom that killed forty-two Holocaust survivors in Kielce on July 4, 1946. In this uncertain environment, over 250,000 Jews remained under U.N. protection in Displaced Persons camps throughout Europe from 1945 to 1952. With the objective of finding homes for the Sh'erit ha-Pletah "surviving remnant" of the Holocaust, Congress passed the Displaced Persons Act of 1948. This Act became the nation's first refugee-specific legislation after the War. By 1952, over 80,000 Jews had come to the United States under the Displaced Persons Act.[12]

In the midst of a global Cold War, Congress passed the Immigration and Naturalization Act of 1965. This legislation eliminated national origins as a determining factor in admissions. Henceforth, potential newcomers were placed into one of seven preferences based on their family ties to an American citizen and possession of scarce job skills. Though linked to the history of immigration, what differentiates a refugee from an immigrant is their potential for persecution. The 1965 Act's seventh preference narrowly defined a "refugee" as a person who, "because of persecution or fear of persecution on account of race, religion, or political opinion fled communism … from any Communist or Communist-dominated country or area, or … from any country within the general area of the Middle East … and is unable or unwilling to return to such country or area on account of race, religion, or political opinion, … or are uprooted by catastrophic natural calamities … who unable to return to usual place of abode."[13] Under this law, the United States consistently favored those being persecuted by communist governments until the collapse of the Soviet Union.

Throughout most of the Cold War era, refugees fleeing communism arrived in the United States under chaotic ad hoc legislation and the controversial parole power of the executive branch. Parole came about as an answer to the Hungarian Uprising of 1956. Reform-minded Imre Nagy had taken power and sought to remove Hungary from the Soviet orbit. The United States engaged in psychological warfare by encouraging the uprising through CIA-sponsored Radio Free Europe broadcasts. Ultimately, the Soviets crushed the revolt, and despite American promises on the radio waves, the United States failed to come to the rescue of the Hungarians. In the aftermath, American policymakers tried to bring these "freedom fighters" to the United States. The nearly 200,000 Hungarians who poured into Austria and Yugoslavia could not be accommodated with the existing refugee policy. The executive branch found a solution in an obscure immigration law that allowed the attorney general to permit entry "temporarily under such conditions as he may prescribe for emergent reasons or for reasons deemed strictly in the public interest." Under this provision, President Eisenhower paroled 40,000 Hungarian refugees. Parole gave the upper hand to the president in refugee policy. With the counsel of the secretary of state, a president asked the attorney general to parole refugees, and this took power out of Congress' hands. Parole forced Congressmen to pass legislation to aid and address the citizenship status of refugees the executive branch had paroled to the United States.[14]

Throughout nearly all of Robert Ray's tenure as governor, presidents continued to lean on this parole process to compensate for the Immigration and Nationality Act of 1965's meager cap of 17,400 refugees eligible for admission under the 7th preference. After the Hungarian Uprising, the United States found itself reacting to refugee crises in Cuba and Indochina with parole and ad hoc legislation. The first wave of 133,000 Indochinese refugees from the Vietnam War came to the U.S. via parole. The president, secretary of state, and Congress rarely had time to thoroughly discuss these emergency measures, so imagine the angst of Ray and fellow governors who wielded no control over who was admitted, and who placed these refugees in their backyards.

Voluntary agencies developed in the twentieth century as a solution to bring refugees to the United States. Since the Immigration Act of 1882, American law had long forbid the admission of those likely to become public charges. Unfortunately, persecution and warfare often stripped refugees of any wealth they may have accumulated. To come to America, refugees needed a sponsor with the financial resources to get the newcomers on their feet. Therefore, the weight of sponsorship fell heavily on one individual's shoulders, which made procuring a sponsor difficult. VOLAGS eased this financial responsibility by distributing this burden among a group of people. Some VOLAGS served religious denominations, such as United States Catholic Conference, Lutheran Immigration and Refugee Services, and Hebrew Immigrant Aid Society. Other VOLAGS, such as International Rescue Committee and Tolstoy Foundation, were not religiously affiliated. Obtaining sponsors and resettling refugees quickly were some of the best attributes of the voluntary agencies' work, a critical attribute in the days of the chaotic parole of refugees. VOLAGS contracted with the State Department and obtained access to federal funds for resettling refugees.

Ray appreciated the humanitarian work of these VOLAGS, but he disliked his lack of control over them in the resettlement process. Representatives from all of the VOLAGS met in New York City and divided up the refugees for resettlement. Ideally, they based their decisions on the religious or previous family ties a refugee had to a VOLAG. Ray and governors throughout the nation lacked knowledge on the numbers of refugees to be brought into their states. Indochinese children unable to speak English could pour into a school district, but governors and public school staffers had little to no warning. VOLAGS had little accountability in the eyes of the governor. If a public official operated inefficiently, Ray might reprimand or fire them, or the public might vote this person out of office. Most irksome to Ray was how the VOLAGS signed refugees up for welfare almost upon their arrival.

A major reason for Ray's establishment of his own resettlement agency lay in his desire to infuse it with his fiscal conservative ideals. Though considered a moderate on most social issues of his day, Ray had always toed the most conservative of lines when it came to economics. Born in Des Moines in 1928, maybe this was the result of Ray's coming of age during the Great Depression or being the only son of a budget conscious accountant. In fact, fiscal conservative ideals had been the primary motivating factor for Ray to get involved in politics in the first place. Said Ray, "Always remember, a Democrat is a guy who does not know all of the answers, but is sure if he raises enough of your taxes, he can find them." From the start, he imparted his political philosophy onto the resettlement of refugees in Iowa. At his 1979 testimony before the House of Representatives on the history of Iowa's refugee program, Ray expressed his displeasure with how VOLAGS signed refugees up for welfare: "We don't like that approach. We think it is far better to start right away from the very beginning with a job and with a sponsor who understands the problems, and with an employer who also understands the problems and will work with the refugee. And we can control that through our own state agency, where we don't really have the control through a voluntary agency."[15]

Ray established his resettlement agency to promote a "work climate" over a "welfare climate." Traditionally, refugee resettlement fell under the jurisdiction of states' existing social services: the distributors of welfare. In contrast, Ray placed the Iowa resettlement initiative under the authority of Job Service. For leadership, he turned to Colleen Shearer, who had led Job Service of Iowa to the number one placement rate in the country. She agreed to become the Director of the Task Force on July 17, 1975. Keeping refugees away from "the pernicious temptation of something for nothing" by putting them to work became their crusade.[16] Bringing the Tai Dam to the Hawkeye state would be a social experiment of sorts, and Ray wanted to wrest control of the lab from the hands of federal officials and voluntary agencies.

Though a few folks are knowledgeable about Governor Ray's part, hardly anyone outside the Tai Dam community understands the crucial roles refugees such as Wing Cam played in bringing their people to the United States. This is because refugees are often portrayed as being mere

Houng Baccam and Colleen Shearer at the White House Rose Garden, circa 1976. Baccam worked for the state's refugee program for more than three decades. Shearer directed the Iowa Refugee Service Center during Ray's governorship. Baccam is in western clothing while Shearer is outfitted in traditional Tai Dam attire. Resettlement was a learning process for all parties involved (Cary Shearer).

victims and numbers to be resettled instead of political actors. Yet before the Tai Dam tried to win over the Governor of Iowa to their cause, they campaigned for admission with governors in Laos and Thailand.

Immediately after the fall of Dien Bien Phu, the Tai Dam in Hanoi planned to relocate to South Vietnam, and many soldiers took their families South, but influential leaders such as Truc Van Lo, San Van Lou, Sinh

Van Hoang, and La Rasavanh discussed the alternative of going to Laos instead. They anticipated an easier transition to Laos because of cultural and linguistic similarities with the Lao. Representatives Binh Baccam and Trong Van Cam traveled to Xiang Khoang Province to persuade Governor Sai Kham to allow the Black Tai asylum.[17]

Governor Sai Kham permitted the Tai Dam entry into Laos because he shared with them an allegiance to the French and a hatred of the Vietnamese. Sai Kham descended from a royal family who once ruled the Phuan Kingdom located at Xiang Khoang, but regional conflict had devastated Phuan by the nineteenth century. In the 1820s, Sai Kham's great grandfather Prince Noi found himself in the middle of a clash between the Kingdoms of Vientiane and Siam. During the conflict, Prince Anou, the defeated ruler of Vientiane, took refuge in Xiang Khoang as the Siamese pursued him. Fearing the might of the invading army, Prince Noi turned Anou over to the Siamese who ultimately tortured and executed him. Sai Kham bore the weight of the treason his relative had committed. Over a century later in Vientiane, the saying "false like a Phuan" circulated. The Lao nobility of Luang Prabang accorded minimal respect to the weak royal family of Phuan, so Sai Kham turned to the French who seemed more likely to recognize his family's status. Sai Kham and the Tai Dam seeking refuge shared the same ally in the French, but perhaps more importantly, the two shared a common enemy: the Vietnamese.

Resembling a young Hannibal being taught to hate Rome, Sai Kham grew up listening to his father tell stories about their ancestors' mistreatment at the hands of the despised Vietnamese. Noi and Anou had been vassals to Minh Mang: the Emperor of Annam. For turning Anou over to the Siamese enemy, the Emperor called Noi to Annam to explain his betrayal. Before arriving in Hue, soldiers captured Noi and took him to the Emperor in a cage. Prince Noi and his family remained there as political prisoners where they suffered greatly. Guards buried Sai Kham's grandfather up to the head in sand, and ultimately, the emperor of Annam executed his great grandfather Prince Noi in 1831. As he came of age, Sai Kham continued to hate the Vietnamese. While studying as a college student in Hanoi in 1934, he refused to associate with the Vietnamese and gravitated towards the French. In 1947, the Vietminh killed his brother, an officer in the French military. When his 102-year-old father passed away just two years before the Tai Dam sought asylum, Sai Kham fulfilled his father's longtime wish to be laid to rest at Kang Na Dau, the site where Prince San had massacred all of the Vietnamese residing in Xiang Khoang in a 1830s revolt.[18]

Unsurprisingly, Sai Kham fiercely opposed Vietnamese expansion into Xiang Khoang during his governorship. In Sai Kham, the Tai Dam found a person sympathetic to their suffering at the hands of the Vietnamese communists; this helped the Tai Dam find sanctuary in Xiang Khoang in the mid–1950s, but they only remained there for about a year and a half because it was on the frontline of the growing military conflict in Laos. This military unrest coupled with a lack of access to good land resulted in the Tai Dam's migration to the relative safety of Vientiane. They rebuilt their lives in the capitol, but the communist menace eventually surfaced once more.

Prime Minister Souvanna Phouma had long tried to play a neutralist role between the communists and their Vietnamese allies and the rightists and their American allies, but the escalating conflict resulted in the erosion of the neutralists' position. By May of 1975, the Tai Dam felt as if the Pathet Lao had gained the upper hand. Tanks appeared in the streets without government permission. On May 9, 1975, communist demonstrators marched through Vientiane. The Pathet Lao denounced leading political and military officials and brought them before people's court to admit their alleged crimes against the Lao people. For the Tai Dam leadership, this demonstration and the flight of an anticommunist general from Vientiane created a growing sense of unease. Apparently, Phouma had lost a grip on the situation. Twenty years after their first exodus out of the Tai Federation, the Black Tai prepared to flee the specter of communism once more.[19]

With great foresight, Wing Cam had overseen the establishment of the Black Tai village of Nong Pen. Kong Le, a paratrooper in the Royal Lao military, launched a coup in 1960. This political unrest in Vientiane led Wing Cam to think to himself, "If it happened again, some kind of disaster, where should the Tai Dam go? What should the Tai Dam do? The idea of building a Tai Dam village closer to the Mekong formed...." As the National Director of Rural Public Works, Cam witnessed the corruption of Lao government officials firsthand, but he never considered himself to be corrupt. However, he decided to engage in corruption to enhance the safety of his people in Laos. Cam recalled, "I took sheet metal from American stock to build the village of Nong Pen ... without any authorization without any orders. The Lao were corrupt already, so how could they denounce my corruption: my corruption for my people?"[20]

Located about twelve miles southeast of Vientiane and just over a mile away from the Mekong River border between Laos and Thailand, Nong Pen had been created as a convenient escape route. Over time, Nong

Pen's Black Tai villagers developed friendly trade relations with the inhabitants of Nong Khai, Thailand. Frightened by the political unrest in the capitol, Cam left Vientiane for Nong Pen on May 9, 1975. From there, Cam, San Van Lou, and T'aoz M'eui met Thai officials to discuss how the Tai Dam might legally find sanctuary in Thailand. A sympathetic frontier police major had been knowledgeable of the circumstances behind the group's flight from northwest Vietnam. The policeman agreed to allow the Tai Dam to pass into Thailand, and he offered several Tai Dam families a temporary place in his home. After these fruitful negotiations, Wing Cam and the other Tai Dam raced back to Vientiane to communicate the escape route to others on May 10. At the urging of their leaders, the Black Tai fled across the Mekong River during the commotion of Laos' National Day celebrations on Sunday, May 11, 1975.[21]

Iowa Tai Dam Timeline

1952
The French airlift anticommunist Tai Dam to Hanoi.

1954
After the fall of Dien Bien Phu, the Tai Dam
relocate to Xiang Khoang, Laos.

1955
Tai Dam have left Xiang Khoang for Vientiane, Laos.

May 1975
Tai Dam flee Laos for Nong Khai, Thailand.

November 1975
The first Tai Dam arrive in Iowa.

Houng Baccam and most other Tai Dam fondly remembered life in Laos until the communist menace grew in strength. Abruptly leaving what had become their second home was not easy. The Tai Dam had earned key positions in the Royal Lao military, private enterprise, and their children obtained schooling: "They considered us as Lao people.... No discrimination.... We were happy and we considered it as our own country, and then the communists came in 1975. And we were afraid. The communists were doing the same business as they do in our country. Kill the officers and the rich people and so on. We fled again to Nong Khai, Thailand." As a young teenager, Mike Rasavanh initially protested his father La's decision to leave Vientiane and join up with Wing Cam at Nong Pen:

> In May I came home from school. He gathered all of us family and kids and he said to us we are going to go up to the countryside and go now. We cannot take anything

with us. It kind of gave me some red flags. I said what is going on ... why can't I change my school cloths to play clothes.... I did not want to get my uniform dirty for the next day. My dad said no you go right now just leave everything ... and I said no. What happened? At fourteen you want to know. My dad just quietly told me the situation in Laos is not good. The communists are going to come and get us. My dad said, "If I do not leave now they are going to kill me. I won't end up on that list." And so I didn't say anything; I just followed him. We got into his jeep, and we drove to the countryside.[22]

After arriving in Nong Pen, La Rasavanh began to help orchestrate the escape into Thailand.

Houng Baccam, then a thirty-four-year-old billing clerk at Shell Oil and owner of a four bedroom brick house in Vientiane, remembered the Lao calling their Tai Dam cousins "crazy" for planning to turn their backs on comfortable lives in Laos. Even if the Pathet Lao took over the nation, most Lao anticipated an easy peace. Many supporters of the Royal Lao Government voluntarily turned themselves in after the nation fell to the communists in December of 1975. Houng recounted, "They did not understand communism. We had the experience" dealing with communism in northwest Vietnam. Sadly, time proved the Tai Dam leadership correct in their decision to flee. Tens of thousands of Lao believed they were to go away to a seminar for weeks. Weeks turned to months and months turned to years. Undernourished and overworked, many never came back; even the deposed King Sissavang Vatthana died under mysterious circumstances while at seminar. This harsh treatment has hindered the healing processes in Laos to this very day. Some Tai Dam in Iowa carry the scars of seminar too.[23]

As time wore on, escape from Laos grew in difficulty, as explained by Dara Rasavanh. Her brother made the crossing in 1975. The bold young man aided people crossing the Mekong River, but one day, the communists captured him: "My mom would not leave the country without him. They took him to northern Laos ... and we never heard from him. And finally in 1978, someone came and told my parents that he died. So my dad decided to come [to Iowa]. In 1979 when we came, we believed that he had died." When Dara took the same path as her future husband Mike, the journey across the Mekong River had exponentially grown in danger. As a twelve-year-old girl, she vividly remembered the experience: "Our family was shot at, but we made it. There were people that I believe died. But we were in the middle of the river already.... They had guards all along the river border and people died every day. That is why the Mekong River was called the River of Blood. There were lots of people who died there."[24] The Tai Dam who fled into Thailand in May of 1975 experienced an easier journey across the Mekong, but they faced the difficult challenge of finding legal sanctuary and building a refugee camp in Thailand.

As the first Tai Dam began to cross into Thailand, Wing Cam, Dr. Thu Van Cam, and La Rasavanh met with Governor Kamphol Klinsukhol of Nong Khai to plead for asylum on Sunday May 11, 1975. Throughout their negotiations with the police major and the Governor of Nong Khai, Cam tried to gain sympathy for the Tai Dam by focusing on their pan-Thai and historic connections. The Governor blamed French colonialism for the separation of the Black Tai from their Thai relatives. By the nineteenth century, the rulers of Siam/Thailand had sought to unite all Tai peoples under their rule, but the French had always been there to block that objective. By the mid nineteenth century, raiders from southern China had swept into Tai Dam country and plundered their way across the region. Known as Black, Yellow or Red Flags based off the standards they carried into battle, these bandits sought plunder and control over the opium trade. During the 1880s, Siam attempted to gain influence over the Twelve Tai Principalities by quelling the widespread banditry in the region. In 1882, Thailand's King Rama V had provided Wing Cam's great grandfather-in-law refuge from these marauders. Cam asked for the same. Swayed by Cam's shrewd diplomacy, the sympathetic Governor allowed the Tai Dam safe haven in Thailand because he "attached especial consideration of the miserable situation of people of the same national origin, separated since the arrival of the French."[25] The Governor set aside a Buddhist temple called Wat Phranou for the group who became refugees once again.

Dinh VanLo, a young man at the time, poignantly recalled those miserable days at Nong Khai: "All I remember in the camp was death as a neighbor, hunger as a friend, and hopelessness as a future ... it was like being in a sinking ship, and you got to go down." This makeshift refugee camp served the Buddhist community as a graveyard. For a people who believed in the power of returning spirits, this mortuary environment mortified them. The Red Cross, Foundation of Saint Paul and Saint Vincent, World Vision, and social services of Thailand had supported the Tai Dam at Nong Khai until the UN began assistance. During those first chaotic days, the Tai Dam packed into Buddhist temples or slept outdoors until more stable tent-like shelter had been completed. The Thai Royal Princess Galyani Vadhana visited to boost their spirits, but it was a difficult transition for the many elites at the camp such as Houng Baccam: "We were used to living in brick houses, driving cars, and living good lives in

Laos. Then when you come there you are living in a shelter with a [tiny] place like this.... The Thai government did not let you out of camp."[26]

At Nong Khai, females focused on providing some semblance of home and food for their families in the camp. In an attempt to gain privacy, women hung curtains between their section of the shelter and other families. To cook meals, women used makeshift wood burning stoves at the base of each tent. As an eleven-year-old girl, the experience of becoming a refugee forced Somphong Baccam to grow up fast. Being the eldest child, her parents charged her with getting her siblings to a bomb shelter in case of an emergency during the family's last months in Laos. She took on adult roles at Nong Khai as well. The Tai Dam needed to hustle to supplement their small rations. While men hunted and children scrounged for resources, Som helped her mother Em Quang earn an income at the local Thai market. Every morning at 5 a.m., they paid a bicyclist to peddle them into town. Mrs. Quang bought foodstuffs from local farmers at wholesale prices, and then she hustled to make money at the local flea market until well into the afternoon. Som reflected on her mother's hard work: "She would have a little basket with plastic [mat] and cutting board and a knife. Every day that is what she took with her ... and she would display on a plastic mat, because she did not even have a table, out in front of the sidewalk and she would put meat or vegetables, whatever she got real cheap, and sell it and make her money that way. That is how we survived being in Thailand for five months." While her mother sold items, Som earned a small income by doing dishes for a local soup vendor. Although she took on adult roles, the young girl still feared being kidnapped while at Nong Khai. Some locals had attempted to abduct two Tai Dam boys. Had their abductors succeeded, these children would have been destined for the sex trade.[27]

While the women focused on food, the men concentrated on the political situation. The Tai Dam males established governorship roles over the camp in the form of committees on security, sanitation, food distribution, education, and foreign relations. The men also had fears as retold by Houng Baccam: "In our camp, we were afraid the communists would come in and sabotage. So we have to make an around the clock watching. We assigned each family to come such an hour to be around." The Tai Dam oral histories conflict as to whether or not the Thai government offered them permanent asylum. Fear of communism and a strong desire to stay together as a group motivated them to seek resettlement abroad. This fear was communicated in a letter former Vice President Quy Baccam sent to nations of the free world in his quest to obtain asylum: "We fought

Tai Dam dancers at the refugee camp in Nong Khai, Thailand, circa 1975. Standing from left to right are Moui Baccam, Kim Baccam, Yenchay Baccam, Luen Baccam, Bounmy Cam, Soa Baccam. Sitting from left to right are Om Baccam, Gnaan Baccam, Vone Baccam, Tiengkham Baccam, Miu Lu, Sommay VanLo. Watching these dancers boosted the refugees' morale. Traditional Tai Dam dancers are still active in Iowa. A troupe recently performed for school students in Shreveport, Louisiana (Sommay VanLo).

against the communists in Vietnam and Laos. We remain their eternal enemies whom they have sworn to exterminate. Under the communist regime the acts of people's courts remain valid for three generations. If we remain in Laos, we will be dispersed, imprisoned, condemned or tortured to death...."[28]

Dinh VanLo emphasized the Tai Dam's philosophy of staying together: "When we left Vietnam, we told each other never leave without your family. Always go in a group. We kept saying that."[29] The Tai Dam did not want to live in Thailand with a communist neighbor, and they feared Thailand itself might fall to communism. As a result, the Black Tai leadership worked diligently to leave Nong Khai as a cluster. On their behalf, Crisfield wrote letters to thirty governors seeking assistance, and he sent an English version of Quy's moving letter to the nations of Australia, Canada, the United Kingdom, and the United States in July of 1975. Additionally, Wing Cam raised funds to send two Tai Dam doctors to France to lobby for asylum.

As the leader of the Tai Dam at Nong Khai, Cam played a pivotal role in campaigning for resettlement abroad. He traveled to Bangkok and knocked at the doors of the United Nations and the U.S. and French embassies. American officials told him that only Vietnamese refugees were being accepted at that time as Laos had yet to fall to communism. In a meeting with the First Secretary of the U.S. Embassy, Wing Cam argued that the Tai Dam must be included as Vietnamese refugees since they originally hailed from Vietnam.[30] Soon thereafter, Robert Ray met with President Ford and Kissinger to obtain an exemption to bring the Tai Dam to Iowa. The American Embassy designated the Tai Dam as refugees that September.

The Tai Dam actively mobilized their resources and then weighed their options for relocating abroad. Early on, the potential resettlement on an Oregon farmer's land presented itself, but this opportunity never materialized. Then, the Iowa opportunity arose. The well-connected Tai Dam who had served both the French and the United States in Southeast Asia had the option of going to either nation. Som Baccam's parents argued over where to relocate. Her father wanted to wait for an opportunity to resettle in France since he had served with the French military, but Em Quang had grown tired of traveling to the market and hustling for food. She dug in, and her husband agreed to go to Iowa. Mike Rasavanh also remembered the circumstances behind his father's decision to resettle in the United States over France:

> One day, he called us up my two brothers my two sisters … and my dad asked all of us where do we want to go. Of course in Laos you study French so all of us wanted to go to France except my older sister…. So four of us said we want to go to France and my sister said no I want to go to America, and my dad said ok we will go to America. I was disappointed because I was studying French and looking forward to going to France after high school…. I asked him why you choose one vote to four; it is supposed to be majority rules right? My dad said this, I could never forget, "France is going to be socialist very soon, and I do not like that. If I go to die, I want to die in a free country. And the only country that I know is going to be free is America. That is the only country in the world that will offer us freedom. I am tired of running away."[31]

Hundreds of Tai Dam who had connections to the French war effort went to France, and an automobile company sponsored some to work. However, most of the Tai Dam then at Nong Khai came to Iowa as part of the 1,200 Ray had agreed to resettle in his first two-year contract with the State Department.

Family separation resulted as an unintended consequence of their resettlement from Thailand. Living in two free countries, at least the Iowa

Tai Dam had the ability to contact loved ones in France, which eased the pain of separation. Sadly, the Iowa Tai Dam were unable to communicate with loved ones in communist-controlled Vietnam and Laos. Some of their relatives who had gone to South Vietnam did not fare as well. Soldiers like Bao Lo Cam and Rang Baccam spent years in reeducation camps. The Tai Dam also lost communication with friends and family who had not been sent to reeducation camps. Not until the late 1980s did a few Black Tai from Iowa begin to visit loved ones in Vietnam. This separation made them appreciate all the more how the Iowa opportunity prevented further breakup of families who came to the United States.

The Tai Dam's desire to stay together motivated leaders like Wing Cam to campaign tirelessly with Thai and American officials. The Black Tai had stuck together after leaving Vietnam for Laos in 1954. For over twenty years, they lived in their own villages under their own local administration. A rallying cry had been to never leave family behind. Over the course of two decades, their shared experience as refugees had only strengthened their bond. It made sense that they sought to leave Thailand as a community. Had the Black Tai not come from anticommunist stock, they would have never set foot in Iowa. However, their falling on the right side of the United States' calculated kindness fails to fully explain how the Tai Dam ended up in the American Midwest; it is equally important to acknowledge the refugees' role in prompting the state of Iowa to get involved in the refugee resettlement business. They orchestrated their escape, and they diligently campaigned for resettlement abroad. In the case of the Tai Dam, refugees must be recognized as more than just pawns and statistics in refugee policy histories. When one looks at the U.S. admissions numbers for 1975, only 300 non-ethnic Lao refugees are listed as coming from Laos, but 633 Tai Dam left Laos for Iowa under the Vietnamese quota.[32] The Tai Dam's important role in creating this inaccurate statistic demonstrates how misleading it is to view them as just a number.

3

The Growing Pains of the Iowa Refugee Service Center

The Governor's Task Force, which later became the Iowa Refugee Service Center, made many mistakes before it matured into a successful resettlement agency. Initially, the Task Force found itself at odds with other voluntary agencies charged with resettling Southeast Asian refugees, particularly the United States Catholic Conference. Part of the problem arose because the Governor's work-first philosophy disparaged the practices of the other VOLAGS. This very philosophy led to an unflattering review of the state's program by the federal Department of Health, Education, and Welfare. The state also did a poor job of understanding the ethnic rivalry between the Tai Dam and the Vietnamese during the early years of the project. Over time, the Iowa Refugee Service Center repaired its relationship with the other VOLAGS. The state's work with the Tai Dam became a unique model of success referenced by others involved with resettlement, especially as the numbers of refugees joining welfare rolls increased throughout late 1970s America.

After Ray designated Colleen Shearer as the head of his Task Force for Indochinese Resettlement, she put together a small team that brought the first group of Tai Dam to Iowa. Before finding a position as an employer relations specialist, Jack Spear had served as a clerk typist in the Army between the Korean and Vietnam Wars. The native of Perry, Iowa, remembered his less than formal appointment to the Task Force: "Now how I got onto the program I am not quite sure. My boss called me in one afternoon, and he said you are going to California tomorrow with Colleen Shearer, and you are going to help her with a refugee project."[1] The next day, Shearer, her secretary Jill Qualm, and Spear traveled to San Clemente,

California. After spending the night in the "Western White House," the small crew traveled to Camp Pendleton to meet with some refugee resettlement officials.

Spear remembered the layout at Pendleton as "a series of these deep gullies ... but in almost every one of these areas there were tent cities of different ethnics. They did not intermingle the different ethnic groups" who had been rivals in Southeast Asia.[2] He saw soldiers off in a distance practicing maneuvers, and he watched a Catholic mass for Vietnamese refugees. Somphong Baccam, a young teen refugee at the time, recalled the camouflage tent cities too. Workers in one tent served out meals at designated times, another tent housed recreational activities such as ping pong, and a woman taught English out of another. However, Baccam best remembered her time at Pendleton because she began to watch Donnie and Marie on her favorite TV show *The Osmonds*.

At Pendleton, Shearer, Qualm, and Spear spent a few days learning the basics of resettlement. Before this project, Spear had never heard of the Tai Dam, "We just didn't have any real idea what we were getting into."[3] For early assistance, the Task Force had been in communication with Department of Emergency Services officials from Washington State. Before Governor Ray decided to relocate the Tai Dam to Iowa, Governor Daniel Evans had resettled 500 Vietnamese refugees by the early summer of 1975. Using the Washington program as a guide, Ray initially decided to bring in a similar number of Tai Dam. Shearer linked up with Washington officials to discuss policy while at Camp Pendleton. From the Washington experience, Task Force members learned the importance of lining up sponsors before refugees arrived in-state, and the important role of the media in promoting resettlement.

After Shearer, Spear, and Qualm returned to Iowa from Camp Pendleton, the Task Force added three more members in Richard Freeman, Tomas Muñoz, and Somsak Saythongphet. Freeman finished his studies at Drake University and soon took a position at Job Service. With his student deferment gone, Freeman's draft number got called soon after he graduated: "Some people thought we should not have been in Vietnam. I probably was as much on that perspective as anybody, but at the same time, if your country calls you, you are supposed to serve. So I did." As an Army combat interrogator, his experience working with Vietnamese allies made him a strong supporter of refugee resettlement: "I knew from my own experience over there that there were a great number of Vietnamese, like the Tai Dam, who had become refugees through no choice of their own and had been very supportive of America's attempts to establish democracy in their country ... and when we just walked away from Vietnam, the country decided enough was enough, we just did not want to send any more of our young men and women over there. I really felt like some of those people were abandoned, and we morally and ethically should give them our support.... I had a very strong feeling about that."[4] When his service in the Vietnam War ended, Freeman returned to his position at Job Service and soon joined the Task Force.

In addition to Freeman, Tomas Muñoz and Somsak Saythongphet became members of the Task Force by August of 1975. After graduating from Drake University with a journalism degree, an acquaintance introduced Muñoz to Colleen Shearer. At this meeting, Muñoz accepted Shearer's offer to join the team as a recruiter of sponsors for the Tai Dam. Muñoz, a Mexican American, tried to "pass" while growing up in Valley Junction, Iowa, "I don't have an accent, and I didn't want to have an accent because I wanted to be like everyone else: white."[5] Later encounters with racism shattered his illusion of being white. By the time he joined the Task Force, Muñoz had been involved in the Chicano movement and was an advocate for civil rights. Helping refugees establish new lives in Iowa fit his personal interests. Shearer assigned Muñoz the job of procuring sponsors for the Tai Dam.

In September of 1975, the Task Force faced the challenge of finding people to help out refugees from America's most controversial war. Many Iowans did not make a distinction between the Vietnamese communist enemies and the incoming Tai Dam. As explained by Jack Spear, "There were some people that were grumbling about refugees, not a lot, but the Vietnam War was a real divisive issue and some people would make some snide comment that I was working with the refugees." Some of the opponents wrongly "felt that everybody that was an Asian was an enemy. Actually, these people were friends. They had supported the American war effort."[6]

Just a few months prior to the Tai Dam's arrival, an August 1975 poll of 600 Iowans showed that 51 percent opposed bringing more Vietnam War refugees to the United States. However, 59 percent of Iowans responded that they would welcome refugees living in Iowa. Young adults residing in urban areas were most likely to support resettlement. Iowans in favor of bringing in more refugees cited humanitarian principles and the need to help out former allies as the most important foundations for their opinion. For some, the need to help out American allies went hand in hand with a sense of war guilt. This war guilt surfaced in the response of the Rev. Delbert Terry of United Methodist Church in Mediapolis, Iowa:

"We made a mistake, what can we do to make some kind of redress? As a symbol, perhaps, we should be able to extend ourselves for them. We extended ourselves in destructive fashion for so many years."[7] Appealing to humanitarian principles and the guilty consciences of Iowans assisted Task Force members in procuring sponsors to aid the Tai Dam. The state targeted religious, civic, and business groups to lend a hand. Muñoz distributed many notices, but at first, he received few replies. For his next round of flyers, he notified potential sponsors that they would receive funding to offset the expenses of resettling refugees. This information led to greater response.

To the great advantage of Iowa's resettlement program, Margaret McDonald, then a co-chair of the Iowa Republican Party, notified state officials about the presence of a well-educated and English-speaking ethnic Lao in Iowa. Somsak Saythongphet attended Sac City High School as a foreign exchange student before graduating with a biology degree from Iowa State University. After earning a master's degree in education, Somsak returned to Laos as an educator. He worked for USAID before returning to Iowa as a refugee. Saythongphet became an indispensable member of the Task Force. Shearer described him as "the perfect cultural bridge; we have many who can interpret the language, but only one who can interpret the cultures in both directions"[8]

For the second time, Shearer and other members of the Task Force traveled to California in October of 1975. The Task Force greeted the first 300 Tai Dam who had arrived at Camp Pendleton carrying all of their possessions in cardboard boxes and garbage bags. In addition to Saythongphet, Faluang Baccam, an agronomist with English-language skills, served as an interpreter. The Task Force faced immense challenges while at Pendleton. They interviewed refugees and grouped closest relatives with the most appropriate sponsors. Each pairing increased in difficulty as the state lost flexibility in matching refugees to sponsors. Shearer explained these difficult yet memorable nights, "We talked ourselves hoarse and shuffled and reshuffled papers—only to repeat the same process the next evening because after calling the sponsors the next day there were inevitable changes." Dick Freeman remembered how the Tai Dam's arrival in California put a great jolt of energy into the team because it put human faces to the job to be done: "I hardly knew what a refugee was when I got asked to participate in this. It was a good educational experience for individuals that were on the team at that time.... It was a good eye-opener as to exactly who they were ... what the size of their families were, and what their hopes and aspirations were."[9]

After this twelve day crunch, the Task Force traveled by car to meet another group of Tai Dam at Fort Chaffee, Arkansas. Wing Cam traveled with the team to help greet the other 320 Tai Dam in early November. In appreciation for helping them flee communist persecution, the group at Fort Chaffee held a traditional celebration to honor the Iowans. Shearer and Jill Qualm crafted makeshift Tai Dam costumes by covering their blue jeans in black cloth, and Tai Dam females ornamented paper pates to serve as fans for a traditional dance. At Fort Chafee, the Task Force repeated the process followed at Camp Pendleton. They learned the camp's standard operating procedure, interviewed refugees, and matched them with sponsors.

Jack Spear traveled to Camp Pendleton, but he could not stay for the duration of the trip. After about one week, he returned to his home in Iowa to attend to his young children, one of whom was sick. Shearer had directed Spear to man the phones in her personal office in Iowa. Though his friends took jabs at him for his being privileged to use the boss' office, Spear had the unenviable task of telling Iowa do-gooders that they had signed up to do more good than they had anticipated: "Most people who volunteered were thinking in terms of the nuclear family: mom, dad, and a couple of kids. Ha, these groups who would come—there were twelve, thirteen, fourteen members of a family we were attempting to resettle!" Sponsors fresh off the phone with the Task Force in California and Arkansas who had learned the true size of the family to be sponsored called Spear to vent, "I would have to take their call and talk them down … we did not have any wiggle room at all for sponsors thinking oh well I cannot deal with a group of that size" because the last sponsor had been procured in the final days before the team left for California.[10] The Task Force returned to Iowa on November 16, 1975. The following day, three planeloads brought the first group of 300 Tai Dam to Des Moines.

The Tai Dam traveled via bus from the Des Moines International Airport to Camp Dodge in Johnston, Iowa. Refugees first met with their Iowa sponsors at this National Guard military post. The Tai Dam and their sponsors had been assigned numbers, and those with matching numbers were paired up with one another. Tomas Muñoz disliked the use of Camp Dodge. Though no Black Tai ever mentioned it to him, Muñoz sensed the police and military presence created uneasiness among the refugees, "They were not very fond of the police to begin with because the police were sometimes worse than the crooks" in Southeast Asia.[11] Shearer preferred to resettle large planeloads of refugees through Camp Dodge because the raw emotion of hundreds of refugees and Iowans meeting for the first time produced great publicity for the resettlement program and had the potential to yield future sponsors. Additionally, Shearer wanted both Tai Dam and Iowans to realize they were not alone in the obstacles to be faced in the coming days.

The state of Iowa's resettlement program ran on the foundation of keeping refugees off welfare; the Task Force's early focus on the Tai Dam eased the logistics of the state's resettlement project. Ray reasoned it would be easier to place one ethnic group into the work force. According to the Governor: "We decided that as long as we were taking x number, why take a few from Vietnam, a few from Cambodia, why a few from Laos. Why not take them from a specific area. That way they'd be compatible. That's how we got mostly Tai Dam."[12] Just days after their arrival, the Task Force put the Tai Dam to work. They wanted zero refugees on welfare by the time federal funding for the refugee program ended. The Task Force, like the other VOLAGS contracted with the State Department, received $500 per refugee resettled in 1975. Initially, the Task Force released $200 per refugee to sponsors; this $200 was to be used for basic necessities such as food, clothing, and shelter. The state held the other $300 in a reserve fund to be used in emergency situations. In case of unforeseen problems, Task Force members inquired whether or not potential sponsors had safety networks, usually in the form of churches. The sponsor and their safety networks formed the first line of defense in keeping the newcomers off public assistance. Sometimes, the Task Force removed Tai Dam from welfare and used emergency funds to provide short-term aid.

Keeping refugees off welfare and good sponsorship went hand in hand. The federal government and Iowa described sponsorship as a moral commitment. Sponsors were to assist the state in finding employment for the Tai Dam. The Task Force wanted Iowans to teach the Tai Dam that real Americans did not use welfare. Staying off cash assistance represented a form of assimilation to Iowa culture and work values. Tai Dam who lacked English skills found employment in factories that required little to no English language ability. Employers demonstrated job duties in front of refugees who then went to work. The Task Force reasoned that refugees could best learn the English language on the job. For assistance, the state had a Tai Dam language hotline. Jack Spear remembered one refugee calling the hotline from Keokuk, Iowa. This man worked as a fish gutter, and he called to say he was quitting due to exhaustion. When the Task Force called his employer, they learned that his boss had been trying to tell the man to slow down his frenetic work-pace.[13] The Task Force paired those without English language skills with Tai Dam who did. So long as one Tai Dam spoke English, this person could serve as an interpreter for fellow Tai Dam coworkers. The Task Force approved of the Tai Dam enrolling in English language classes only if they did not conflict with their full-time work schedule.

Shearer also reasoned that employment positively influenced refugees' mental health. First, she wanted all heads of household employed. Next, the state linked up secondary wage earners with job openings. For females and the elderly, Shearer hoped to create cottage industries for ethnic handcrafts. Getting driver's license materials translated became a high priority so the Tai Dam had transportation to jobs. With hard work, the Tai Dam would gain self-worth and the respect of Iowans. She reasoned, "Busy hands make happy people."[14]

By the end of 1975, the state had resettled seventy-seven families for a grand total of 633 Tai Dam. In less than six months, the Task Force found employment for every designated head of household, and seventy secondary wage earners supplemented family income. The state placed the Tai Dam into a myriad of occupational fields: auto mechanics, sewing, clerical, cleaning, restaurant, farmhand, carpentry, construction, domestics, and many more. Though Iowa used a cluster resettlement of the Tai Dam as opposed to the federal government's dispersal policy, the Tai Dam were scattered across the state of Iowa. The group lived in thirty-six of the state's ninety-nine counties.[15] The Task Force located in Des Moines, Iowa, used Job Service offices to reach Tai Dam throughout the entire state. When sponsors learned a refugee intended to sign up for welfare, they were to discourage them and notify the Task Force.

Similarly, social service employees had been told to alert the Task Force when any Tai Dam registered for aid. Shearer received a computer printout with the names of each refugee on cash assistance and then attacked each case accordingly. One printout showed the names of refugees drawing assistance. Beside each name, Shearer wrote whether or not the circumstances justified the family's use of welfare. Next to the names of three family members Shearer noted to Governor Ray's aide Dennis Nagel: "These are the three I told you about. They needed no welfare; several have jobs; they live in two of Colacino's *very nice* apartments; head of one of families has a new car." The linkage between finding a refugee work and the evaluation of a sponsor is evident in Shearer's notes: "This sponsor was just trying to get all the dollars he could get for his refugee family. They could have made it without welfare. Sponsor should have known better," appeared next to one refugee's name. Other notes revealed how the removal of one sponsor led to the desired effect of the removal of the refugee family from the cash assistance printout. One Tai Dam had a solid job at John Deere in Waterloo, Iowa, fall through because of calcium deposits on his lungs. Later, he found employment at Gerald Sulky Company. Shearer had mixed feelings on this Tai Dam's sponsor who had been "more apathetic and less creative" in keeping his charge employed. All refugees receiving assistance needed to be registered to work with Job Service and to accept any job offered. One refugee man focusing on education instead of employment told a *Wall Street Journal* writer, "They chew me out every day for being on that list."[16]

On this printout, one finds the name of Un Van Quang of Story City, Iowa. In her notes, Shearer designated him as being in need of financial aid because he had a broken leg. Though nearly all the Tai Dam in the United States had resettled in Iowa because of their own campaigning and the generosity of Governor Ray, they lived in counties throughout the entire state of Iowa. In November of 1975, the Quangs represented the lone Tai Dam family in the small and predominantly white community. The absence of fellow Tai Dam caused Un Van Quang to grow lonely while in Story City. He desperately wanted to communicate with a Tai Dam friend in Ames, but he could not speak English to the phone operator. While his wife and children attended church one Sunday, this loneliness drove Un Van Quang in February of 1976 to get on a bicycle and pedal all the way to Ames, Iowa. Once in town, he linked up with his friend and enjoyed good company for the day. Late into the evening, Un still had not returned from his trip, causing his wife and children to worry. His family learned from their sponsor that Un had been hit by a drunk driver while on his return ride home. He broke his leg and hip, and spent days in intensive care. Un had never wanted to come to the U.S. This accident only compounded his frustrations trying to adapt to a new culture, and it caused the family great hardship.[17] The state of Iowa had tried to use cluster resettlement to combat the kind of loneliness that compelled Un to bicycle all the way to Ames in the middle of winter.

In addition to using Job Service offices, the Task Force sent workers throughout the state of Iowa. Initially, the workers interviewed heads of households, but they interviewed more family members in future visits. Tomas Muñoz fondly remembered making these trips with fellow team member Somsak Saythongphet: "Somsak and I were traveling around the state, we would be behind [schedule] in some cases … as soon as we walked in I could smell food, the aroma ahhhh, and we had just ate and my god they had everything on the floor, like a blanket in the living room.

The Quang family celebrating Christmas, Story City, Iowa, 1976. On the couch left to right are Un, Em, and Somphong. Kneeling left to right are Vanlop, Daungta, and Paivahn. Somphong was recently elected as a Polk County Public Hospital Trustee, and she attended the 2016 Democratic National Convention as a delegate. Her career in politics has been motivated by a desire to repay the state and former governor who welcomed the Tai Dam (Somphong Baccam).

The Rev. Clement Gisselquist, Story City, Iowa, 1968. Good sponsorship was one of the main pillars of the state's refugee resettlement program. Through the Immanuel Lutheran Church, the Gisselquist family cosponsored the Quangs. Clement died in 1979, leaving behind his beloved wife Borghild. When Un Quang died in 2000, Mrs. Gisselquist kindly gifted two burial plots to his widow Em. Clement and Un rest in peace in the Gisselquist family plot at Fairview Cemetery in Story City, Iowa (Somphong Baccam).

They were cooking there. Immediately we had to sit down and immediately they gave us the dish and immediately I'd say oh my god I can't eat anymore. I'd take a taste of that and hey give me some more. It was tremendous. They treated me like a king."[18] The goal of these visits was to keep the lines of communication open and "put out brushfires" before they became big problems, says Muñoz. The state encountered its most troubles not with the Tai Dam, but federal reviewers and the Catholic Church.

In April of 1976, the U.S. Department of Health, Education, and Welfare reviewed the resettlement programs in Iowa, and their final report offered strong criticism of the state's overzealous work-first philosophy. For this review, HEW officials interviewed sixteen Vietnamese and nine Tai Dam families for a total of 191 refugees. HEW correctly identified a rift between the state of Iowa and the other VOLAGS. The Governor and his Task Force arrived as the new kid on the block, and they boasted that they would resettle refugees more efficiently than anyone else. No Tai Dam would be on welfare. Other VOLAGS resented these boasts. HEW acknowledged that the 8.5 percent of Tai Dam receiving cash assistance was far lower than the overall state average of 24 percent. However, HEW's findings suggested the state had attained this efficiency through draconian tactics: "Some refugees have been told that they would have no respect in their new home if they accepted cash assistance; some needy refugees have not applied for assistance out of fear of angering their sponsor." According to HEW, the Task Force's obsession with keeping refugees off welfare caused some Tai Dam to "suffer unnecessary deprivation." In March of 1976, HEW noted 130 cases of refugees refusing assistance for which they had been eligible. The report implied this refusal came out of pressure from the Task Force.[19]

Governor Ray and Shearer disputed the legitimacy of this report. In a scathing response, Shearer demanded to know by name which refugees had not been enrolled for "badly needed" financial support. She wanted to know who, where, and when did any representatives from the Governor's Office claim that zero refugees would go onto cash assistance? She challenged HEW's finding that the Task Force blocked the enrollment of Tai Dam onto cash assistance and food stamps.[20] In some respects, the Iowa program represented a threat to HEW. It was an alternative model that called into question HEW's oversight of the U.S. refugee resettlement process. Though this potential bias must be noted, HEW's findings seem to corroborate how the state dealt with other Iowans eligible for welfare during the Vietnam War era.

This strong dislike of welfare must be seen as being more of an Iowa ethos than a narrow attribute of the Iowa resettlement program and the fiscally conservative governor who launched it. Prideful Iowans identified themselves as belonging to a state with a strong work-ethic. This hard work went hand in hand with Iowa being one of the leading agricultural producers in the world. When Premier Nikita Khrushchev wanted to improve agricultural production in the Soviet Union, he traveled to Roswell Garst's farm in Coon Rapids, Iowa. During this 1959 visit, Khrushchev observed cutting-edge agricultural technology. Iowans have always been proud of their agricultural prowess and ability to feed others. So imagine the shock a *Des Moines Register* headline caused readers in October of 1976, just a few months after the HEW report on refugees had been finished. The state of Iowa had received the dubious distinction of being on a "failure to feed" list as reported by the American Friend's Service Committee, a Quaker organization. In 1976, about 100,000 Iowans received food stamps, but 78 percent of eligible Iowans had not been enrolled in the federal program overseen by the U.S. Department of Agriculture. One social worker in every county needed to devote at least 10 percent of their job duties to enrolling the 300,000 plus needy individuals who had not been registered. Vernon Woodard, the coordinator of Iowa's food stamp program, acknowledged the state had not been diligent enough in registering Iowans. Part of the problem lay in overcoming the stigma attached to being poor and the state's strong-work ethic. Woodard and company had sent 200 letters to churches seeking volunteers to help register the poor for food stamps. However, only three individuals responded.[21] In tough times, people were to make do in Iowa. Several years later, Iowans would question Ray's decision to bring in more refugees when rural poverty continued to exist at home.

The work-first philosophy and very existence of the state's resettlement project alienated the other six VOLAGS operating in Iowa. The biggest rift occurred between the two most active resettlement agencies: state of Iowa and the United States Catholic Conference. Just over a year after the fall of Saigon, about 2,500 Indochinese had resettled in Iowa. The Catholic Church had brought in 701 mostly Vietnamese refugees and the Task Force had resettled 633 Tai Dam. The work-first philosophy annoyed USCC representatives who thought the Task Force exploited refugees for political gain. In contrast, the Catholic Church had been more willing to sign refugees up for welfare. The Governor's Task Force also meant competition. If a Catholic family wished to sponsor Tai Dam for the state of Iowa, this meant one less sponsor for the USCC. Turf wars for sponsors could result.

Hints of this early division between the Task Force and the USCC appeared in the HEW report. In its early history, the Task Force ran a resettlement program separate from the other VOLAGS. Part of the problem lay in the state's original decision to focus their efforts on bringing just the Tai Dam to Iowa, and unintentional problems arose as a result of that decision. When the Vietnamese sought assistance from the Task Force, the state seemed unwilling to provide financial assistance. The Task Force offered a twenty-four-hour information/help hotline in the Tai Dam language, but no such service existed for Vietnamese. However, Vietnamese seeking financial help represented the biggest source of tension. The Task Force received State Department funds to bring in the Tai Dam at $500 per refugee. This prevented the state from providing assistance to the Vietnamese whose own VOLAG had received $500 on their behalf. The state argued that the original resettlement agency had the financial obligation to look after their own refugees, but the Vietnamese interviewed by HEW interpreted the state turning them away as favoritism towards the Tai Dam, "The close follow-up provided to the Tai Dam is perceived by many Vietnamese refugees and sponsors as a lack of state concern for the 2,000 Vietnamese residents of Iowa."[22] Additionally, the state of Iowa had hired three Tai Dam to work for the Task Force, but the Vietnamese lacked any representation, which upset some Vietnamese living in Iowa.

Correspondence between Janet Baker of Boone, Iowa, and Dennis Nagel, Administrative Assistant to Governor Ray, reveal the state's narrow focus on the Tai Dam. Baker wrote to Governor Ray seeking help for some Vietnamese being mistreated by their sponsors. Too proud to beg, these Vietnamese went hungry. Nagel responded, "While the State of Iowa has been involved with the Tai Dam, we have not had an active role in the resettlement of the other refugees in Iowa. Instead, all other refugees have been sponsored by voluntary agencies such as church and community groups. The primary responsibility for assisting the refugees rests with these sponsors."[23] Early on, an "us versus them" mentality began to form between the state and its Tai Dam charges and the Catholic Church and their Vietnamese charges. In October of 1976, Shearer made controversial remarks that exacerbated an already tenuous relationship.

On October 21, 1976, the *Des Moines Tribune* ran a story where Shearer, the Director of the Governor's Task Force, criticized Vietnamese refugees in Iowa for taking advantage of welfare. Shearer stated some of the Vietnamese simply did not want to work. Speaking about the subject of welfare fraud, Shearer commented, "The Vietnamese themselves are wise in the ways of this." Far from being innocent victims, Shearer personally believed refugees who had been survivors of some of the most corrupt governments had more than enough skills to defraud the American welfare system. She told the *Tribune* writer about the case of one Vietnamese man whose $16,000 of personal wealth prevented him from collecting welfare. The man overcame the system by putting his wealth into a trust fund for his children in order to collect assistance. Shearer believed that many Vietnamese who came to the United States immediately after the Vietnam War had been those with the most wealth to buy their way out. She recalled how banking representatives showed up at the military processing centers at Camp Pendleton, California, and Fort Chaffee, Arkansas; these banking officials bought the gold refugees had brought to America. Shearer even hinted that some of the Vietnamese refugees owned Swiss bank accounts. As of October of 1976, she estimated that 900 out of 1,900 Vietnamese in Iowa received welfare. In contrast, the Governor's Task Force oversaw a program in which hardly any Tai Dam received welfare. Finding employment for the Tai Dam had been a joy, but her working with the Vietnamese had been "very different—more frustrating," stated Shearer.[24]

Immediately after Shearer made these controversial statements, Iowa's Vietnamese community responded. Pastor Phan Van Hein wrote to Governor Ray and many other important figures challenging the notion that the Vietnamese who came to the United States were affluent gold hoarders: "Mrs. Shearer has undervalued the search for freedom of the Vietnamese refugees…. She did not know that we had to leave behind our homes, our properties, our family members and our homeland because of FREEDOM. As you are aware, most of us came to the U.S. empty handed, this is well known by the U.S. Congress…." The Vietnamese community leaders also asked, "What has she done for the Vietnamese refugees" that would permit her to make a judgment that "working with the Vietnamese was very different—more frustrating than working with the Tai Dam?" In addition to the pastor's letter, the Vietnamese Association of Iowa criticized Shearer and the state's favoritism toward the Tai Dam. If the director of Job Service and the head of the Task Force did not already favor the Tai Dam in job placement, then at the very least her remarks "intentionally created a very bad impression of the Vietnamese refugees to the American public and in particular to the actual or prospective employers…. It is not fair to downgrade the Vietnamese refugees on purpose to publicize the Task Force's project of resettlement of the Tai Dam."[25]

The sponsors of the Vietnamese also fired back at Shearer, none more so than Father John Zeitler of Holy Trinity Parish in Des Moines, Iowa.

Zeitler had grown close to the Vietnamese after overseeing the Catholic Church's resettlement of thirty-five families. His angry letter to Ray marked the height of the tense relationship between the Task Force and the other VOLAGS operating in the state: "Let me laud you for accepting the [Tai Dam] Laotians to Iowa. But I dismissed as ludicrous the earlier statements by Ms. Shearer that their resettlement was any model of success. The offering of a $200 bounty to the sponsors, the absence of the screening of the sponsors, the poverty of the programs offered combined to make the Laotian resettlement program in Iowa a very poor program that was saved only by the determination of the Laotians and the open heartedness of the Iowa citizens. It worked in spite of Ms. Shearer." Shearer met with the Vietnamese community on November 21, 1976. Instead of an apology, the Vietnamese received a "lecture on the shame of being on welfare" instead. This annoyed Zeitler who urged Ray to shut down the state's Task Force because the Vietnamese could not work with Shearer. Like Zeitler, Mary Ann Pederson had been involved in the sponsorship of Vietnamese, and Shearer's comments infuriated her. In a letter, she asked Shearer, "Why do you continue to harass the Vietnamese?" Pederson felt guilty about the Vietnam War's devastation and uprooting of these people, "It is my somewhat informed opinion that every Southeast Asian still in that tortured part of the world could be put on full welfare benefits and it would be less expensive than fighting the obscene war in which so many were victimized."[26]

Publicly, Ray backed Shearer throughout the criticism. After all, she had only been carrying out the Governor's work-first philosophy. The *Cedar Rapids Gazette* quoted his reflection on the matter: "If the Tai Dam come in and none of them goes on welfare, it would seem that if the Vietnamese had been handled in the same way, fewer of them would be on welfare…. We understand the first thing some sponsors of the Vietnamese did was to take them down and register them for welfare."[27] The public outrage over her comments dumbfounded Shearer. She reasoned that middle-class American sponsors felt implicated because they too readily signed their refugees up for welfare. Furthermore, Shearer did not understand the deep and combative history between the Vietnamese and the Tai Dam. Her comments inverted the traditional social order of Southeast Asia, which helped fuel the Vietnamese outrage.

Scholars have addressed how the immigrant's world can get turned upside down in their new environment. For example, language and cultural barriers caused Vietnamese professionals to fall into lower class jobs in the United States. The Director General of the South Vietnamese Ministry of the Interior became a yard worker, an Air Force Colonel became a newspaper delivery night watchman, a medical doctor became a limousine driver, another medical doctor became a dishwasher, a bank manager became a janitor at a bank, a professor of literature became a furniture assembler, a three star general became a maître d, the ARVN chief of staff became a waiter; all of these examples represented a tragic loss of status for Vietnamese refugees. A 1975 Interagency Task Force survey concluded that 73 percent of Vietnamese professionals became blue collar workers in the United States, and only 10 percent took jobs on par with those they held in Vietnam. Similarly, gender and age inversions took place. Refugee women might find access to higher paying jobs than their spouses, challenging the traditional patriarchy of Southeast Asian families. Indochinese refugees also went from cultures praising the elderly to a land where youth is venerated.[28] Though scholars have addressed inversion with regards to class and age, they have not addressed how the inversion of ethnic group status can occur in the United States.

In French Indochina, a hierarchy of race existed with the Vietnamese or Kinh on the top. Since the beginning of French colonial rule in the region in the late nineteenth century, the French viewed the Kinh as being intelligent and hardworking. For this reason, colonial officials used Vietnamese civil servants to help govern Laos. In contrast to the ambitious Kinh, the ethnic Lao had the reputation of being polite and easy-going but inefficient workers in need of civilizing. The French believed the Tai Dam to be similar in manners as their ethnic Lao cousins. In Vietnam, the Kinh had long looked upon the Tai Dam and the other fifty-plus recognized minority groups as inferiors. This sentiment continued in Iowa. William Johnson, the head of Des Moines Area Community College's adult basic education program, acknowledged that some Vietnamese students refused to take courses with Tai Dam. Phuong Baccam of Des Moines angrily recalled how the Vietnamese "look at us as if we are slaves."[29] Shearer's comments caused such a stir among the Vietnamese because, in part, they inverted the traditional social order of Southeast Asia. Imagine black American refugees being praised over white American refugees in a new homeland. It was bad enough Shearer criticized the Vietnamese community, but her praising the Tai Dam only added to their outrage.

To this day, the Tai Dam and Vietnamese have a distant relationship in Iowa. Some Tai Dam have blamed Vietnamese nationalism and communism as the catalyst for their becoming refugees twice over. In 1948, the French attempted to use the Tai as a counterweight to Vietnamese national interests by establishing the semi-autonomous Tai Federation in northwest Vietnam. Some Iowa Tai Dam equated the Tai Federation with being an independent Tai nation, and its collapse resulted in the Tai Dam becoming refugees in the 1950s. In 1975, the Pathet Lao seized power in Laos with the crucial aid of their Vietnamese communist allies. This event made the Tai Dam into refugees once more. Vinh Nguyen, an educator in the Des Moines public school system and member of the Vietnamese community, believes that the Tai Dam and other Southeast Asians continue to view the Vietnamese as being aggressors because of the history of the region.[30] In Vietnam today, the Tai Dam live in poverty. Their lands have been overtaken by Vietnamese migrants, and Vietnam has built large hydroelectric dams in Tai Dam country, further angering some of the Tai Dam in present-day Iowa.

Over time, the state's resettlement agency mended its relationship with the Vietnamese and other VOLAGS and became an alternative model for refugee resettlement. To quell the charges of Tai Dam favoritism, The Task Force hired Vietnamese representatives and assigned five of its four-

Governor Ray is presented with a traditional rice basket at the Tai Dam Freedom Festival in Des Moines, Iowa, 1978. Pictured from left to right are Wing Cam, Somsak Saythongphet, Colleen Shearer, Governor Ray, Inngeu Baccam, and Ny Baccam. The Tai Dam's successful transition to life in Iowa led to the continuation and expansion of the state's resettlement program (Houng Baccam).

teen members to serve on a Vietnamese team. The formation of the Vietnamese team signaled a shift in the state's operations. Though the Task Force continued to resettle Tai Dam in the greatest numbers, it branched out to coordinate all of Iowa's refugee resettlement activities. In the first two years of its existence, the Task Force resettled about 1,200 Tai Dam in the state. After its first contract expired in September of 1977, the Governor's Task Force reformed into the Iowa Refugee Service Center.

Shearer desired a name change to protect Governor Ray. Having his name attached to an issue that remained controversial could cause future political problems. Also, Shearer wanted to signal to the Tai Dam that the state now had the responsibility of working with all refugee groups in Iowa. Four divisions comprised the Iowa Refugee Service Center: employment and social services, education and resettlement, communications and publications, and volunteer and grants coordination. A total of fifteen individuals directly worked for the IRSC. Funding for Iowa's resettlement program came from two main federal sources. The U.S. Department of State paid the center for each individual resettled. During the 1970s, this amount fluctuated from a low of $350 to a high of $500. Congress allocated the other main source of funding through its Indochinese Refugee Assistance Program (IRAP). The IRSC obtained this funding by purchasing services from the Iowa Department of Social Services. In contrast to the early HEW criticisms of the state's narrow focus on the Tai Dam, the IRSC became a clearinghouse of information for other voluntary agencies and all refugees in Iowa.

To coordinate the resettlement effort, the IRSC formed the council of Iowa Joint Voluntary Agencies in April of 1979. Representatives from each of the VOLAGS in the state attended periodic meetings and kept the lines of communication open. The IJVA tried to prevent the duplication of services and to share strategies for resettlement. They kept one another informed of the numbers of Indochinese to arrive under their auspices. These rough numbers allowed the state to prepare for the employment of adult new arrivals, and the IJVA informed school districts about the number of Indochinese students that might be added to their districts.

Nowhere was the coordination of the IRSC and other service providers more apparent than in the creation of Iowa's unaccompanied minors program. Unaccompanied minors arrived in the United States without parents or guardians, but they were not necessarily orphans because their parents might still be alive in Southeast Asia. To find the solution to this legal dilemma, Iowa's VOLAGS consulted with one another, the Polk County Court, the Attorney General, federal refugee resettlement officials, and individuals from the states of Illinois, Michigan, Florida, and Colorado. Iowans interested in becoming foster parents of unaccompanied minors inquired with one of the state's voluntary agencies and became licensed as foster parents by Social Services. Next, the Iowa VOLAG received a case from the American Council of Voluntary Agencies in New York. Then, the state of Iowa took custody of these children through the Iowa Attorney General who next transferred guardianship to the Iowa Department of Social Services. The first unaccompanied minors arrived in Iowa on July 15, 1979. Though complex, this process showed the maturation of the IRSC.

The state's communication with other VOLAGS improved drastically, but old conflicts in philosophy persisted while new problems arose between the IRSC and other VOLAGS. Initially, the Task Force alienated VOLAGS by its very existence, competition for sponsors, work-first philosophy, and separate program tailored to the Tai Dam. By the late 1970s, the IRSC became a center that assisted all refugees seeking help. If the state had not resettled a refugee, it still refused to offer direct financial assistance because this violated their contract with the State Department. However, the IRSC referred these individuals to appropriate service providers and offered other services. Charlene Heggen, an IRSC staffer, informed Ray in a monthly report how Catholic Social Services signed up refugees for welfare immediately, and other VOLAGS passed off their responsibilities to the IRSC. One refugee arrived in Iowa at 10:00 p.m. and was signed up for welfare by 10:00 a.m. the next morning! Instead of working independently as in the past, IRSC staffers resented the other VOLAGS for pushing their refugees onto the state. Wayne Johnson, a former Lutheran Immigration and Refugee Services worker, admittedly recalled passing on his charges to the IRSC sooner than he should have. The state simply had more resources. This passing the buck problem frustrated Charlene Heggen:

> More and more refugees are landing on our doorstop. When the USCC families find they have no one except the small Catholic Charities staff to turn to, they come to us for help. When the Lutheran sponsors find there is no one to help them, they come to us. All of this increases dramatically the work load of our staff. We clearly feel an obligation to help all refugees in the state, but it is becoming increasingly clear that the other agencies rely upon us to take over a responsibility which should be their own, and if an agency such as ours did not exist, the welfare statistics would climb higher and higher ... a problem we foresee for the entire resettlement effort nationally.[31]

Heggen described two other examples of the IRSC helping refugees sponsored by the USCC. The state had to take children to the doctor to remove sutures and assisted another group of youngsters going barefoot and wearing coats indoors to brave an Iowa winter without heat or electricity. With the Governor's strong advocacy for Indochinese refugee resettlement, when any refugee went on cash assistance, the public assumed they had been brought in by the state. The growing numbers of refugees on welfare reflected badly on the IRSC more so than the actual VOLAG who had sponsored them, causing frustration among IRSC staffers.

In June of 1979, the Governor's Office of Volunteerism and the IRSC jointly launched what became the largest volunteer tutoring program for refugees in the United States. The state had long tried to keep refugees off welfare by placing them in jobs. Ray and company reasoned that working on the job exposed Indochinese refugees to American culture and values. Refugees also absorbed some English-language skills at the workplace. While children picked up language skills in the public schools, adults in the workplace, the elderly, particularly females, remained isolated from U.S. culture and the English language. The volunteer tutoring program offered an alternate route to learn English.

Those interested in becoming volunteers contacted the Governor's Office or the IRSC. Tutors ranged in age from young teenagers to the elderly. Next, a prospective tutor took a brief training from the Iowa Department of Public Instruction on how to teach English as a second language. After passing, the tutor linked up with a refugee for what was usually one on one tutoring in the refugees' homes two or three times weekly. Local area community colleges supplied language materials for the tutors and about two dozen volunteer tutor coordinators helped manage the program. In one month alone, a tutor in Osceola, Iowa, had volunteered 105 hours of instruction to five refugees. During one session, a tutor taught a refugee family the word emergency. After learning the meaning of the word, the head of household stood up, cried out "emergency," and directed the tutor to a bedridden child. Medical authorities were called, and the child received treatment for a high fever. By Ray's last year in office in 1982, the volunteer tutor program had served over 2,700 refugees with over 100,000 hours of instruction, and 560 tutors operated out of eighty-five of the state's ninety-nine counties.[32]

Despite the state's best efforts, the numbers of refugees receiving welfare increased dramatically throughout the 1970s. Shearer blamed the VOLAGS and the federal government's policy of "front-end loading." The front-end loading philosophy held that enrolling refugees in vocational and English language programs, supplemented by cash assistance, would reap future dividends. In line with this philosophy, the federal government in 1979 provided refugees a stipend if they attended ESL classes. Shearer described how the state's Tai Dam went onto welfare rolls, "Once they became independent and moved beyond the frequent advice and help of their sponsors and IRSC they began to be persuaded by the system."[33] Even with the setback, the Iowa program remained an alternative model for bringing in refugees more efficiently. In February of 1980, the Select Commission on Immigration and Refugee Policy asked Shearer to provide insights into Iowa and federal refugee policy.

In her testimony, Shearer gave her opinion as to why the refugee resettlement program had gone awry. First, the oversight of the federal program had been placed under the jurisdiction of HEW, later known as the Department of Health and Human Services, the traditional dispensers of welfare. Upon arrival, refugees had easier access to public assistance because of the very structure of the federal refugee program. To Shearer's dismay, inefficient VOLAGS played too much of a role in the resettlement process. After establishing numbers to be admitted and appropriating funds for refugees, the "federal government loses control of the entire program ... the government hands the control and the money over to private 'companies' to accomplish the resettlement." Congress provided VOLAGS large sums of money to resettle refugees, but the VOLAGS too readily signed them up for welfare. These private organizations lacked accountability. To Shearer's horror, some of these VOLAGS did not use individual sponsors for their refugees. Instead, they simply designated one of their local offices as the sponsor. In response, the federal government had to dump more and more money into its refugee program, and they created special programs for refugees. These special programs and the growing numbers of refugees caused resentment among disadvantaged groups such as African Americans and the elderly; many in the American public viewed these newcomers as a liability and resented the use of their tax dollars to support foreign refugees from a controversial war. Federal reimbursement to states was temporary. Afterwards, states had to pay for their share of public assistance to refugees. As a result, state officials grew angry because they lacked control over the federal government's resettlement process.[34]

Shearer's calls for reform centered on giving other governors the same type of control Ray exercised over resettlement. She wanted the Iowa model to be adopted by all states. Each state's Governor's Office could oversee the resettlement process with the cooperation of their respective job services. The refugee program needed to be removed from the jurisdiction of the Department of Health and Human Services and placed under the Department of Labor. This restructuring would keep more refugees off welfare. Shearer viewed assistance to refugees not as welfare but as a type of temporary unemployment insurance. These folks should be seen as workers transitioning to employment in their new nation. Shearer wanted to limit voluntary agencies to the role of procuring individual sponsors for refugees. VOLAGS should play no further role in resettlement because they lacked accountability and placed their charges onto welfare too readily. Serving in this limited capacity, the State Department could reimburse VOLAGS only a fraction of the $500 they had been allotted per refugee resettled in the past. Shearer also called into question the primary factor in determining the placement of refugees. VOLAGS used family reunification to determine where to send refugees. Family reunification and secondary migration resulted in large numbers of Indochinese in states such as California and Texas. These large numbers overwhelmed these states' existing social service systems and often caused tensions in the affected communities. Instead of family reunification, Shearer argued that the job market should play a decisive role in determining where to place refugees.

Personally, Shearer believed refugees provided an important source of cheap labor, tax revenues, and job creation. Refugee labor could keep jobs in the United States instead of having companies relocate in search of cheap labor abroad; as wage earners, refugees became better consumers, which created jobs for Americans. States gaining control over the resettlement process and placing refugees into the workforce would have allowed the American public to view refugees as an asset instead of a liability.[35]

Though Shearer's calls for reform went unheeded, the crisis in refugees receiving welfare vindicated the Iowa program. The early HEW criticisms had caused the state's refugee program to reflect and reform its narrow focus on the Tai Dam and to communicate better with VOLAGS throughout the state. However, the IRSC held firm to Ray's work-first philosophy. As more Indochinese refugees went on welfare and costs for the program rose so too did the value of having the Iowa program as an alternative model for resettlement. The states of Michigan, New Jersey, Florida, Wisconsin, Colorado, New Mexico, Idaho, North Carolina, South Dakota, and Vermont all contacted the IRSC for advice on resettling refugees as they flirted with the idea of establishing their own resettlement programs. The IRSC developed an international reputation. When the Federal Republic of Germany wanted insights on how to resettle refugees, they sent a delegation to Des Moines to consult with the IRSC in 1979. Australian resettlement officials spoke with IRSC staffers and created a volunteer tutor program modeled after Iowa's.

The state's resettlement program meant state pride to many who had been involved in the effort. For many Iowans, this pride came from having a governor take a stand to help others in need during a humanitarian crisis following the wars in Indochina. For the staffers of the IRSC, state pride came not just in the act of bringing Indochinese refugees to Iowa, but also in the efficiency of resettlement. IRSC officials gloated when they read about others praising the state's program in national newspapers and in many other publications on resettlement. Iowans contrasted the strong presence their governor had in alleviating a humanitarian crisis with the hands off approach of most of the nation's other governors.

Part of the reason for the positive reputation of the state's program lay in the dedicated staff who worked for the IRSC. These men and women faced ups and downs in their own lives while serving the refugee community. A lone monthly report Shearer sent to Governor Ray in 1979 provided a glimpse into just how much these employees had to balance their personal and professional lives. Somsak Saythongphet lost his wife Vientha to leukemia in 1978, and his young fourteen-year-old daughter fell into a deep depression and required hospitalization. Throughout this turmoil, Somsak was still "everywhere at once.... Somask has been torn in so many directions it's difficult to describe. He is one of the strongest and wisest human beings I've ever met," noted Shearer. Tom Thorup worked as an employment specialist for the IRSC. The 6'3" 200-pound man lost thirty-five pounds from a stomach ulcer and worry over a child custody battle, but he took outpatient treatments in the early mornings so as to not cut into his work schedule. Doctors diagnosed Charlene Heggen with cancer in 1979, and she underwent a mastectomy. Throughout this surgery and rounds of chemotherapy, Heggen missed work only sparingly.[36] These dedicated staffers deserve much of the credit for helping the Indochinese adjust to Iowa. Their interaction with refugees invigorated these Iowans through their own personal hardships. They knew the importance of their work and the traumas being endured by their clientele. As we shall see in the next chapter, the refugees' background also must be examined in order to understand how Iowa's resettlement program took the course it did.

4

Tai Dam as Professional Refugees

A dedicated governor, state employees, sponsors, volunteers, and employers deserve much credit for reestablishing the Tai Dam without the major problems experienced elsewhere, but the Tai Dam's history, politics, and culture must be examined to fully comprehend their adjustment to Iowa. A transnational approach is necessary because the Tai Dam, like all immigrant groups, constantly referred back to their own culture while trying to understand their new environments.[1] Though they resettled with little in the way of material goods, the Tai Dam possessed a lot of human capital that they and the state of Iowa used to their advantage. Urban living, education, communalism, and strong leadership aided the Tai Dam's adaptation to Iowa, but their coming from a tropical climate, expectation of having "American" sponsors in "American" homes, and patriarchal culture made the transition difficult at times. Conversion to Christianity, often considered to be a form of assimilation, can still be an expression of traditional culture and influenced by the Tai Dam's history. Addressing the Tai Dam's background demands that we view them as being more than just numbers; they were decision-makers whose past and culture helped to influence the positive outcome of their resettlement in Iowa, which in turn influenced Governor Robert Ray's decision to increase the Iowa Refugee Service Center's intake of other refugees.

At the Nong Khai refugee camp, the Tai Dam frequently listened to the Voice of America radio station. One spring day in 1975, Houng Baccam remembered the news being announced over the radio station: "The state of Iowa has accepted Tai Dam to become farmers. We were very very happy.... We knew nothing of Iowa. When we received the news, I rushed to town looking for a map of the United States. Where is Iowa?" The Tai Dam only had heard of larger American cities and states, and they desperately sought any sort of information on their potential homeland. Siang Bachti, a USAID employee, remembered how the Tai Dam seeking admission to the United States anticipated becoming farmers in Iowa:

> Some American officers gave us a brochure.... It was about agriculture: Iowa. Somehow that brochure focused on sheep; how to raise sheep. Inside, we saw a lot of people taking the sheep to the hills or the plains and raising sheep. Everybody said, "Ah, we are going to Iowa; we are going to raise sheep!" Ha ha. Everybody said oh that is easy. It is a lot easier than pigs. Pigs are dirty. Oh yay, it will be fun. In the morning we will go and take all of the sheep to the fields until nighttime we will come back. That is easy work because nobody spoke English ... just 10 percent maybe.... Everybody was happy.... When we came here, we did not see any sheep! Just pigs and cows![2]

Dinh VanLo refused to believe the literature U.S. officials gave him. How could cornfields stretch as far as the eye could see? Skeptically, he figured this must be "propaganda." American officials had wrongly categorized all the Tai Dam as being farmers, and they assumed the Tai Dam would farm in Iowa. Moreover, the Tai Dam added to this mischaracterization as they strategized to improve their chances of coming to Iowa.

Tai Dam soldiers who had fought against communism, those who had worked for American enterprises such as USAID, and professionals had the strongest potential to be relocated to the United States. For all other Tai Dam, they figured the best way to improve their chances of acceptance to Iowa, an agricultural state, would be to say that they were farmers. Siang Bachti recounted the uneasy and now humorous exchanges between American officials and Tai Dam "farmers" seeking admission to Iowa going something like this:

> IMMIGRATION OFFICIAL: "What do you farm? Do you do rice fields?"
> TAI DAM: "No. We raise livestock."
> IMMIGRATION OFFICIAL: "How many cows do you have?"
> TAI DAM: "No cows."
> IMMIGRATION OFFICIAL: "How many buffalo do you have?"
> TAI DAM: "No buffalo."
> IMMIGRATION OFFICIAL: "So what do you raise?"
> TAI DAM: "We have two pigs and a dozen chickens."

"Almost every Tai Dam family said I am a farmer.... Maybe that is why Governor Ray took us," reflected Bachti.[3] Though limited, their stating their occupation as farmer demonstrated some agency in the Tai Dam seeking admission to Iowa. They told the immigration officials what they wanted to hear. Indochinese refugees tried to influence the admissions process in others ways too. When listing family relations, friends became cousins and cousins became siblings. Some refugees used their idea of an extended family to try to enhance the likelihood of bringing loved ones to the United States. However, while in Iowa, some refugees used the American nuclear family definition to collect multiple welfare checks while living at the same residences with extended family.

American officials figured the Tai Dam, an agricultural people, would make a great fit in Iowa, an agricultural state. Traditionally, farming formed the very foundation for Tai Dam life in their homeland in northwestern Vietnam. They cultivated wet rice in the highland valleys, and some also practiced slash and burn agriculture, but to characterize the Tai Dam who ultimately came to Iowa as being farmers would be inaccurate. Those Black Tai deemed important enough to be airlifted out of northwest Vietnam to Hanoi in 1952 were not common farmers, but political and military officials and their family members. Similarly, political and military elites and their relatives comprised the evacuees who fled from Hanoi to Xiang Khoang, Laos, after the fall of Dien Bien Phu to the communists in 1954. Just as American officials expected the Tai Dam to become farmers, so too did Lao officials. In Xiang Khoang, the land proved difficult to cultivate. Part of the problem lay in the inadequacy of the soil but also in the Tai Dam's lack of farming expertise. The situation appeared so bleak that Suc Baccam, the head of the Tai Dam faction that went to Xiang Khoang, looked into the possibility of leaving Laos for South Vietnam. Lao political leader Souvanna Phouma found the migrants in dire straits when he visited them in the mid–1950s. Souvanna realized the newcomers had not farmed for a living previously and could not farm in Xiang Khoang. However, he scoffed at the notion of the Tai Dam leaving for South Vietnam. He reasoned that they should remain with their Lao cousins instead of relocating among the Vietnamese. Souvanna arranged for them to be airlifted into the capital of Vientiane to find employment in other sectors.[4]

The Tai Dam who arrived in Iowa came from higher social status and had been exposed to urban living while in Vientiane, which helped the group transition to life in the United States. Generally speaking, the first 130,000 Indochinese refugees paroled into the United States immediately after the fall of Saigon possessed more human capital than later arrivals. Many of these early arrivals were literate in their own language and had been exposed to urban living and Western culture by working for the U.S. military and U.S. businesses in Indochina. In December of

1975, the Interagency Task Force for Indochina Refugees compiled statistical information on 30,628 heads of households. They discovered that only 1.3 percent had no schooling whereas nearly 48 percent had some secondary education. About 23 percent of these early arrivals had attended a university.[5] In contrast, later Indochinese arrivals such as the Hmong were often illiterate in their own languages and came from rural backgrounds.

The Tai Dam who came to Iowa fit the profile of the initial wave of Vietnamese; many had been part of the anticommunist political and military elite. Though no statistics exist, it is highly likely that the literacy rate of those who came to Iowa in 1975 would be much higher than the literacy rate of the Tai Dam population who remained in northwest Vietnam. Traditionally, the leading families like the Lo Cam and Luong kept histories about their respective *muang* and the exploits of their ancestors; they also carried out religious ceremonies that required reading from the *Kwam To Muang*. Some Tai Dam political figures and soldiers had the ability to read and write in Tai Dam, Vietnamese, and French. When the group relocated to Vientiane, their multilingualism proved useful for the Royal Lao Government. Later, these language skills also eased the job of the Task Force in resettling the Tai Dam throughout Iowa. Possessing literacy in another language greatly aided their learning the English language.

In addition to this elite background, Tai Dam experiences in Vientiane eased their transition to modern society in Iowa. By 1975, over 200,000 people lived in Vientiane, making it comparable to the population of Iowa's capital of Des Moines. In Vientiane, the Tai Dam worked in many different fields. In his letter to Ray, Arthur Crisfield mentioned the numerous jobs held by the Tai Dam while in Laos: a professor, engineers, accountants, electricians, carpenters, interpreters, tailors, seamstresses, cooks, gardeners, and lastly, farmers.[6] Some joined the Royal Lao military. The Black Tai's history of fighting communism made them trusted allies of the political right of Laos. Wing Cam lobbied fellow rightists to be more aggressive in fighting communism. By the late 1960s, he had overseen the formation of a Tai Dam guerrilla unit that planned to launch offensives into their former homeland in northwest Vietnam. Women like Dinh VanLo's mother did contractual labor for the military by sewing clothing for soldiers. Other than military service, a few Tai Dam found employment in Lao government. Wing Cam served as the National Director of Rural Public Works. Some Tai Dam like Siang Bachti worked for USAID and American businesses. Foreign officials employed many Black

Tai as limousine drivers, domestics, and interpreters. Some farming was done by the villagers outside of the capital, but very few of the Tai Dam who came to Iowa had been farmers in Laos.

Their varied occupational background helps to explain part of the reason why the Tai Dam did not become farmers in the American Midwest. Tending to garden plots was the closest many came to being farmers in Laos. While in Iowa, the Tai Dam visited farms and were taken aback by their size: "We saw thousands of cows and thousands of pigs…. When we came here we saw that farming is hard, not like in Laos, so we decided not to farm and everybody moved to Des Moines," recalled Siang Bachti. The Tai Dam and American officials underestimated the sheer capital and skill set necessary to succeed as agriculturalists in 1970s Iowa. In 1955, the year after Dien Bien Phu's fall, Iowa's 195,000 farms averaged 179 acres in size at a value of $238 per acre. The year the Tai Dam arrived in Iowa, the average farm size had increased to 251 acres, and the average cost per acre had skyrocketed to $1,095.[7] Tai Dam refugees had very little in the way of capital to startup farming ventures in their new homeland. Even if they had the finances, they still lacked the skill set to farm; they did not understand modern industrialized agriculture. Moreover, Iowa's twentieth-century mechanized farming had long limited the need for landowners to have hired help.

The first wave of resettlement had brought 633 Tai Dam to Iowa, but only three of these seventy-seven families lived on farms. Raymond and Ruth Walker owned a 500 acre farm near Rose Hill, Iowa. Their son Leland served in South Vietnam and sent pictures back home. Viewing images of a Vietnamese orphanage compelled the Walkers to send assistance to the children. This preexisting connection to the people of Southeast Asia and their desire to help out their beloved Governor Ray motivated the Walkers to sponsor two Tai Dam families. In contrast to the Walkers, Tomas Muñoz remembered one farm family's sponsorship going less than smoothly. The sponsors thought room and board to be adequate enough compensation for their refugee field hands. Muñoz and the IRSC had to compel the farmer to pay the refugee family a wage.[8]

Although few farmers sponsored refugees, many Tai Dam initially resettled in rural communities. Traditionally, many histories of immigrants have focused on rural people adjusting to their new urban environments. This happened with Indochinese refugees coming to Des Moines, but the opposite process happened as well. Indochinese from urban environments found themselves trying to adjust to lives in small town Iowa. The First Reformed Church of Hull, Iowa, sponsored Dinh

Dinh VanLo in his dorm at Dordt College in Sioux Center, Iowa, 1976. VanLo was one of the few adult Tai Dam who immediately attended college. The state's resettlement program demanded refugees find employment. State officials believed English language learning should take place on the job; college courses should be taken outside of regular work hours (Dinh VanLo).

VanLo, a brash twenty-something soon to be college student. VanLo remembered his first impression of the tiny northwest Iowa town of predominantly Dutch ancestry as being less than up to par with Vientiane: "I came from Vientiane: the capital of Laos. I know more than these [Iowa] people. These people are farmers. They know nothing. I came to small town Iowa, a thousand people. I said my god.... Can you believe it. How arrogant you are when you live in this big town Vientiane, the capital of Laos, and what is Iowa to you.... Iowa was nothing to me. Iowa was small potatoes."[9]

Though he did not speak English, the Iowa Refugee Service Center provided tuition assistance because VanLo had studied at a prestigious French school in Laos. He attended Dordt College and appreciated all those who helped him complete his studies. VanLo believed that his placement in Hull aided his assimilation. He needed to speak English and to interact with "Americans." However, he yearned to be with other Tai Dam and preferred city life: "When I came to visit Des Moines, I saw some black haired people. I was so excited. I lived in a small town with no black haired peoples.... It made me feel so good to see Asians.... When I came to Des Moines, I said I like it. You can hide without anybody knowing who you are. Over there [in Hull], if you cut grass on Sunday, you are in big trouble."[10]

VanLo's story of relocating from a rural Iowa community to Des Moines was not unique. Throughout the 1970s, the Tai Dam gravitated towards the urban locales. The Iowa Refugee Service Center estimated that in July of 1981 nearly 70 percent of the Tai Dam lived in cities and or cluster areas. Of the 2,400 Tai Dam in the state, almost half lived in Des Moines. Marshalltown, with a mere 137 refugees, ranked as the second largest Tai Dam cluster in the state. A desire to relocate to be closer to family and the availability of entry-level jobs pulled the Tai Dam towards the city of Des Moines. According to Siang Bachti, the saying "the money pot" has tipped in Des Moines circulated among the newcomers.[11] Opportunities for jobs existed for those who wanted them, but before long, these opportunities might be lost. The Tai Dam wanted to be active consumers in a market economy. In their new city, they had access to commodities like never before. Marv Weidner and other IRSC staffers joked about the number of Trans Am Firebirds bought by the refugees. Dinh VanLo described the dilemma facing young adult Tai Dam. Many wanted to work to buy goods like electronics and vehicles, but this consumerism, coupled with language barriers, prevented many from going to college.

Just months after the Tai Dam resettled in Iowa, the Task Force boasted the material gains made by the newcomers. Within half a year of their arrival, all seventy-seven Tai Dam families had at least one wage earner. Forty-three individuals had purchased vehicles and five families became homeowners. After nearly five years in Iowa, the Tai Dam averaged two vehicles per family and an astounding 80 percent of all Tai Dam had become homeowners.[12] The state's work-first philosophy deserves partial credit for these amazing statistics, but the Tai Dam's historical and cultural background must be taken into account as well.

Historically, the Tai Dam have always had strong family units because of their spiritual beliefs. The group maintained detailed family genealogies in order to venerate deceased relatives. If they did not venerate these ancestors, they might return as bad spirits to cause harm to the living who neglected them. Worshipping common ancestors created strong kin ties among the Tai Dam families: the Cam, Lo, Vi, Lu, Leo, Luong, Ka, Tong, and Quang. Each one had specific taboos affecting only their family. For example, consumption of the vegetable *kam tanh*, shoots of bamboo called *sen kam* and *lay lo*, and the pulp of the *lang kam* tree would result in the loss of teeth for the Lo Cam family. Similarly, the Lo could not eat certain birds, and the Luong could not eat mushrooms growing on logs. Using the *may tong tree* in home construction would mean disaster to members of the Tong family.[13] These genealogies and taboos reinforced family identification.

For centuries, marriage customs and ties also bound Tai Dam families. Upon engagement, the male needed to compensate his in-laws for taking their daughter. If a man married into an elite Lo Cam family, he might have to work his father-in-law's fields for eight to upwards of ten years. This period of bride service and the marriage bonded the families. If a bachelor married into a family that lacked males to do fieldwork, the man immediately married his bride, and then the groom moved into his father-in-law's house. Usually, eldest sons inherited the father's house. Younger sons established new residences with their wives, but sons were expected to live nearby their fathers.[14] Religious ceremony also tied families together. Traditionally, the eldest son-in-law performed the last rites for the deceased, and the son-in-law guided the spirit of the dead back to Tai Dam country. Even in the afterlife, those from certain families went to live in certain villages for a certain period of time.

Tai Dam had long used family ties to cope with the hardships caused by their many displacements in Indochina. For instance, those with the same surname lived near one another in the same village on the periphery of Vientiane. In Iowa, they sought to do the same. The Tai Dam attained the high rate of vehicle and homeownership by pooling their family resources. Seventy-seven families comprised the first 633 Tai Dam arrivals for an average family size of over eight persons. These larger family sizes pushed the Tai Dam to look for homes instead of renting out small apartments. Extended families lived together at the same residence, and these multiple wage earners shared the burden of paying mortgages. At his 1981 testimony before the Senate Subcommittee on Immigration and Refugee Policy in Des Moines, Iowa, Houng Baccam cited family support as the reason for the Tai Dam's high homeownership rate: "If a family wanted to buy a house and didn't have enough money for the down payment, the head of household could go to the relatives for the contribution of some money to make the down payment. Next time, it will be his or her turn to pay back without interest."[15]

In addition to family support, the Tai Dam joined mutual assistance associations to benefit community members. In 1976, with the help of the

IRSC, the Association for the Positive Promotion of Lao Ethnics (APPLE, Inc.) came into being. The organization served the Lao, Tai Dam, and Hmong refugees in Iowa. APPLE organized Lao New Year festivities and taught the community about the peoples and cultures of Laos. By 1977, the IRSC had helped to create the Society of Tai Dam-American Friendship with the goal of preserving Tai Dam culture and guiding its members to prosperity in Iowa. Other self-help groups popped up without the support of the IRSC, but each association helped the IRSC in keeping refugees off welfare and promoted active citizenship among its members. As one of the earliest MAAs to form in the United States, groups across the country asked for APPLE's charter and other tips when trying to form MAAs of their own. Though its future looked bright initially, Richard Murphy, one of the founders of APPLE, recalled ethnic tensions dividing the association. Some Tai Dam wanted their own organization as did some Hmong. Lowland Lao, Tai Dam, and Hmong often fell into disagreement over issues such as when to celebrate the New Year.[16] Each side had big personalities, none more so than the Tai Dam.

The Tai Dam's creation narrative divinely ordained the Lo Cam family to rule over the Tai Dam people. In the late nineteenth century, French imperialists tried to break up the ascribed authority of these families, but to no avail. The people still elected the Lo Cam and deferred to them as their leaders. If other families took power, they would not be able to carry out the proper ceremonies to ensure the health of the *muang*; disaster would ensue. French imperialism and over twenty years of exile did not weaken the hold these families had on leadership positions within Tai Dam society. Soon after the state of Iowa established a resettlement agency, officials realized the power traditional leaders of the Tai Dam wielded. They harnessed the influence of these leaders to the cause of resettlement. Three individuals stood out for their important roles in the resettlement process: Wing Cam, Houng Baccam, and Faluang Baccam. It should come as no surprise that the three men were from the Cam family, the traditional political and religious elite of the Tai Dam.

The three men who joined the Task Force had been figures of importance in the Tai Dam community before they ever heard of Iowa. Wing Cam had orchestrated the Tai Dam's flight from Laos. With his elderly father-in-law Quy Baccam in frail condition, Cam had been the spokesman for the Tai Dam for years. He made the decision for the Tai Dam to leave Vientiane in May of 1975, and thousands followed him into Thailand. Cam, an engineer who studied in Paris and the United States, served as the National Director of Rural Public Works in the Lao government, and he headed the Lao Lumber Company. The Task Force recognized Houng Baccam as the second in command. He also studied in France. Houng worked as an accountant for Shell Oil, and he had been the point man for the Tai Dam who came through the Fort Chaffee refugee camp. Faluang might have been one of the few refugees who understood industrial farming in Iowa. He had been trained as an agronomist and studied in Thailand and Japan. These three individuals joined the Task Force and used their influence to communicate the state's resettlement ideals. Shearer hoped to employ these influential figures for a short while and to let them go after a couple of months. Houng Baccam became the most important liaison between the IRSC and the Tai Dam. Initially hired on a three month contract, he would go on to work for the state's resettlement program for nearly thirty-five years, longer than any other individual.

These three traditional leaders played important roles in the successful resettlement of the Tai Dam. They traveled throughout the state and spoke with community members. Neth Rasavanh's sponsorship broke down rather quickly in the mid–1970s. Her sponsor lacked adequate resources to care for her charges. Rasavanh does not even remember the community in which she first resettled. However, she does remember being so miserable living in a rundown hotel that she wanted to return to the refugee camp in Thailand. Her children made a fire in the parking lot

Task Force members at a retreat in Minnesota, circa 1979. Left to right: Wing Cam, Houng Baccam, Colleen Shearer, Somsak Saythongphet, Tomas Muñoz, and Faluang Baccam. The group visited Shearer's cabin in northern Minnesota. Wing, Houng, and Faluang were the three most important Tai Dam leaders; the state used their influence to assist the resettlement process (Houng Baccam).

of the hotel, which alerted state officials. Ultimately, Houng Baccam made provisions for the family to relocate. Baccam believed his visits boosted the spirits of fellow Tai Dam, especially those living in rural communities. In addition to outreach, the three translated important information like driver's test materials, emergency information, and a Tai Dam/English newsletter. In case of emergencies, they manned a twenty-four hour hotline. William Johnson, the head of adult basic education at Des Moines Area Community College, helped supervise a Southeast Asian radio station, and Baccam became one of the hosts. He communicated important information to the Tai Dam community, and played traditional music that brought both joy and sadness to homesick listeners. According to William Johnson, the best way to work with the Tai Dam was to gain the ear of powerful figures in their community. The IRSC employed the same methods to pressure and shame welfare abusers as described by Shearer: "The IRSC has conducted an evening meeting with approximately seventy-five heads of households from the Tai Dam community to explain in detail the attitudes of the American people toward unnecessary cash assistance. The increased awareness appears to be helping the overall welfare situation and it is felt that peer pressure will be more effective than some of the rules and regulations, for the refugees know which among them are the abusers of the system."[17] The important power wielded by traditional ethnic leaders undeniably aided the Tai Dam's transition, but their gender roles often conflicted with those of Iowa.

In Tai Dam culture, the oldest male is the head of household and major decision-maker. Men partook in business and politics while women looked after the family in the home; not a single woman made up the leadership of the Tai Dam refugee community in exile. Even though women practiced fortunetelling and faith healing, the men of the Luong family remained the most important religious authorities, and the oldest son-in-law guided spirits of the deceased to the afterlife. Parents desired to have sons to carry on the family name as well as keeping a family altar to ancestors. Some of the Tai Dam who came to Iowa as adults had male relatives with multiple wives, a common practice among leaders in the old Tai Federation.

In 2009, Monsoon United Asian Women of Iowa conducted an oral history project with refugee victims of sexual assault. This project, titled *Unburdening Our Mothers' Backs*, vividly illustrated the patriarchal history of the Tai Dam, and how this power structure sometimes facilitated violence against women. At age sixteen, Tai Dam women were expected to marry. If a woman refused to marry and sought more education, she would be labeled as "no good." One elderly female described attitudes towards educating women, "They said if you are smarter, meaning if you knew how to read and write, then your husband would die." Patriarchy dominated marriage decisions as well. Fathers often decided who their daughters were to marry. In some cases, bride capture took place whereby a man kidnapped a woman he yearned for, raped her, and gained the support of the female's family, who out of shame consented to a marriage. Traditional Tai Dam leaders could and sometimes did abuse their power. According to one female elder, some Tai Dam elites took attractive women as lovers, whether the women wanted the relationship or not, and the community never challenged these authority figures.[18]

As part of the Monsoon project, two Tai Dam women in their eighties told their sad stories to interviewer Don Southammavong. One of the Tai Dam participants we will call "Em" recalled her first marriage at the age of sixteen. A Tai Dam soldier saw her and told her parents he wanted to marry their daughter. When asked if she wanted to marry this man, she responded, "I don't know. That is what my parents told me to do, so I did it. I married him." Upon marriage, the groom paid a dowry in the form of a pig to "Em's" family, and he took up residence in the bride's home. "Em" then recounted what happened next: "I was only sixteen when I married him. I didn't know what to do when he married me. When we got married, he wanted to get on top of me, but he was very fat and I was scared. I thought he was going to crush me and I would die." Em's reservations about having sex may have been alleviated if her mother spoke to her about sex and menstruation, but Tai Dam mothers rarely talked to their daughters about these topics. "Em" continued:

> I didn't want him to get on top of me at all. So I fought him and then he was not nice to me…. He hit me in my face and hit me in my vagina many times. I didn't want him to be on top of me, so I pushed him off. He got so mad that he went to get the stick that I sweep the floor with and hit me in my vagina. He just kept hitting me there over and over again. It hurt very bad. I had to just lie there because I knew if I got up, my mom and dad would yell at me to go back to my husband. Then he tried to put the stick in me. So I grabbed my skirt and held it in between my vagina so the stick would not go in me and I turned on my stomach so my back was only showing. Then he hit me in the butt. I think he got so tired, he just stopped and went to sleep…. I tried to be very quiet when it was time for me to get up to make breakfast before he went out to the fields. It was hard because everything hurt….

Unfortunately, traditional Tai Dam marriage practices could isolate female victims of spousal abuse. After marriage, a son-in-law sometimes moved in with his new bride's family to pay off a bride debt. Lacking healthy adult sons of their own, "Em's" family desperately needed the labor of their new son-in-law; they would have to repay the expensive dowry of a pig if the husband left. "Em" explained her parents' response to the attack: "When I went to get some food, my mom came with me and she was very mad at me. She told me that I should have not fought him. That is what wives are supposed to do, to let their husband get on top of them to have sex. I didn't know. I didn't like him yet.... I was scared, I told her that I didn't want him to do that to me. Then she said that tonight I would have to open my dress for him so he can have sex with me no matter what. She said that my dad would get mad at me and beat me too if I did not open my dress for him."[19] Ultimately, "Em's" husband left her, angering her parents. Sexual violence against women occurred at refugee camps in Thailand as well. Out of fear of bringing shame to their families, women who had been sexually assaulted often had nobody to talk to, or blamed themselves. The Tai Dam women from the Monsoon project tried to bury these painful moments in the past.

By 1976, the Task Force created an English/Tai Dam Newsletter to communicate its work-first philosophy and provide general information to the refugee community. In *Newsletter No. 10*, the Task Force tried to inform the Tai Dam about the different gender roles observed in America. Other than being wives and mothers, American women worked in many fields, including as business professionals: "Her great versatility has led her to believe that she deserves as much respect as her husband. She considers herself the intellectual equal of her husband or any other man. You may feel that the American woman is too independent but she wants the same respect as any man." The newsletter continued by informing the Tai Dam about the proper treatment of women in America. The passage's author demanded Tai Dam men assimilate to American gender norms. The author continued in a patronizing tone: "In the United States, it is not respectable to date someone when you are already married. A man dating behind his wife's back is looked upon with scorn in America. In Asia, this practice is acceptable but in America it is taboo! This is because in America, women are more respected than in Asia and they are not treated as mere possessions but as a human being, equal in every way to their husbands. Remember, if you live in America, it is wise to live by the American customs. Treating women equal to men is one of these customs."[20] Male authority figures in the Tai Dam community had to adapt to these new gender roles, especially since the "headman" of the resettlement program was a woman. Wing Cam denied any difficulties working under Colleen Shearer. Studying in France and the United States and collaborating with refugee relief organizations while at Nong Khai had brought him into contact with female leaders of social services. Nevertheless, Jack Spear sensed some tension among the Tai Dam males who had to listen to a woman. He believed that some Tai Dam leaders would have preferred to have had a direct line of communication with Governor Ray. Of course being the female head of an agency in 1970s America had its challenges as well. Shearer handled them gracefully.

Tai Dam males also encountered new expectations required of fathers in the United States. The consensus among the male Tai Dam interviewed for this project seemed to be that childrearing was more difficult in Iowa than in Southeast Asia. American fathers had to be more present in their child's upbringing, and language barriers often proved difficult for Tai Dam to help their children adjust to American culture. Houng Baccam explained:

> In Laos you just leave teaching to the teachers at the school.... Here you have to go and listen to the teacher about your children at the teaching conference. Over there, they do not care.... Raising children here is very difficult. The children go to school here ... they become more Americanized quicker than their parents. For us, education in our country and raising children, you just leave to the village. Your children are growing up in the village ... and so you do not pay much attention. But here, you have to pay more attention to the children. You have to ask them what happened at school. What happened in your language but as they do not speak English how can they do it? They do not know how to counsel their children. They leave the children to just learn whatever they can.

Khouang Luong argued that childrearing was more difficult in the United States because parents could not spank their children: "My parents had more freedom raising us. Here we have to follow the law. So it is a little hard for us to adjust ourselves into the surrounding. Here everything seems to be like no no.... We had a little hard time because we grew up a different way. Our parents treated us the way they do it over there, and we got used to it in the head, but when we came here, it is still in the mind, but we cannot use that way."[21]

In contrast to the males, female elders Neth Rasavanh, Em Quang, and Nga Baccam agreed that raising children in Southeast Asia had been more difficult. According to Nga Baccam, "In Laos, it was difficult to raise children.... Technology here in Iowa and the United States is amazing. It really helps save time. For example, disposable diapers are so much easier. In Laos, we only had cloth diapers. They took so much time to wash and clean. If the kids came home sweaty, we'd have to take them to an area that had water to bathe them. That all took time." Rasavanh also emphasized how timesaving appliances made rearing children in Iowa easier. In Tai Dam country, Rasavanh sewed her family's textiles and washed dirty clothing by hand, but Tai Dam parents in Iowa have access to readymade clothing and washing machines. Rasavanh described the difficulties of cooking for her family in Tai Dam country: "We never had ovens or any type of the technology that we have today.... I would have to search for wood to burn for fire to cook our foods, and the smoke would get in my eyes. No matter how much I suffered, we had to do this. We used oil for lighting. We had to squeeze the juice of a fruit called *ma laan* for oil. We'd then put it on a piece of fabric and burn it, and then we were able to see while we cooked. We never had electricity in Tai Dam country or Laos either."[22]

In addition to technology, the female elders noted how access to medicine, education, and toys has helped Tai Dam parents raise children in Iowa. Without medicine, Tai Dam parents relied on traditional faith healers who communicated with spirits. Rasavanh never believed in the power of these healers. She recalled a homemade remedy used for healing her children: "For medicine in Tai Dam country, we'd take the feces of a female hog to roast for medicine for an advanced cough. They'd take the roasted feces and mix it with water. We'd tell the kids that it was some type of fruit. It worked to relieve coughs. The French never provided us with any medicines. We had never even seen a hospital in Tai Dam country. Only the seriously wounded soldiers on their death beds would be taken there." Baccam and Rasavanh agreed that Tai Dam children in Iowa have more educational opportunities, especially women. Rasavanh remembered girls being discouraged from studying in Tai Dam country: "I never received any type of education. Most girls were forbidden to go to school. Girls were only encouraged to work the fields and create textiles. Parents told girls that they cannot make a living or support a family if they took time for education and do not learn how to work the fields and create textiles."[23]

In Iowa, Tai Dam parents entered a land of plenty, and children benefitted from this access to goods. Neth compared her rudimentary childhood playthings to those of Tai Dam children in Iowa:

> We only played with the dirt and puddles and created games from them. We just played with anything that was available, which wasn't much of anything at all. We'd roll around in the dirt and puddle and would get so dirty. There was absolutely nothing at all. Now with this new generation, they have way too many toys. We had nothing for our children to play with in Tai Dam country at all. Sometimes we'd just go up to the mountains and come back really dirty. We hardly had enough clothes to wear. Some people didn't have clothes. We'd just have to keep patching up the clothes we had sometimes. And then we came to Iowa and the United States: the land of plenty.[24]

The Rasavanh family in Vientiane, Laos, 1957. Houng "Roger" wearing hat, Neth (left) and La seated, Phaymone Low, Chanda Cavan, and Xieng "Jim" in front row from left to right. Neth Rasavanh believes it is easier for Tai Dam mothers to rear children in Iowa. In Tai Dam country and Laos, parents did not have access to washing machines, disposable diapers, and medical care (Neth Rasavanh).

Tai Dam mothers had long balanced work and childrearing in Laos. Many had labored as domestics for Lao and American officials. In Iowa, Tai Dam women continued to be the primary caretakers of children, and many entered the workforce. American technology made their balancing act easier.

Whether male or female, all Tai Dam faced a difficult adjustment to Iowa's winter climate. In April of 1975, the last full month the Tai Dam spent in the capital, Vientiane had an average high of 96 degrees. January, the coldest month of that year, showed an average *low* of 68 degrees. While going through processing at Camp Pendleton, Somphong Baccam believed weather in Southern California to be a little chilly but livable. She expected the same kind of weather in Iowa, but would be disappointed. Initially, the Tai Dam received a warm welcome. When the first Black Tai arrived on November 17, 1975, Des Moines' 70 degree temperature was uncharacteristically high. Iowa's true winter soon revealed itself to the newcomers. In 1976, their first full year in Iowa, December had an average low of 11 degrees, a full 58 degrees beneath the average low of Vientiane's coldest month during their last year in Laos. On New Year's Eve, the mercury dropped to minus 12 degrees.

Arthur Crisfield provided the Task Force a brief overview of the Tai Dam shortly after Ray agreed to bring the group to Iowa, and he predicted adjusting to Iowa winters as one of the biggest hurdles facing the newcomers. In their tropical homeland, the Tai Dam bathed outside, left doors and windows open, and rarely had to heat their homes. With the exception of downpours during the rainy season, the Tai Dam were outdoor bodies. Crisfield correctly predicted cabin fever would develop among the Tai Dam. When Siang Bachti first arrived in the winter of 1975, she compared Des Moines to her tropical homeland: "In Thailand and Laos, people live outside. People walk. It is noisy and so on all the time." During that first Iowa winter, "Nobody walked on the streets. Just cars and houses just like a deserted town. Oh, where did all the people go? We did not see anybody at all." During those first couple of Iowa winters, the Tai Dam bought cheap vehicles while trying to establish new lives in Iowa. These cheap vehicles often broke down in Iowa's bitter cold. Khouang Luong learned about mechanical problems upon arrival: "We came here in January the third week, the twenty-fifth, and it was very cold. As a matter of fact my cousin went to pick us up from the airport, and his car was stuck in the snow and it was my first time pushing a car away from the snow."[25]

During their resettlement, the Tai Dam experienced many refugee moments. These missteps occurred as a result of the refugee not understanding their new environment. Though these moments might be embarrassing and or even painful when they took place, as the refugee learned more about their new culture and reflected back, these moments became humorous. Many early refugee moments took place because of a lack of understanding about Iowa weather. On sunny winter days, some Tai Dam women hung their cloths outside to dry. To their surprise, they returned to their lines and found the clothing soaking wet although the sun had been out all day. Similarly, Tomas Muñoz spoke of one Tai Dam who went outside to shovel snow: off his rooftop!

Other than problems with winter, the Tai Dam had refugee moments because of a lack of understanding about Iowa culture. Siang Bachti, a Catholic, came into contact with priests and nuns frequently in Vientiane, but she had not seen any men and women of the cloth early in her resettlement. One day, an excited Bachti spotted a priest walking in downtown Des Moines. She called out to him several times, but he walked by. Later, Bachti realized she had tried to get his attention by calling "daddy, daddy, daddy" instead of father. In Vientiane and in their travels abroad, most of the Tai Dam had experience using most modern appliances. However, the inhabitants of Laos ate rice, not bread. When her toaster shot the bread up after toasting, it "surprised" and "startled" Bachti.[26] Dinh VanLo remembered eating a Big Mac. He enjoyed the sandwich and tried to recreate one at home. He tried it again but did not like it. VanLo realized he had put French salad dressing instead of catsup onto his burger. Mike Rasavanh tried to explore Des Moines as a young teenager. He had ridden the bus before, and he decided to take the bus to travel around Des Moines. He thought all of the buses went on the same route. Lost and confused, he had to ask the driver for help on how to get him home.

On a more serious note, the Tai Dam did not fully comprehend the full range of diversity to be experienced in Iowa, and their ignorance and prejudice towards blacks made for tense moments. The Tai Dam assumed their sponsors would be white "Americans." Gateway Opportunity Center was an African American community organization that sponsored roughly seventy of the first wave of Tai Dam refugees. These seven Tai Dam families received six months of free room and board at a Gateway-owned apartment complex on the Northside of Des Moines, Iowa. Tensions existed in Shearer's acceptance of the Gateway sponsorship from the start. In Shearer's opinion, racial discrimination against African Americans resulted in a dejected and impoverished group who had taken to welfare. Set apart by their race and again by their use of welfare, African Americans had become a "double minority." Shearer's goal with the Tai Dam was to prevent them from becoming a double-minority like African Americans. Shearer understood that Asian features made the Indochinese perpetual foreigners.[27] No matter how many years they lived in the United States, Asian Americans would be looked at as being outsiders because of their physical differences from "Americans." Shearer could not change the Indochinese refugees' race, but she could do her best to keep them off welfare.

Initially, the Gateway initiative proved trying for all parties involved. Shearer knew the "shock waves which would go across the white community" for her agreement to the Gateway sponsorship in the first place. Accepting Vietnam War refugees had been controversial from the start. Even some supporters of Ray's decision to bring refugees to Iowa disapproved of black sponsorship. They assumed that white hands would help assimilate the Indochinese to American life. So too did the Tai Dam. They had expectations of having white "American" sponsors and living in nice "American" residences. The Tai Dam moved into a Gateway apartment complex in the more rundown part of Des Moines, Iowa. Jack Spear reflected on the early misunderstandings between the Tai Dam and their African American sponsors: "The furnishings weren't the best. When the families came in ... they complained to their leaders." The refugees asked the Task Force if they could find someplace else to live. Spear remembered their desire to leave insulted the folks at Gateway, one of whom said, "We don't want a bunch of racists living with us.... They were pretty offended that these people did not want to live there."[28] The Gateway representatives' charges of racism might have been justified.

Dara Rasavanh came to Iowa as a young girl a few years after the first group of Tai Dam. She remembered "hearing horrible stories from our people that the black people are bad ... oh do not go near them. That is a black neighborhood they will steal your stuff. They are bad people." Rasavanh theorized that some Tai Dam may have feared African Americans because of physical size differences. The smaller Tai Dam wanted to warn their friends, but this warning passed along a negative stereotype of black people. In the early days of resettlement, Tai Dam lacked information on African Americans. Nga Baccam and Neth Rasavanh mistakenly believed that all Americans were Caucasians before they arrived in the United States. Well before coming to America, some Tai Dam had formed attitudes about African soldiers in Southeast Asia, and their opinions of these African soldiers influenced their ideas and therefore relationships with African Americans in Iowa. For example, Khouang Luong associated blacks with soldiers in Laos: "When we saw a black, we called them

French … a black French. I found out there are black Americans. So there
are many kinds of blacks. I did not know anything about Africa. I just
called them French." Houng Baccam admitted that he associated blacks
with rudeness and violence. His initial opinions of African Americans
had been molded by the image of African soldiers who served French
imperialism in Indochina.[29]

Europeans had long believed Africa to be a godless land populated
by ferocious, lustful, and lazy savages well before the French colonial effort
began there in the nineteenth century. For example, even Enlightenment
thinkers Voltaire and Montesquieu thought poorly of Africans. The French
hoped to harness the supposed savagery of Africans when they created a
battalion of African soldiers in 1857. These *tirailleurs senegalais* policed
French possessions in Africa. Requiring less pay than white soldiers, having more resistance to tropical illnesses, and taking the blame for outbursts
of colonial violence were among the advantages of employing these black
fighters. By 1910, Colonel Charles Mangin lobbied the public to let African
soldiers protect the French mainland. Several years later, the French played
on the violent image of the African to her advantage by mobilizing the
tirailleurs senegalais as shock troops against the Germans during World
War I.

Inherent tensions emerged from France's decision to use African soldiers. Deploying a race Europeans deemed primitive and inherently violent struck natural fear into the opposition. However, exposure to France's
civilizing mission should have uplifted African soldiers from their bar-
barism. By the interwar years, French colonial officials tried to replace
the violent image of the African soldier with the image of them being
children, but World War II and conflict in Indochina witnessed a quick
resurgence of the violent African soldier stereotype. In Indochina, sixty
thousand *soldats africains* served under the French. Most were stationed
near small villages and interacted with local inhabitants. The Central
Office of African Affairs investigated a high number of complaints about
black soldiers serving in Indochina from 1952 to 1954.[30] Tai Dam experiences with and stories about black soldiers, at least in a couple of instances,
informed their early opinions of African Americans in Iowa.

The tense start between the Tai Dam and their African American
sponsors continued for both the Task Force and the Tai Dam. Richard
Freeman recalled having to check Gateway's books often. Rumors circulated that Gateway had diverted federal funds intended for refugees to fix
up their apartment complex. In a memo to Kenneth Quinn, Shearer
recounted how one refugee informed her that young black children had

thrown rocks at Gateway Opportunity Center, causing panic among some Tai Dam. Shearer raced to Gateway: "We all feared it might be a reaction from the black community. I had to go and find out for myself ... and I couldn't trust hearing the story from a refugee who could hardly speak the language ... and no rocks were thrown ... and I learned that the black kids were only mad because they'd been sent home from the center because they were too noisy one night." Shearer walked at the head of a column of frightened Tai Dam from their apartment to the Gateway Center to show that there was nothing to fear from the black community. When a *Washington Post* reporter asked to learn about any downside of Governor Ray's resettlement initiative, Shearer advised him to go alone to Gateway to investigate for himself. The reporter noted that the Tai Dam refugees sponsored by Gateway had been the happiest he encountered because they all lived together.[31] Over time, the relationship between the Tai Dam and their Gateway sponsors improved. So too did Houng Baccam's opinions of African Americans. He realized that African Americans were different than African soldiers. He laughed at his earlier opinion of blacks, a population he learned to work with and live next to amicably for many years.

Both their new surroundings in Iowa and homeland histories have influenced Tai Dam spiritual beliefs in America. Since arriving in the state forty years ago, many Tai Dam have converted to Christianity for a multitude of reasons. Some Southeast Asian refugees felt pressured to convert by their Christian sponsors. Yet many Tai Dam willingly attended church services out of respect for their sponsors, especially those who had done so much to aid their resettlement. For example, a teenaged Mike Rasavanh remembered church being a place to get help, and this sparked his interest in the faith. Under these circumstances, some Tai Dam became Christians, but in name only. They did not fully comprehend or believe in the Christian faith until years later, if ever.

In addition to conversion to the faith of their sponsors, the Iowa climate influenced Tai Dam spiritual beliefs. Tai Dam studied in 1950s Laos attributed supernatural spirits as the main cause of illness. In the early 1980s, Iowa State University researchers surveyed and interviewed female Tai Dam about healthcare practices, and the participants listed weather as the main cause of illness in Iowa.[32] It is highly likely that weather's prominent role in illness causation among the Iowa Tai Dam can be attributed to the refugees moving from tropical Southeast Asia to Iowa's four-seasoned climate. In addition to the changing seasons, the sheer range of Iowa weather would be difficult to adjust to and have the potential to reshape traditional attitudes about illness causation. In 1975, 70 degrees separated Vientiane's low of 34 and high of 104 degrees. In 1976, 109 degrees separated Des Moines' low of minus 12 and high of 97 degrees.

Changes to Tai Dam spiritual beliefs in Iowa must be seen as a continuation of an earlier process. Separation from the Tai Federation and traditional farming had long disrupted the spiritual practices of the Tai Dam. In her homeland of Muang Sai, Nga Baccam's father used to sacrifice a water buffalo to ensure a good harvest for the village. After the Tai Dam fled to Xiang Khoang, they no longer had access to good land and livestock to perform these traditional ceremonies. Years later, the ceremonies returned but on a much smaller scale. According to traditional healer Khouang Luong, "We dropped a lot of things. We prayed for Earth Mother or Sky Father. Or before you go to somewhere, you pray first. Now we do not do that anymore. If you went from town to town before, they would pray for the spirit ancestor to help him … we do not do that anymore."[33] As they became distanced from farming, the Tai Dam dropped ceremonies that ensured good harvest, though Luong knows of a family in Hawaii who still holds the old ceremonies for this very purpose. Luong himself is the personification of the diverse set of beliefs held by the Tai Dam because of their history of upheaval. On top of being a traditional healer, he described himself as a Presbyterian Christian who attends a Buddhist temple.

In addition to sponsors, climate and occupation, the Tai Dam's cultural background must be taken into account when studying why some converted to Christianity. Somphong Baccam is a practicing Christian, yet she still maintains an altar to her ancestors. Like so many others, she interprets Christianity through the lens of traditional Tai Dam beliefs. Venerating ancestors is like the Fifth Commandment requiring people to honor their parents; they do not worship their ancestors, but they honor them. She equates ancestor veneration to American Memorial Day. People visit cemeteries to talk to loved ones passed, but not to worship them. Siang Bachti, a member of the Catholic Church, has analyzed Tai Dam spiritual beliefs and tried to make comparisons to Christianity. The Tai Dam creation narrative has gained credence for her because the Christian faith also describes a catastrophic flood.

Phuong Baccam and Dinh VanLo converted to Christianity, but their past experiences in Southeast Asia were part of the reason for their conversion. Baccam missed the communal living of his childhood. At mealtime, the entire family gathered together as one, and they all ate the same meal: sticky rice. In Iowa, he laments that family members eat at all different times of the day, and they eat all different types of foods. A sense of unity through community was an aspect of the Christian faith that appealed to Baccam. He disliked each Tai Dam family's venerating their own relatives at different times throughout the year. He enjoys seeing diverse peoples from different areas gathering together for worship on Sundays; they are all unified in their faith in Christ. It would make sense that the biblical story of Joseph appealed to Dinh VanLo. Like Joseph, VanLo suffered from family separation. His father died at a young age, and VanLo's mother remarried and moved away, "If you have no father you are nothing" in Tai Dam society. For twenty years in Egypt, Joseph maintained his Israelite identity. Likewise, VanLo spent twenty years in Laos and maintained his Tai Dam identity. Like Joseph: "I was poor, I was nothing, and I wanted to be somebody who could help my people. Joseph is one of my idols. He goes to Egypt and helps out all of the people."[34]

The Tai Dam's encounter with Christianity helped some to rationalize their escape from communism, and Christianity helped some to cope with the lingering problems of wartime trauma. In 1975, Dara Rasavanh's brother had been captured by the communists while crossing the border between Thailand and Laos. As a result, Dara's mother refused to leave the country without her missing child. After receiving news of her brother's death, the family decided to flee Laos in 1978. While in Sioux Center, Iowa, the family learned that her brother had survived and escaped communist captivity, "That is how my parents became Christians because they had just started praying for him, and it was not too long until we heard from him so that is why they believed that God answered their prayers."[35] Neth Rasavanh converted because she believes that a higher power guided her and fellow Tai Dam from their many wartime troubles. Similarly, Nga Baccam says praying helps her fall asleep at night.

Although conversion to Christianity helped some Tai Dam cope with traumatic pasts, their conversion still resulted in some tensions in the Tai Dam community. The Tai Dam had long privileged maintaining their identity while in Laos. Some believed failure to worship ancestors and conversion to Christianity represented an assault upon Tai Dam identity; Dinh VanLo's relative questioned whether or not Dinh could oversee traditional funerary rites for a loved one because he had converted to Christianity. Mike Rasavanh, currently a pastor at LifeSong Open Bible Church in Des Moines, Iowa, recounted his father La's near death experience a few years ago. La's near death experience demonstrated the anxieties that conversion to Christianity could bring about. La dreamt that he had traveled up to heaven. There, he found an angelic figure behind a gate, but he and other Tai Dam could not get in because they had not fully accepted

Eber "Lloyd" and his wife Ruth German with Neth and La Rasavanh, Des Moines, Iowa, circa 1975. After the Rasavanh family's first sponsor failed them, the Germans offered to help. Lloyd served in the Coast Guard during World War II and worked for Anderson Erickson Dairy. The Germans were dedicated members of the First Church of the Open Bible and helped introduce the Rasavanhs to Christianity. Today, the Rasavanhs' son Mike is pastor of Lifesong Church of the Open Bible in Des Moines (Neth Rasavanh).

Christ. After this near death experience, La testified to fellow parishioners. His experience reinforced his belief in Christ, and his faith in God helped him prepare for his last days in his new land.[36]

The Tai Dam made it to Iowa and flourished not because of divine providence. The IRSC deserves some credit for the successful resettlement of the Tai Dam. Success may be defined in many different ways. Lower numbers of Tai Dam went onto welfare, and many more bought homes than other Indochinese refugee groups throughout the state. Additionally, no major conflicts between the general populace and the refugee community occurred. In the Galveston Bay Area of Texas in 1979, competition between local white and Vietnamese fishermen led to an alteration that left one Texan dead and Ku Klux Klansmen rallying in the streets. That same year, Denver, Colorado, witnessed a heated housing dispute between the Indochinese and Mexican Americans. Part of this success lay in the role of Governor Ray in advocating for refugees and using the weight of his office to promote their successful resettlement throughout the state. Additionally, partnerships with Job Service and the Department of Instruction, and novel programs like volunteer tutoring helped the Tai Dam adjust. Yet, the Iowa Refugee Service Center resettled the Hmong using similar methods, but they did not have the same success with this group. Part of the reason for this explanation lay in the historic experiences and backgrounds of each group. Many of the Tai Dam who arrived in Iowa had experienced urban living and had obtained literacy in a language. They also held a diverse array of jobs in Southeast Asia. Likewise, the Tai Dam transitioned to Iowa well because they had migrated before. By the time Ray agreed to bring the Tai Dam to Iowa, the group had become "professional refugees." In fact, the Tai Dam relocated to Laos before USAID began supporting similar flights from communism. No such thing as welfare existed for the group in Laos.

In their many upheavals from the Tai Federation to Hanoi to Xiang Khoang to Vientiane to Nong Khai to Iowa, family support and making do helped them through these trying times. Family separation always haunted the Tai Dam, as recalled by Houng Baccam in 1981:

> When I was young, the same age as my older son, my father showed to me a picture in the newspaper of orphan kids victimized by the Korean War in 1951. He was scared about family separation like in the picture. In 1952, we fled our country to North Vietnam. When North Vietnam became communist, we fled to the country of Laos. In 1975, on the eve of South Vietnam's collapse to the communists, it happened to me to see on the *Time Magazine* a picture published on the cover—two Vietnamese children in the baby-lift program. I showed the picture to my children, the same as my father did 24 years ago. I was scared with the same feeling like my father. In May 1975, I had to take my family across the Mekong River to escape communism in Laos.... Only Gov. Robert Ray responded to our appeal by accepting the first Tai Dam group into Iowa. Six hundred were accepted by Iowa. The rest remained in the camp and many families were separated. Left behind were close relatives such as parents, grandparents, sons, daughters, brothers, sisters, etc.[37]

Whereas the state had the goal of keeping refugees off welfare, the refugees had the goal of aiding and reuniting with family members who had been left behind. Their desire to help and reunite with family left in Southeast Asia best explains why Tai Dam went to work so willingly in the early years of resettlement. They needed extra income for their families in Iowa, but they also took any job offered and worked hard to help their relatives in Nong Khai. From their very arrival in November of 1975, these refugees thought about their loved ones still languishing at the refugee camp. Siang Bachti remembered thinking that the leafless Iowa trees were dead, and these trees could have provided so much needed firewood to loved ones back in Thailand. They sent money to family and friends. When Nong Khai burned to the ground a few years later, the Tai Dam pooled their resources and sent assistance.

Ray had agreed to bring in hundreds of Tai Dam, but there had been no guarantee that all of the others back at Nong Khai would be able to join them. The Tai Dam wanted there to be no doubts about their worthiness of being resettled in Iowa. The refugees often refused welfare benefits they qualified for because they feared their acceptance of this assistance would prevent their loved ones from joining them.[38] They accepted dead-end jobs and wrote to Governor Ray and the State Department in the hopes of bringing more of their loved ones to Iowa. Their aggressive campaigning to be resettled as a group had resulted in Ray accepting them as refugees, and once in Iowa, their hard work persuaded the Governor to bring in more Tai Dam. Overall, the state's experience with the Tai Dam went smoothly. This influenced Ray's decision to take action when confronted by another Indochinese refugee crisis in January of 1979.

5

The Boat People Come to Iowa

During its first two year contract with the State Department, the Iowa Refugee Service Center resettled 1,200 Tai Dam. By the late 1970s, the state's Tai Dam project neared its end. For fiscal year 1978, the IRSC resettled 179 refugees, most of whom were Tai Dam reuniting with family. IRSC officials anticipated bringing in another 200 refugees for fiscal year 1979, but a humanitarian disaster caused Governor Ray to amend this number. In its haphazard exit from Vietnam, the United States left behind many former allies. The communists sought to "reeducate" all who had collaborated with the Americans. Fear of reprisals along with economic and political factors resulted in a mass exodus from Vietnam. Refugees packed onto small vessels and took to the sea to escape communism. Seeing the plight of these refugees compelled Ray to announce in January of 1979 that Iowa planned to admit an additional 1,500 Indochinese refugees, but the Tai Dam also influenced the Governor's decision.

Ray's increasing admissions demonstrated once again how he influenced Indochinese refugee policy more than any other governor in the nation. Some Iowans who opposed greater intake of refugees questioned whether or not Ray had the power to make this decision. In their letters to the Governor, Iowans opposed resettling the boat people for a myriad of reasons: economic competition, racial animosity, and the bitter legacy of the controversial Vietnam War figured most prominently in their letters. Some Iowans favored Ray's increasing refugee admission out of a sense of guilt over the abandonment of former Vietnamese allies. Other Iowans supported resettlement because of their Judeo-Christian beliefs and or personal experiences with Southeast Asians. Many Iowans took pride in their Governor's humanitarian efforts on behalf of their state.

The United States delayed the evacuation of Saigon until late April of 1975. They feared news of an exit plan might leak to the public, which would have caused a panic and therefore quicker collapse of the South. Ultimately, about 130,000 Vietnamese fled South Vietnam for the United States that April. However, the delayed and chaotic U.S. exit resulted in many former allies being abandoned. When evacuation efforts ceased on May 1, 1975, the United States left behind as many as 30,000 agents trained by the Central Intelligence Agency for the Phoenix program and over one and a half million soldiers, policemen, and public officials of the toppled Republic of Vietnam. To make matters worse, the communists obtained American computer data containing the list of thousands of the United States' Vietnamese allies. After the communists seized power, more than 200,000 political and military figures who had cooperated with the United States went to reeducation camps.[1] Dau Truong of Davenport, Iowa, was just one of the many Vietnamese punished for working with the Americans.

Dau Truong served as an interpreter for Marine Lt. John Judge of Albia, Iowa. The two men worked for the CIA's Revolutionary Development Cadre program with the objective of improving village infrastructure and assisting with village security. Dau also worked for the Provisional Reconnaissance Unit under the CIA's famous Phoenix program. His mission was to infiltrate and eliminate Vietcong infrastructure near I-Corps. As the war ended and the communists advanced South, Dau's wife Thuong burned all of his American service related documents. Unfortunately, the communists still discovered Dau had worked for the U.S. military.

As punishment for aiding the Americans, Dau toiled in a reeducation camp for seven years. The communists oversaw these prison camps which were often located in mountainous regions throughout Vietnam. Prisoners worked eight hours per day clearing forests and harvesting crops. Indoctrination sessions often followed work. Detainees received a meager daily ration of three or four bowls of rice. Hunger ravaged the prisoners who scavenged for food. For the foragers grasshoppers became a delicacy. Consuming anything that seemed edible, prisoners often fell ill with stomach aches. They drank detergent to ease their pain. Many never made it out of these camps. Dau remembered this difficult time in his life: "It was very hard control. Sometimes we worked under bad weather and most of the people did not eat enough, but we worked eight hours in the fields. We had to go to the forests to cut the trees to build houses. In my camp there were over a thousand people.... It was a very bad situation."[2]

Dau survived his imprisonment with the aid of his dutiful wife Thuong. In addition to taking care of their children during his absence, Thuong also helped her husband survive reeducation. She walked long distances to sell items on Vietnam's black market. With her extra income, Thuong purchased supplemental rations and brought them to her husband in the camp. After Dau left reeducation, the communists kept a close watch over him, and they initially refused to let him go back to his hometown in Tam Ky. Later, he moved to Saigon and worked as a waiter and interpreter at a friend's restaurant. In Saigon, he planned to escape the country as so many others had done while he was away in camp.

Other than northerners who had migrated to South Vietnam over the years, many southerners lacked information about communism. Initially, many families happily reunited and enjoyed the conclusion of the war. Unfortunately, the joy lasted only a short while as the communists gained control over the South. Kiet Tran, an ethnic Chinese born in Saigon, recalled learning about the bizarre workings of the new government.

> We did not know about communism. After about one year they gave every family a paper. They told you to record what you have—diamonds—everything. If you have never experienced communism, it scared the hell out of you and your family. They sent out all of the young people ... and they handed you the paper and your family had to fill out I have twenty ounces of gold, diamonds, whatever. They say it is for your sake the government will keep [your possessions] for you. Everybody ran away and hid their things.... After the report, they suspected you. 'You are lying. You did not report.' And they sent twenty people to search. They took everything out to see if you hid something. If they found something, you are going to jail.... Every family was confused in this society.

The Hoa, or ethnic Chinese in Vietnam, numbered about 1.7 million, and 1.4 million of these lived in South Vietnam. Because of their heavy involvement in the South's business sector, communist economic policies adversely affected the ethnic Chinese community the most. As the communists gained control, Hoa private businesses collapsed. On March 23, 1978, the government closed thousands of businesses and confiscated their assets. Kiet Tran's father owned a restaurant in Saigon, but by 1978 the family business shut down. If not a communist insider, people in Saigon lacked job opportunities. "You just walked around and sold everything so you can eat," reflected Tran. Kiet also found it odd that the government changed the currency so frequently. When the people went to exchange their old money for the new currency, communists accused those with money of robbing the people, and they threw them in jail for their treachery.[3]

In the past, Vietnam had been one of the world's top rice producers. From 1976 to 1978, Vietnam's per capita rice availability declined from 159 kilograms to just 129. Part of this can be blamed on the economic policies of the communists. Farmers lacked incentives to produce crops. The government promised cash for their crops but instead handed farmers IOUs. Authorities told farmers to take these IOUs to the local communist party office for cash, but many refused out of fear of being arrested as "exploitative capitalists." Even the heavens seemed to conspire against Vietnam. From July through October of 1978, typhoons and flooding damaged agricultural output. Then a young school student from Saigon, Vinh Nguyen remembered the economic situation deteriorating soon after the communists seized power. Nguyen's diet noticeably worsened. He recalled bread lines and a meager monthly ration of one pound of meat for an entire family. Nguyen and many others endured this change in lifestyle because "when we were young, we did not realize it because the propaganda at that time was we were rebuilding the country. We did not know any better."[4]

Kiet Tran and Vinh Nguyen soon learned that their new government observed their every move. Tran remembered youngsters wearing AK-47s and watching over him in the streets. Nguyen recalled being one of the watchers in this society: "When we were young, we were trained to be the listeners. I went to the market, and I pretended to be out there buying stuff, but my job was to listen to people to see if anybody was talking about organizing an escape." In school, communists indoctrinated youngsters. Children wore red scarves, stared at portraits of communist heroes, and everybody joined clubs such as Ho Chi Minh Vanguard Youth. As they came of age, Nguyen and his peers soon learned about the realities of communism: "We began to understand we were being controlled but had no control. I am watching you and you are watching me. Somebody else is watching us."[5]

Aside from economic factors and a dislike of the new communist regime, Vietnam's conflict with Cambodia and China created a panicked atmosphere that compelled many to flee. Vietnamese support had been integral to the establishment of the communist Khmer People's Revolutionary Party in the early 1950s. After the 1954 Geneva Accords divided Vietnam in two, nearly half of the 2,000 KPRP's officials went to communist North Vietnam. By the 1960s, a rift emerged between Cambodian communists who had studied in Vietnam and or adhered to Vietnamese advice and those who detested Vietnamese influence over the revolutionary path of Cambodia. Ultimately, Pol Pot's anti–Vietnamese faction prevailed. Racist policies influenced the course of the Cambodian revolution, which resulted in the ethnic-cleansing of Vietnamese and other non–Khmer.[6] As Vietnam's relationship with the Khmer Rouge soured, border warfare broke out by April of 1975. On Christmas Day of 1978, the Vietnamese led an invasion of Cambodia and placed Heng Samrin into power.

Vietnam invaded Cambodia in part because it feared a two front war with Cambodia and China. Vietnam had long feared the power of her northern neighbor. The roots of Vietnamese nationalism can be found in resistance to Chinese dominance. As World War II neared its conclusion, the French, Vietminh, and Chinese competed for influence over Vietnam. Ho Chi Minh preferred to deal with the French because of Vietnam's long history of being dominated by China. Ho once said, "I would rather sniff French shit for five years than eat Chinese for a thousand."[7] Though both adhered to the same political doctrine, tensions between communist Vietnam and China soon emerged. A rift in the communist bloc occurred after Nikita Khruschev denounced Stalinism in 1956. Khruschev's de-Stalinization resulted in the deterioration of the Soviet Union's relationship with China. The Soviets withdrew their technicians from China and began courting a closer relationship with Vietnam. Eventually, the Soviets and Vietnamese formed an alliance in opposition to the Chinese and the Cambodians. When Vietnam invaded Cambodia, China responded by attacking northern Vietnam in February of 1979.

The reasons for the exodus out of Vietnam were many. Former allies of the Americans lived marginal lives in Vietnam. They and their families faced imprisonment in reeducation camps and discrimination. Those with American ties were refused jobs and barred from university training. Communist economic policies caused great hardships for many, especially the Hoa. As their relationship with China worsened, so too did Vietnamese treatment of her ethnic Chinese population. The Vietnamese communists viewed the Hoa living within their borders as a fifth column ready to support China when called upon. As a result, many Chinese lost their jobs. Vietnam's communist state also sought to conscript young men into her ever growing military as border warfare with Cambodia and China commenced. In addition to job loss and conscription, the state relocated some Chinese and former political prisoners to New Economic Zones. There, they performed labor on isolated agricultural communes. Many Hoa from the city viewed relocation to New Economic Zones as a death sentence.[8]

For these reasons, hundreds of thousands like Kiet Tran and Vinh Nguyen took to the sea to escape.

Tran and Nguyen recalled their decision to flee Vietnam. In Saigon, Tran's brother worked for the Bank of Tokyo. In 1977, the communists arrested his brother for involvement with the CIA. This sent Tran into a panic: "After they took my brother, I dared not go home. If I go home, they are going to catch me too. So I lived around the city. [I stayed with] this friend one week this friend another week. Then, I looked for some way to escape on some boat."[9] Nguyen's family decided that he should try to leave because he did not have a family of his own. If he failed, Nguyen's capture would have caused the least amount of hardship to family members.

In order to escape, Tran and Nguyen entered a duplicitous market where people tried to buy their way out of Vietnam; they relied on relatives for financial support. In July of 1979, the State Department estimated one adult needed 7.26 to 12 ounces of gold to buy one place on a ship. The State Department's report *Vietnam's Refugee Machine* accused the Vietnamese government of profiting from this refugee trade. The Public Security Bureau approved passenger lists, collected fees, and arranged departures of boats. *The Far East Economic Review* estimated that Vietnam's government made $115 million off the boat people trade in 1978 alone. Quite often Hoa formerly in private enterprise in the South served as the middlemen for the boat people and the government. These middlemen negotiated the exit price to be paid and procured the boats, most of which ranged from about fifteen to twenty-five meters in length. At every step, boat people might be swindled out of their money. The political police sometimes collected gold and then refused to let the buyer leave. Coastal patrols stopped boats and demanded additional payments. Furthermore, middlemen conned boat people out of their gold. In his first attempt at escape, Tran dealt with tricksters who took his deposit, but never showed up at the rendezvous point. Nguyen remembered the nervousness of leaving, "We left my life up to somebody I did not know, but that was how it worked."[10] Yet for all of its troubles, finding a way onto a boat proved far easier than the ordeal that occurred while at sea.

In 1978, Tran left Vietnam in a ship he estimated to be about eleven meters in size. Seventy-one persons of ethnic–Chinese descent, including Tran's sister and nephew, packed into this small boat. During their trip, boat people lived at the mercy of the sea and the disposition of those they encountered on it. Tran's group desired to sail to Malaysia because Thailand held a poor reputation for keeping refugees in camps for many years.

However, those aboard Tran's boat did not understand navigation: "We just drove around and around in the Thailand Bay. Our boat was leaking water. All these people tried to put the water away and finally we met a Thailand fishing vessel, but the Thailand fishing boat was Chinese. They had M-16s ... but they were real good." The Thailand fishermen gave Tran's group directions to an oil rig. As the boat neared its destination, Tran remembered seeing a huge fire in the middle of the ocean. An American oversaw the operation of the rig, but many Chinese worked there as engineers. Employees at the oil refinery called the Malaysian Navy which picked up the refugees. Tran spent about one week at sea: "Everybody got sick ... when you got off the ship you could not eat anything. All threw up.... Our ship made it safe. We were lucky it was a Thailand peace boat but a lot of Thailand 'peace boats' robbed and raped those women and kidnapped them to sale.... We were lucky or else all would have died in the ocean.... A lot of people died in the sea. A lot."[11]

In comparison to Tran, a worse fate awaited Nguyen's group while at sea. Pirates viewed the boat people as easy targets; these refugees carried on their persons whatever wealth they managed to retain after paying to exit Vietnam. Nguyen recounted the hardship endured by the roughly 135 members of his boat:

> We got robbed and raped and caught by the local fishermen many times. One time we got stopped by real pirates ... but I tell you this—the very last time we got robbed—just imagine this—when you are being robbed and raped by somebody and you cry [for those who are harming you] can you imagine how bad they looked.... We were not human at that time after so many days of being robbed and raped and tortured and stripped naked.... I guess many of them who were fishermen at the time probably would not have a day of good sleep in their conscience. It was really tough, and we were not the only boat.

In spite of experiencing such trauma, Nguyen recognizes he was fortunate to have survived: "Statistically, half of the Vietnamese who escaped by boat died. So I am lucky. It is all luck." Estimates on the number of boat people fatalities differ. Political scientist R.J. Rummel estimated that 500,000 boat people perished, but the United Nations High Commissioner for Refugees stated that about 250,000 boat people died and 929,600 found safe haven.[12] Regardless of the actual number of deaths, the boat people's suffering was incalculable.

Even after landfall, survivors such as Vinh Nguyen and Kiet Tran still witnessed traumatic events while awaiting resettlement abroad. At Sonkla, Thailand, Nguyen recalled the difficult decision facing many women: "We saw people being carried to the camp who could not even walk they had been raped so badly so many times. They had to take med-ication so they did not carry the pregnancy.... It is sad but a few people carried the pregnancy through. They did not have the heart to kill the baby." Southeast Asian nations of first asylum often despised refugees for overwhelming their limited resources. Some villagers stoned to death incoming boat people; the impoverished villagers resented their nation's having to take care of these illegal aliens. The boat people also presented potential security threats to Southeast Asian governments that feared com-munist infiltration. As a result, the naval and police forces of Singapore, Thailand, and Malaysia all turned some boat people away from landing at one time or another. Sailors might have offered food, drink, and or repairs to distressed boat people, but they still towed these vessels back to sea. While a refugee at Palau Bidong, Malaysia, Tran remembered the navy firing shots at unauthorized boats: "We saw a lot of ships. If they wanted to get on the island, the policemen fired at you, and the people were scared and ran away. Next thing all those died in the ocean." Tran guessed about two or three thousand refugees lived at the island camp of Palau Bidong upon his arrival. By the time he left in April of 1979, the number had risen into the tens of thousands. At his tightly packed camp, sanitation became a problem, "A lot of people sat there and died ... too many people."[13] As January 1979 approached, nearly 62,000 boat people awaited resettlement in refugee camps throughout Southeast Asia.

As the boat people crisis unfolded, a talented aide began working for Governor Ray's refugee resettlement initiative. Kenneth Quinn met Ray through the Tai Dam project. To celebrate their first year in Iowa, the Tai Dam held a freedom festival in November of 1976. Governor Ray invited Gerald Ford to the event, but the President could not attend and sent Quinn in his place. Quinn worked as a Foreign Service diplomat in Viet-nam from 1968 until 1974, and he had served under Henry Kissinger and Richard Holbrooke in the National Security Council and the State Depart-ment. Being raised in Dubuque, Iowa, and specializing in Southeast Asian affairs resulted in Quinn taking an early and special interest in Iowa's resettlement program. Appreciating Quinn's expertise on refugee issues, Ray began recruiting him after the two men met at the Tai Dam festival. In September of 1978, Quinn started working with Iowa officials while on loan from the State Department. Though Quinn and Colleen Shearer had kept the Governor informed of the escalating crisis, it took seeing the tragedy unfold on camera to compel the Governor to take action.

In January of 1979, Governor Ray planned to end his workday after attending a Drake University basketball game, but Quinn urged the Governor to return to the office to watch a *60 Minutes* special on the boat people. Ed Bradley's powerful report provided a glimpse into some of the hardships suffered by the boat people as they landed in Malaysia. Frightened children screamed while being pulled from the sea, and exhausted adults collapsed to the ground and gave thanks that they had survived. Bradley spoke of how some boat people had been stoned to death by Malaysians, and many others had been turned away by the police. The boat people profiled in the *60 Minutes* report ended up at the island of Palau Bidong. At this camp, tens of thousands of refugees lived in a densely packed area less than one square kilometer in size. Many of these refugees appeared on camera while a spokesman pleaded to Bradley for the United States to accept them as refugees: "We hope we will get the help of the government of the United States. Please help us to survive so that one day we can live in freedom again as you all. The United States is our only hope."

On January 17, 1979, Governor Ray announced through a press release that the Iowa Refugee Service Center planned to resettle an additional 1,500 Indochinese refugees. Ray cited the *60 Minutes* broadcast as being the catalyst for his decision. The Governor believed these refugees deserved resettlement in the United States after fleeing communist rule, and Americans had a moral obligation to help save lives. Drawing on state pride, the Governor pronounced, "Iowa is not only a state in the heart of the nation, but also a state with a heart." As a nation comprised of immigrants, Ray asked Iowans to empathize with the boat people by asking themselves what "if their immigrant forefathers had been denied entry to the country." As the decision to bring in more Indochinese refugees unfolded, Colleen Shearer worried that America's Vietnam War guilt had waned. In her opinion, this guilt had been one of the primary motivators for Americans to support Indochinese resettlement. She confided in Quinn, "My gut feeling is that it's going to be a tough battle this time around."[14] She was right.

All of the Governor's aides received mail, but after the boat people announcement, no aide received more mail than Kenneth Quinn. He remembered, "We were flooded with letters. They all would come to me. I had a pile this high of those who liked it, and honestly, the pile of those who opposed was about the same height." On September 30, 1979, the *Des Moines Register* published the results of a poll that asked Iowans the following question, "Do you favor or oppose the resettlement of the 'boat people' in Iowa?" Whereas only 40 percent of Iowans favored resettlement, a majority of 51 percent of respondents opposed the Governor's decision.

Shearer tried to interpret the poll results with optimism by comparing them to an earlier poll. In August of 1975, the *Des Moines Register* had asked Iowans if they approved or disapproved bringing South Vietnamese to the United States. Forty-one percent of those polled favored and 51 percent opposed resettlement. Shearer believed holding the same level of support four years after the controversial war represented a win.[15]

From the collapse of Saigon through the boat people crisis, Iowans opposed resettling Indochinese refugees for similar reasons, but a closer comparison of the two polls reveals a decline in support for resettlement. According to the 1975 poll of 600 individuals, lower class, elderly, and rural Iowans were most likely to oppose resettlement. Sixty-four percent of Iowans who made $10,000 a year or more favored resettlement whereas only 46 percent of Iowans who made less than $5,000 a year favored resettlement. In addition to annual earnings, elderly and rural Iowans usually desired a closed door policy to the Indochinese. In fact, only 48 percent of elderly Iowans polled favored resettlement in comparison to the 70 percent of Iowans aged eighteen to twenty-four. Only 45 percent of Iowans living in rural communities approved of resettlement in comparison to 65 percent of Iowans living in large cities.

This same demographic—lower class, elderly, and rural Iowans—also figured prominently in the 51 percent of Iowans who opposed resettlement of the boat people in 1979. Although the 1975 poll also revealed that 51 percent of Iowans opposed bringing South Vietnamese to the United States, nearly 60 percent of Iowans stated they would welcome Vietnamese who resettled in their local communities. In contrast, the 1979 poll showed that only 40 percent of Iowans would welcome Indochinese to Iowa. Also, three out of ten Iowans wanted to prevent all boat people from coming to Iowa, but only one in ten favored bringing in greater numbers of boat people.[16]

Many Iowans questioned Governor Ray's power to admit refugees. In the 1970s, the president decided how many and which refugees to parole to the United States, Congress allocated special funding for their support, and voluntary agencies resettled these refugees in states without input from their governors. From start to finish, the workings of American refugee policy left the nation's governors feeling powerless. In 1975, Ray had established his own state refugee resettlement agency in part to gain some measure of control over this federally dominated process, but the very same frustrations and powerlessness that Ray once felt simply shifted to some of the citizens he governed. Mrs. Phyllis Hansen opposed resettlement because the decision had not been made democratically: "I question your right to offer to relocate these people to Iowa. I think it should be decided by the people in the state ... by those already in our country who need our help ... but most certainly not you as an individual."[17]

Ray Ford of Des Moines, Iowa, concurred with Mrs. Hansen's opinion. Ford thought Ray acted out of self-promotion, not the best interests of Iowans, "I question if you are really doing something that the people want you to do or if you are trying to build a name for Robert D. Ray?" In June of 1976, Ray had helped write the Republican Party's platform at their national convention in Kansas City. Serving as chairman of the platform committee showcased Ray's political ability, and many Republicans began to see Iowa's Governor as a viable

Anti-Ray political button, circa 1980, Iowa. While advocating refugee resettlement in 1979, Ray testified before congressmen in Washington, D.C., participated in the U.N. Conference on Indochinese Refugees in Geneva, Switzerland, and toured refugee camps in Thailand. Political opponents argued Ray had been elected to serve Iowans, not refugees. One correspondent said Ray had outgrown Iowa, and another referred to the Governor as "Ambassador Ray" (State Historical Museum of Iowa, Des Moines).

Vice Presidential candidate for Gerald Ford. However, Ford eventually chose Robert Dole as his running mate, and the pair lost a close election to Jimmy Carter and Walter Mondale. Critics of Ray as a Vice Presidential candidate noted that the Governor did not have international experience. The question of whether or not Ray became involved in refugee affairs to make himself a more appealing candidate for higher office is a fair one, but it must be noted that Ray never actively campaigned to join Ford's ticket. Ray believed if Ford wanted him to join the ticket, Ford would have asked him. In addition, the Governor had already started a refugee resettlement agency in 1975, nearly one year before the Republican National Convention and Vice Presidential rumors circulated. Still, the Governor's involvement in international affairs angered some Iowans who felt Ray to be out of touch with his constituents. Mrs. Alice Hemsted, a struggling farmer from Hills, Iowa, had been a longtime Ray supporter, but she wrote to inform him he had lost her vote because "you have outgrown Iowa" by focusing on international affairs. Similarly, E.B. Fredrickson, a retiree from Onawa, Iowa, demanded that Ray realize Iowans disapproved of resettlement before he ran off to try to become president. Alan Bulluck of Waterloo, Iowa, addressed the Governor as "Ambassador Ray" because he gallivanted across Southeast Asia and Europe to attend to international refugee affairs instead of the needs of Iowans. Bullock argued that Ray should help alleviate the plight of Iowa's rural poor.[18]

In the hundreds of letters mailed to the Governor's Office, economic considerations appeared with the greatest frequency for those opposed to resettling Indochinese refugees. These correspondents argued that charity must begin at home. In October of 1976, the American Friend's Service Committee labeled Iowa a "failure to feed" state because 78 percent of Iowans eligible for food stamps had not been enrolled into the program. Shortly after the Governor's decision to admit 1,500 additional refugees, Sherry Ricchiardi of the *Des Moines Register* started profiling rural poverty throughout the state. In her moving article "The Hidden Poor of Rural Iowa," readers confronted images of hungry blond-haired and blue-eyed children in their own backyards. Kevin Beauvais, the Director of the Woodbury County Community Action Agency, tried to promote awareness by speaking to Ricchiardi: "To most Iowans, the poor are the boat people of Southeast Asia, or natives on the dark continent of Africa. They don't realize it's the Widow Jones out in the boondocks of Iowa who might not have enough to eat. The great majority of Iowans are totally unaware of the rural poverty in this state." According to the U.S. Census Bureau, 72 percent of Iowa's poor lived in rural communities. Only twelve states registered a higher rural poor population than Iowa's 225,000. Decatur County had ranked as one of the poorest fifteen counties in the United States, and the 1979 census stated that roughly one in five residents of Davis, Decatur, and Ringgold Counties lived in poverty.

For her articles, Ricchiardi spoke with representatives from Iowa's Community Action Agencies. Workers for these nineteen federally funded agencies provided social services to the rural community, and they shared their "horror stories" related to the rural poor. One elderly and physically disabled man lived in a small shed in the middle of a farmer's pig lot. He survived on a Social Security income of $114 per month and by working odd jobs for area farmers. Without electricity or running water, the man remarked that even the dogs on these farms lived in better circumstances. One elderly woman ate dog food to save money for fuel for the upcoming winter. She maintained $900 in her bank account at all times to spare her the shame of having a county burial.

The impoverished rural Iowans profiled by Ricchiardi all felt the stigma of being poor, yet the author portrayed them as proud and resourceful individuals worth helping. The destitute often went without assistance because they did not know they qualified for it, or they refused aid because of shame or mistreatment by county welfare workers. Unfortunately, religious institutions failed to aid the destitute in their communities. Many rural poor could not attend church because they lacked transportation. Others refused to attend services because they felt embarrassed wearing ragged clothing and being unable to donate to the church collection plate. Rural pastors, overburdened with serving multiple congregations and working part-time jobs, failed to take a leading role in ameliorating rural poverty. According to the author, these Iowans often fell into abject poverty because of divorces, deaths, and or accidents, not because of laziness; the rural poor were more likely to be employed than their urban counterparts. Many Iowans found the rural poor in their own backyards to be more deserving of assistance than the foreign Indochinese refugees.[19]

The elderly and their supporters represented the most vocal segment of Iowans who criticized Ray's decision to admit 1,500 additional refugees. Out of all of the negative correspondence received by the Governor's Office, elderly women proved to be the most forceful opponents of resettlement. According to data from the National Rural Center in Washington, D.C., elderly Americans had high representation among the rural poor, and elderly females comprised the largest number of rural poor living alone. Whether they lived alone or with spouses, elderly women often performed household budgeting duties. When their bills outpaced their limited income, they wrote their governor in protest.

Class tensions appeared in the letters elderly females sent to Ray. In their opinion, the Governor seemed out of touch with Iowans' disapproval of resettlement, and Ray's upper-class status prevented him from empathizing with the financial woes faced by the elderly. Mrs. Hugh McLean of Traer, Iowa, wondered why the government "taxed to death" McLean and other average Iowans. She charged Ray with "sitting there pretty easy" in his governor's chair while the elderly lived on a sparse income. Etta Sluter compared Ray's large $60,000 a year salary to her struggle to survive on a meager $122 monthly Social Security check. Mrs. Estella Jones of Dakota City, Iowa, made a similar comparison. Ray and other government officials received large salaries, but elderly Iowans had to live on monthly grocery budgets less than what Ray and other politicians received in daily stipends for their numerous travels.[20]

For the elderly women who wrote to Ray, it came down to a question of fairness. In their opinion, aged Iowans deserved better treatment than foreigners. Mrs. Estella Jones stated, "I know elderly people who have lived here all of their lives, and they live in shacks not as good as the average garage or chicken house—nobody seems to care about them, but we are asked to take people from their countries and help them." Vesta Rhea of Sumner, Iowa, demanded that Ray's humanitarian efforts serve native Iowans instead of foreigners. In her shaky penmanship, the eighty-four-year-old commented: "I seen you looking at the dead in China. You could of seen dead in Iowa last winter when they turned heat off in old people home and [they] froze to death." Kathy Rees, a resident of Fort Dodge, Iowa, alleged refugees received special treatment in the form of cheap loans and tax exemptions while the elderly froze to death: "Americans should at least receive equal treatment; the same privileges as the oriental immigrants." Mrs. McLean asked why the Indochinese received Social Security benefits immediately when her generation had paid into Social Security by working low paying jobs for decades. In fact, some Indochinese refugees provided older ages to immigration officials in order to receive Social Security benefits sooner. Mrs. George Hamilton, a native of Elwood, Iowa, questioned why Ray let refugees abuse the welfare system while her fellow elderly made due "on fixed incomes too proud to ask for food stamps that their taxes have made it too easy for other people to receive and use for luxuries, rather than necessities." Mrs. Levi Jacobsen of Harlan, Iowa, fretted over finances, "I'm a senior citizen and I'm sure it won't be long before my life savings will be gone with the high utility and medicine bills."[21] Elderly women like Mrs. Jacobsen viewed the newcomers as competitors for limited resources. In their opinion, the governor diverted funds from aged Iowans to support refugees in Iowa.

Racist animosity towards the Indochinese appeared in the writings of some Iowans. Mrs. Pauline Wright, an elderly woman from Des Moines, Iowa, informed Ray he had lost her support because he let "all these dirty uncivilized gooks come over here" and provided them handouts. To Wright's great annoyance, her sister experienced financial woes, but these "refugees have everything, nice houses, new cars and each kid has a new expensive bicycle. I am so irked I cannot even write. Why didn't you leave that trash over there, and take care of your elderly aged sick people here in Iowa.... Every time I see them on the street I could spit in their faces. They are like the Japs—they can't be trusted." Another Iowan accused Ray and Shearer of being traitors to their race for helping Asians come to Iowa: "I don't know what kind of a breed of people you are but you sure are a hell of a breed. I know you can't be American because you want to bring all the Vietnamese here to Iowa.... I do know if an American here in Iowa was starving and needed a crust of bread to keep him alive you and Shearer would turn your back on him because he would not be one of your yellow Vietnamese.... Ray you and Shearer too low to be in Iowa why don't you two go to Vietnam and live with your kind I mean yellow people rats. P.S. You two must be fish eaters people I mean the worst kind." In his 1979 press release, Governor Ray asked the public to remember their own immigrant roots and support refugee resettlement, but this plea failed to persuade Forrest Warner of Newton, Iowa: "Yours and my ancestors came from Europe. We do not need Asians or Africans. Refugees. No. No. No."[22]

Indochinese refugee resettlement drastically altered Iowa's population, and many Iowans reacted negatively towards their state's changing demographics. In 1970, Iowa's Asian population stood at 3,420, but from 1975 until Ray left office in 1982, more than 8,000 Indochinese refugees resettled in Iowa. In 1970, no Vietnamese lived in Iowa, but 2,476 Vietnamese lived in the state just ten years later. Iowans of a provincial outlook worried their state might lose its Midwestern charm and become more like the states on the coasts. Some residents from small towns might have welcomed refugees with open arms, but others feared foreign intrusion from this Yellow Peril that allegedly brought to Iowa disease, crime, and unassimilable cultures. A nativist individual from Moorland, Iowa, advised Ray: "This Iowa is ours keep it that way. We don't want those foreigners coming here and taking over." S.A. Ruber disliked Vietnamese women challenging white racial hierarchy in small town Iowa. Ruber recounted how one Vietnamese woman had the audacity to ask for maids to serve her in Monona, Iowa, "That yellow broad thought two white women were going to wait on her." Ruber also wrote about how one war bride in Guttenberg, Iowa, expected the same treatment from her white mother-in-law. Sargent Robert Jackson feared the consequences of Iowans interbreeding with a supposedly inferior race: "I am proud to be from Iowa.... The people of Iowa are hearty and do not need our blood thinned with the blood of Vietnamese. I know these people—I've been there. They are parasites."[23]

Of those correspondents who self-identified as African Americans, career prospects figured important in their arguments against refugee resettlement. Some African Americans argued that the state favored Indochinese refugees over African Americans. Derrick Davis of Waterloo, Iowa, applauded Ray for his humanitarianism, but he felt the Governor lacked concern for African Americans in the state: "How is it that you can find, (create), fifteen hundred jobs for non-residents, or should I say residents who have not yet arrived, but seemingly have so little, or no concern about tax paying Iowans? I take issue with your preferential treatment of these people.... It really makes it clear, or at least easier to see, which politicians support and sustain the anti–Black system, which makes it virtually impossible for qualified Blacks to move into the economic mainstream. Frankly, I am glad that you are not running for Governor again. Ready to riot, Derrick E Davis."

Some African Americans resented what they deemed to be the state's special treatment of Indochinese refugees. Ray formed his resettlement program with the goal of keeping refugees off welfare. For this reason, the Governor asked Colleen Shearer, the Director of Job Service of Iowa, to lead the program. Initially, Job Service worked diligently to find jobs for the Tai Dam, but they eventually expanded services to all Indochinese refugees in the state. When a refugee applied for cash assistance, social workers sent this information to the IRSC. The IRSC immediately tried to place these individuals into the workforce and held employability conferences. At these conferences, refugees receiving aid signed an agreement to take any employment offered to them. Iowa's seventy-two Job Service centers helped find work for refugees throughout the entire state, and at each of these centers, one staffer specialized in finding employment for unemployed refugees on cash assistance.[24] The Governor invested political capital in resettlement; the state needed to employ this population because Indochinese on welfare reflected badly on Ray.

In this context, the IRSC earned a reputation for keeping the Indochinese off welfare, but their close attention to refugee employment alienated some African Americans. Community leader Arzania Williams oversaw Gateway's sponsorship of the Tai Dam. At a 1981 congressional inquiry into refugee resettlement, Williams voiced his displeasure with the special treatment received by the Indochinese that seemingly came at the expense of African Americans. At the hearing, Williams quipped, "If black people had a Colleen Shearer working for them, every one of my people would have a job." Williams also resented what some scholars have described as the "model minority" myth attributed to Asian Americans who as a race have been stereotyped as "intelligent, gifted in math and science, polite, hardworking, family oriented, law abiding, and successfully entrepreneurial." By the 1970s, Asian Americans had earned the praise of many in the white community for overcoming racism and poverty through hard work and education. Both Ray and Shearer endorsed the model minority myth. They believed it tragic that Asian refugees arrived in America with a strong work ethic, high intellect, and obedient demeanor only to be pushed onto welfare by inefficient resettlement programs run by VOLAGS. The *Des*

Moines Register surveyed employers of Indochinese refugees and found that refugees arrived on time, worked diligently, and sometimes labored through lunch breaks, further reinforcing the model minority myth. Out of fear of looking poorly in comparison, some native Iowans had to tell their refugee coworkers to slow down their work pace.[25]

The model minority myth has many flaws. First, the myth lumps diverse cultures together under one Asian category. For example, the experiences and general socioeconomic statuses of Cambodians and Japanese in America differ significantly. In addition to this generalizing, the model minority myth has been used to attack African Americans. If Asian Americans have been able to overcome racial discrimination, then African Americans' failure to do so rested on their own shortcomings. To promote resettlement, the state projected a positive image of the refugees to media outlets and through presentations to the general public. The IRSC told employers about the refugees' hardy work ethic and advertised employers' high satisfaction with their new workers. Whereas Asian Americans have been held in high esteem by whites, African Americans have been stereotyped as drug pushing thugs.[26]

Arzania Williams compared the job search environment for refugees to that of young blacks in Iowa. Employers vigorously recruited the Tai Dam Williams helped to sponsor. "We were amazed at how quickly we were able to get them jobs," Williams said. "Employers took them much quicker than they would the black male. Americans have opened up their hearts to these people." In contrast to the refugees, Williams said that employers never asked him to "give me those black people you've got; we've got jobs for them." Whereas Iowa boasted a low unemployment rate of 4 percent in 1979, Williams lamented that in the black section of Des Moines, Iowa, 40 percent of young blacks could not find work. Williams stated, "I'm not saying don't do anything for refugees. It's just that charity begins at home and spreads abroad."[27]

Overall, African American responses to resettlement seemed to have been muted in comparison to groups such as the elderly and or rural poor. For example, the state's African American newspaper the *Iowa Bystander* provided no coverage of Gateway's Tai Dam resettlement initiative and Ray's decision to admit 1,500 more Southeast Asians. Allen Ashby, a longtime sports columnist, was one of the few *Bystander* commentators on the Indochinese in Iowa, although this came as an aside to his main article about the closure of a drop-in center for the elderly in Des Moines, Iowa. The decision to close the drop-in center and build a fast food restaurant resulted in Ashby's feeling like a powerless outsider: two defining characteristics

Gateway Opportunity Center sponsors and Tai Dam refugees, Des Moines, Iowa, 1975. Director Arzania Williams (pictured smoking) believed the state favored Asian refugees. He was quoted in the *Washington Post,* "I know the Governor is sincere and I don't have anything against helping these people. But, damn, it just burns me up that refugees always seem to be raised above blacks.... I wish we had come as refugees, but we came as slaves. Everybody still sees us as inferior." Would Ray and Iowans have accepted black refugees with such open arms, wondered Williams and other African Americans (Houng Baccam).

of the African American experience. He compared Iowa's warm reception and integration of Asians into their community with their mistreatment and rejection of African Americans: "You read about the small towns welcoming hundreds of Asians into their community and providing them with jobs and a chance to buy or rent living quarters until they can get on their feet. Your first thought is would this same community take in even twenty-five blacks on the same basis. For us the cry comes even from kids, 'Go back where you came from.'"[28]

Although the *Bystander* sparsely commented on Indochinese refugees in Iowa, article after article criticized and called for an end to South Africa's shameful system of apartheid. The *Bystander*'s coverage of post–Vietnam War fallout centered not on refugee issues but on black veterans being unable to find good jobs because they had received less than honorable discharges from the military. According to African American community leader Edna Griffin, one out of seven black veterans did not receive an honorable discharge, and discrimination might have played a factor in white military officers' punishment and demotion of black soldiers. Griffin wrote to her local American Legion post and to President Jimmy Carter asking for the nearly 800,000 veterans to have their less than honorable discharges removed from their permanent records. She asked President Carter why he pardoned draft dodgers in January of 1977, but allowed those who served to have their career prospects ruined by their military records.[29]

That so few African Americans like Derrick Davis and Arzania Williams criticized the Governor's resettlement program comes as a surprise because the numbers of African Americans living in poverty had been on the rise throughout Ray's tenure as Governor. In 1969, 26.5 percent of Iowa's African Americans lived in poverty. By 1979, the same year Ray made his boat people announcement, black poverty had risen to 28.2 percent. In contrast, the state's elderly poverty had dwindled during Ray's governorship from 28.3 percent in 1969 to just 13.3 percent in 1979.[30] The decline in elderly poverty can be attributed to Congress' adjusting Social Security payments to account for inflation starting in 1972.

Iowans opposed Indochinese resettlement mostly because of economic considerations, but in their letters, remembrances of the Vietnam War frequently appeared. The two arguments cannot be easily separated because Iowans often piled on the legacy of the Vietnam War alongside of their economic arguments against resettlement. These Iowans believed themselves to be more worthy of assistance than a group they deemed as poor allies—if not outright enemies—in the only war ever lost by the United States.

Many Iowans opposed resettlement because they viewed the Vietnamese as poor allies responsible for the United States' loss in Vietnam, and several correspondents emasculated South Vietnamese men. In her letter to Governor Ray, Etta Sluter blamed the American defeat in Vietnam on Vietnamese allies: "I guess you forget we were helping them fight their war. They weren't helping us. Where were your bleeding hearts when you sent all those American boys to their deaths and destroyed the lives of so many others?" A native of Armstrong, Iowa, also scapegoated Vietnamese allies for the American defeat. He wrote, "If they would have helped out our boys over there they could of got results." The anonymous correspondent also charged the South Vietnamese soldiers with exploiting U.S. military financial support and then using these funds to buy their way out of Vietnam. Ray Ford of Des Moines, Iowa, agreed that the Vietnamese rode the U.S. military's "gravy train." Ford spent time in Vietnam and held negative opinions of the Vietnamese, "I know the people well and you don't spend your life dealing in the black market, stealing and begging, lying and cheating, selling your brothers and sisters and expect things to change." If they needed to leave so badly, Ford explained, true Vietnamese refugees would have done so when Saigon fell nearly four years earlier. Marvin Fawcett, a Navy veteran from Goldfield, deemed Vietnamese refugees unworthy of resettlement because they refused to fight to save their own nation. If they could not fight to save South Vietnam, Fawcett reasoned, the Vietnamese migrants would never fight to protect America. Similarly, Esther and James Merrill only wanted people who could "stand up for themselves" in United States, and they did not want to reward "cowardly" boat people who had deserted their own country by taking to the seas. Mr. and Mrs. Merrill accused Ray of being insensitive towards Vietnam veterans in his decision to admit more Indochinese, "It is really asking them and their families to overlook a great deal."[31]

Instead of simply being poor allies, some Iowans considered all Vietnamese to be the enemy of the United States. During the Vietnam War, American soldiers often fought against an opponent that employed guerrilla tactics. The Vietcong engaged larger U.S. forces then retreated, often blending in with the local population. Under these conditions, American combatants had difficulty determining friend from foe. Mrs. Anthony Riley of Cedar Rapids, Iowa, suspected that many "allies" coming to America had been the enemies of the United States: "How many of these refugees were hurting and even killing our men while we were in Vietnam? You can't possibly suggest each and every one has been screened." Marilyn Krueger of Griswold, Iowa, associated all Vietnamese with being adversaries, and she considered Ray's resettlement program to be insensitive to veterans, "Evidently you did not have a member of your family over in Nam fighting and being shot at by women and children as well as men." Gary Ohls, a youth living in Des Moines, Iowa, also associated all Vietnamese with being the enemy, "We fought these people for how long, and [we] killed our people doing it and then this is the thanks we get to live with them."[32]

Some Iowans criticized resettlement because they had simply burned out from the Vietnam War. The war was a continuing nightmare for the American people. When the United States withdrew from Vietnam in 1975, some Americans accepted refugee resettlement as a duty to former allies. The first 130,000 refugees paroled into the United States represented a sad ending to American military involvement in Indochina but an ending nonetheless. For some Iowans, the boat people crisis of the late 1970s reopened old wounds. Alan Bullock, a resident of Waterloo, Iowa, expressed some of this Vietnam War fatigue in his letter to Ray, "I think it is a crying shame the American people have to fight the Vietnam War for fifteen years *and now* they are being asked to finance *and bring* these 'poor and unfortunate people' over here to give a better life." Some Iowans argued refugee resettlement represented a continuation of the Vietnam War in another form. Boat people resettlement had the potential to make Vietnam look bad in the court of public opinion and drain her of talented individuals. Clifford Rushton, an army veteran whose brother served in Vietnam, challenged resettlement because it represented a continuation of the Vietnam War. He wrote: "I realize the present administration is peopled largely by Vietnam Warhawks and some of them have a severe case of guilty feelings. One poor, irrational decision has simply triggered another one, equally poor." Rushton informed Ray that military veterans of the war considered resettlement "a slap in the face."[33]

On the whole, those critical of Ray's boat people decision were not bad people; these Iowans crossed paths with refugee resettlement during vulnerable moments in their lives. Their letters hold more value than mere poll numbers. Their letters provided glimpses into the daily struggles of Iowans who wrote the Governor's Office to vent about these struggles as much as about Ray's resettlement decision. As Mrs. Cletus LeBarge and her husband entered their twilight years in Logan, Iowa, they prepared themselves for an uncertain future: "We are retiring age. Why did we do all of this? Now we can't afford to retire-can't buy gas to go anywhere if we did and then pay taxes to keep boat people.... I used to be one of the first to want to help. But like so many others, I am so tired of it.... I'm sorry but I am a very tired and bitter gal that really was looking forward to a little enjoyment and rest when I retired. Now, thanks to people like our good hearted governor, I have no hope."[34]

Desperation also appeared in two Des Moines mothers' letters to the Governor's Office. Mrs. Griffin fell in love with an Iowan and moved to the state from Pennsylvania, but hardships endured in her new state made Mrs. Griffin regret the decision. She had recently given birth to her son Douglas when her husband Earl injured himself on the job. The Griffins tried to make do on a mere $140 a week in workers' compensation. In her letter, Mrs. Griffin listed her monthly bills that totaled $487.50. Angered at being denied food stamps which seemed to be so easily dispensed to refugees, Mrs. Griffin wrote to Ray in protest of his giving to the Vietnamese instead of her hungry family. Ms. Gay Van DeBoe also struggled raising a child and believed refugee resettlement adversely affected her family. Budget cuts resulted in the cancellation of Ms. DeBoe's developmentally disabled son's usual thirty day respite care at Woodward State Hospital School. If the state had the funds to resettle refugees, "Why can't Bill have this one program available to him and to us? I don't feel like I'm asking too much of the State of Iowa for thirty days respite.... This state has a $50 million dollar general fund surplus—any monies spent on making my son independent is money well spent."[35]

Governor Ray anticipated his boat people decision would cause controversy. To prepare for those who argued refugees stole jobs from native Iowans, Ray had staffers count the wanted ads in local newspapers. One Sunday, Ray personally responded to a critic of the refugee program. The Governor explained to the out of work man that the latest Sunday *Des Moines Register* had advertised 1,029 jobs. Ray told this individual and other unemployed opponents of the refugee program, "Look, you have got the whole hundred yards in front of you right now. Go get the job and no refugee will take it from you."[36] Though Ray personally contacted some detractors, he charged his aide Kenneth Quinn with responding to all inquiries relative to refugee issues. Quinn replied to hundreds of letters and answered hundreds of phone calls with the goal of turning public opinion in favor of resettlement. For letter responses, Quinn worked from a general template that countered the most common criticisms of the program. He then customized these letters accordingly.

When Iowans complained about refugees stealing their jobs, Quinn provided current statistics on all of the jobs advertised in the *Des Moines Register* or by the Iowa Department of Job Services. Mrs. Joan Laverty of Carlisle, Iowa, questioned Ray's motives for announcing Iowa's acceptance of more refugees. She thought Ray acted out of self-promotion and desired national attention. Quinn countered by stating Ray acted out of humanitarian concern because "innocent men, women, and children are dying. Over four hundred died in one week alone in December. I trust you agree with the Governor that we cannot turn our backs when human lives are at stake." In her letter to the Governor, Mrs. Delores Marshall of Estherville, Iowa, sarcastically asked if Ray planned an upcoming Christmas dinner for refugees instead of elderly and disadvantaged Iowans. Quinn responded that in 1978 the Governor "spent over $70 million in aid to the elderly, over $112 million in support for the handicapped, and established a new Department of Veterans Affairs." After Howard Grobe of Dubuque, Iowa, protested his neighborhood's becoming a "dumping ground" for diseased foreigners, Quinn retorted: "As one who grew up in Dubuque with friends of German, Irish, Scandinavian, and other ancestries, I cannot help but wonder where we would be today if your philosophy were followed one hundred years ago. In Iowa in the 1850s many people used your very words in opposing immigration by many European peoples. Our forefathers were given a chance to start new lives. Can we deny these same opportunities to these new immigrants?" For those who charged the Governor with favoring refugees over other disadvantaged populations in the state, Quinn responded that the state could help save lives and improve the lot of needy Iowans. Of the many critics of the refugee program, one stood out the most for Quinn. Alan Shaffer of Des Moines, Iowa, returned an American flag sent to him while serving in Vietnam. Shaffer witnessed the deaths of too many American boys over there to approve letting the Vietnamese come to Iowa.[37]

Like Shaffer, Quinn also spent time in war torn Vietnam, but Quinn's involvement there made him into a strong proponent of refugee resettlement. Quinn fit the profile of a generation of junior Foreign Service officers who advocated for Vietnamese resettlement because of their personal experiences with the Vietnamese people. Quinn fell in love with and married a Vietnamese woman, and his brother-in-law died in the struggle against communism. Warfare forged strong bonds between Americans and their Vietnamese allies as explained by Quinn:

> The experience of Foreign Service officers and military officers working out in the provinces and in the development area brought you face to face with individual human suffering. It is difficult to overstate how important that was on a generation of military officers and Foreign Service officers who came to Vietnam as fairly young professionals.... It is different to talk about problems in general than it is to see people up close and personal and deal with individual situations ... seeing what happened when there was fighting in a village and places that were destroyed ... that made a deep personal impression: personal human suffering. Those of us who were there, we felt a commitment to the Vietnamese who had fought with us and that we cannot abandon them. The war was lost, but we had to do something to try to help them.

Gaylord Thayer, a Vietnam War veteran from Milo, Iowa, also had positive experiences with Vietnamese allies. He fought and ate alongside them, and Thayer knew these people deserved a chance at freedom.[38]

State officials believed that the personal interactions of Iowans and refugees naturally fostered goodwill for resettlement. Amongst IRSC staffers, a slogan circulated, "The refugees sell themselves."[39] From its very inception, individual sponsorship of refugees had been one of the defining characteristics of the state's refugee program. These sponsors kept refugees off welfare, but they also became allies of resettlement. Many sponsors benefitted more from the relationship than the refugees they aided. Sponsors learned about their charges' family and friends still in camps throughout Southeast Asia, and these Iowans often recruited family and friends to sponsor Indochinese as well. Iowans also formed positive bonds with refugees while providing services such as volunteer tutoring or working alongside refugees. As model students and employees, the Indochinese earned the support of many Iowans.

One Iowa woman felt uncertain about supporting the Governor's resettlement program because she did not want to betray Vietnam War veterans. She had followed the war closely. In her letter to the Governor, she related the story of Laurent Gourley, a pilot who went missing in action during the conflict. When U.S. naval pilot Larry Spencer also went MIA, she wore a bracelet with his name engraved in it as a show of support. She had been uncertain about supporting refugee resettlement in Iowa because she did not want to betray these veterans. However, her interaction with refugees at church changed her mind. During the holiday season, her pastor and a foreign exchange student sang one verse of *Silent Night* in German, then a refugee family sang a verse in their tongue, and finally, all sang in English. This powerful moment led this woman to realize that all mankind is one, and Iowans should open their homes to Vietnam War refugees.

Ray's resolution to increase refugee intake is a prime example of how a governor influenced refugee policy, but the actions of Indochinese refugees in Iowa also figured prominently in his decision. The successful resettlement of the Tai Dam undoubtedly influenced Ray's boat people declaration. His acceptance of 1,500 extra refugees approximated the number of Tai Dam the state had resettled by 1979. In a great irony, the Tai Dam came to Iowa because an American found a loophole to classify the group as Vietnamese, their ethnic rivals. Nearly four years later, many Vietnamese boat people arrived in Iowa because the Tai Dam had done so well in their new nation. Ray did not take tremendous stock in unemployment numbers when making his decision because he believed refugees accepted minimum wage jobs Iowans refused to work. Still, Iowa's unemployment rate stood at just 4 percent on the eve of his boat people announcement. In 1979, Iowa also experienced a record crop harvest. After Ray personally witnessed one of the worst human tragedies unfold in October of 1979, he asked Iowans to share their bounty with starving refugees in Southeast Asia.

6

Iowa SHARES and
the Cambodian Refugees[1]

"To keep you is no benefit. To destroy you is no loss."
—*Khmer Rouge Slogan*
"In a world where there is hate, there is more
reason to love. In a world where there
is hunger, there is more reason to share."[2]
—*Governor Robert Ray*
to Iowans, Christmas Eve 1979

The two above quotes seem so different, yet they are intricately linked. Those who espoused the Khmer Rouge slogan created a world of misery and depredation for millions of Cambodians. Half a world away, Governor Robert Ray promoted and inspired ordinary Iowa men, women, and children to make tangible gifts seeking to alleviate that misery. Through their wholehearted support or strong opposition, Iowans interpreted Iowa SHARES in diverse ways. Far from being a simple story of Iowans giving to Cambodians, Iowa SHARES meant many different things to many different people. This chapter explores this multiplicity of meanings.

As Governor, Robert Ray confronted three refugee crises: the Tai Dam and boat people episodes and the Cambodian tragedy. Though the Tai Dam had been resettled by the time he began working for Ray in 1978, Kenneth Quinn played an important role in the last two refugee crises. While on loan from the State Department, Quinn oversaw emergency preparedness and relief, coordinated security for Pope John Paul II's visit to the state, and helped Governor Ray overhaul the leadership of the Iowa National Guard after a scandal. Yet Quinn's greatest value lay in his expertise

133

in Southeast Asian affairs. While a Foreign Service officer in Vietnam, Quinn had interviewed refugees fleeing Cambodia. In 1976, he published "Political Change in Wartime," an article which described the true political character of the Khmer Rouge. Quinn was the first outside observer to accurately describe the nightmarish situation that had developed inside Cambodia. Initially, scholars accused Quinn of embellishing his findings, and only a few took his work seriously. In Iowa, Quinn played an integral role in Ray's refugee relief program for Cambodians.

The third refugee crisis, which inspired Ray to his final and most extensive activism, stemmed from the 1970–75 civil war that had ravaged Cambodia, as the Communist forces led by Pol Pot fought the backers of the Khmer Republic led by General Lon Nol. Making matters worse, from 1970 through 1973, American forces dropped 539,098 tons of munitions onto Cambodia in an attempt to weaken Vietnamese supply lines. Vietnamese communists invaded Cambodia in 1978 to overthrow Pol Pot, but meanwhile, 1.7 million Cambodians lost their lives to the communist forces of Pol Pot. Between 1975 and 1979, 20 percent of the country's population died in an orgy of violence. One former Khmer Rouge soldier later recalled that he had slit so many victims' throats that he developed arthritis in his wrist and forearm from the repetitive motion.[3]

The violence seared the survivors who later arrived in Iowa. As teenagers at Des Moines' Hoover High School, Monyra Chau and Pa Mao wrote essays recalling the horrors unleashed upon them by the communists. Chau, whose father was killed by the Communists in 1979, remembered:

> It was strange. They were wearing black cloths and black caps. They carried guns all over the places. Some of them went into people's houses and took their properties … they told the people to leave their homes and town. Everybody had to go to different places. The people had to work on the farms, nobody worked in the city. People had to work hard and do whatever they said. If somebody did not follow them, they killed him. We didn't have much food to eat either…. They let people eat like animals. We had to get up to work at four o'clock in the morning. When people told them that they were sick, they wouldn't believe the people. They had to take the people to go to work.

Mao, who had also lost her father to communist violence, recalled the starvation that drove her family to escape to Thailand in November 1979: "We got up very early before sunrise and walked 40 kilometers a day. We took pottery, rice, food, and only the clothes that we wore. We walked three days and nights that seemed like one very long day because we didn't sleep. We were too afraid of the soldiers, so we didn't walk on the road, we walked through the jungle...."[4] Hundreds of thousands of war ravaged and starving Cambodians made the same decision to flee to Thailand, but as Iowa Governor Ray saw first-hand, refugees' arrival in Thailand did not ease their misery.

In October 1979, Ray and five other American governors toured communist China as part of the normalization of relations between China and the U.S. Since his Task Force first began resettling Indochinese refugees in 1975, Ray had an interest in refugee issues. He suggested that the small delegation take a side tour of Cambodian refugee camps in Thailand. Ray, his wife Billie, his aide Kenneth Quinn, and the other governors were shocked and haunted by the camp's horrible conditions. As Ray later described it, they saw over thirty thousand people packed together: "Have you ever stood in a small muddy spot about two hours while five people died around you? I did, two days ago, at the Cambodian border camp of Sa Kaeo. Those deaths were only part of the more than 50 that died in that one camp, on that one day. To see little kids with sunken eyes and protruding tummies trying to eke out a smile will bring a tear to the eyes of even the most calloused."

On his flight from Asia back to Iowa, Ray began to compose a speech to deliver a short time later at the General Assembly of the Christian Church in St. Louis, Missouri. In that talk, Ray referred to Pope John Paul II's recent appearance at Des Moines's Living History Farms to emphasize the message that Judeo-Christians had an obligation to work to alleviate world suffering and relieve crimes against human rights. On his trip, Ray said he had been struck by China's tremendous poverty and recent struggles to modernize agriculture. However, life in China "was like a walk through the park compared with our last stop" to the refugee camps in Thailand. He compared the suffering of the refugees of Indochina with the plight of the Jews during the Holocaust. Ray declared that the world had missed an opportunity to provide help to the Jews; the world failed that test but now faced a new crisis of mass distress:

> I believe that we can never live with a clear conscience if we turn our backs on dying human beings who cry out for a touch of life. There is no way I can describe the misery and human suffering and anguish of these people—God's children. It's indescribable. But try if you will to imagine what it would be like to run, hide and scramble through wet and rough terrain for weeks, day after day, in an attempt to escape communist torture and death. Add to that the fact that you were leaving your home, your belongings, your family, or that your spouse, or children or parents had already been killed. And, that if you reached a border you would have no assurance you wouldn't be thrown right back into the path of the pursuers.

Ray told the congregation that as people from a prosperous nation, Americans needed to take action. He added that even critics who opposed resettling refugees in the U.S. still should aim to relieve their immediate suffering, "We're talking not where these people are going to live—but whether they are going to live." Ray appealed to Christian principles, while adding a rhetorical link to his St. Louis hosts:

As we meet here tonight in Missouri, the "show-me state," I sincerely believe that Jesus is saying to our church:

> —Don't tell me of your concerns for human rights, *Show Me*! Don't tell me of your concerns for the poor, the disenfranchised, the underprivileged, the unemployed, *Show Me*! Don't tell me of your concerns for the rejected, the prisoner, the hungry, the thirsty, the homeless, *Show Me*! Don't tell me of your concerns for these people when you have a chance to save their lives—*Show Me*! Don't tell me how Christian you are, *Show Me*! *Show Me*![5]

Ray's concern for refugees resonated with other Iowans, as the international crisis attracted growing publicity. After the Iowa delegation returned from the camps, the governor handed his undeveloped photos from the trip to David Yepsen of the *Des Moines Register*, which devoted a number of articles and editorials to documenting the crisis. After reading the piece "Let's Bomb Cambodia. This Time with Food," fourth graders at Brooklyn-Guernsey-Malcolm elementary schools wrote to the Governor in November 1979. Most of these youngsters enthusiastically volunteered suggestions; several suggested using airplanes, boats, or trains to bring food to the desperate. Student Donita Nicklas recommended putting cartoons of milk and juice onto an airplane, and added, "Why don't we take a boat with fruit and go down there with tractors and medicine." David Hawkins stated, "If I was governor I would make a bridge to Cambodia and take a lot of food for them." Lynn Huddleson asked, "Why don't you try getting food by submarine?" She insisted, "I'd like you to do something about the people starving in Cambodia. I hate looking at the half-starved person with no clothes on. I hope you do something about it."

Both reflecting and deepening Iowa's relationship with the Cambodian refugees, teachers helped these and other young people engage powerful issues such as starvation and controversial politics. After recognizing Americans' relatively privileged position in the world, fourth-grader Dale Henry Goodrich declared, "I wouldn't eat for a week if I could get the food I was suppose to eat to them." In writing to Governor Ray, students engaged in active citizenship, perhaps for the first time. Ada Marie Weiermanny asked, "Are the Cambodians going to live? I hope so. Because it

Khmer woman with emaciated child, Thailand, 1979. A small group of Iowans visited the Sa Kaeo refugee camp for a mere two hours. During that short time, the Governor witnessed five people die. Ray, an avid photographer, took numerous pictures. When the Iowans returned in late October, Ray handed his film to a *Des Moines Register* reporter. David Yepsen titled his article, "I Watched Refugees Die, Gov. Ray says." This trip prompted Ray to create the Iowa SHARES program, with Kenneth Quinn overseeing the project. The *Des Moines Register* also lent its support through advertising and further reporting on SHARES (courtesy Robert Ray).

isn't right for the Vietnams to try to kill them when they didn't do nothing to the Vietnams." Students generally blamed communist Vietnam for the plight of the Cambodians, overlooking the genocidal role of Pol Pot and the Cambodian communists. But while these fourth-graders missed much of the complexities of recent Asian turmoil, several specifically suggested that America itself bore some culpability for the misery, since U.S. forces had devastated Cambodia during the Vietnam War. Danny Allen and Donita Nicklas wrote, "Iowa has spare money we should give it to Cambodia it was half our fault," and "Why did we attack them? My teacher said we bombed them once."[6]

In his St. Louis speech, Ray had not yet proposed a specific mechanism to channel Midwest aid to refugees, but in a November 1979 press release, he announced the formation of Iowa SHARES: Iowa Sends Help to Aid Refugees and End Starvation. Again citing the teachings of Pope John Paul II on his recent visit to Des Moines, Ray declared that Iowans had a special role as "stewards of the earth with an obligation to share the fruit of our land with all mankind." The program's structure creatively drew upon Iowa's pride and duty as an agricultural state, calling on Iowans to help the people of Cambodia by sharing the state's record harvest of 1.6 billion bushels of grain. For practical reasons, Ray did not plan to actually ship Iowa's crop to Cambodia. Instead, his program appealed for donors to buy a "SHARE in humanity"; each share cost $2.20, the equivalent of a bushel of corn. Ray aimed to raise a sum equal to the price of 52,500 bushels, representing one barge full of Iowa grain, which he said "would be a mighty symbol of Iowa generosity and an important example for the rest of the world." Although SHARES accepted large donations from corporate donors such as Pioneer Hi-Bred International Inc. of Des Moines, Ray and Kenneth Quinn primarily envisioned SHARES as a grassroots project that would engage the entire community and inspire contributions from individual Iowans. Ray declared, "Many times in the past we have proved that ours is not just a state in the heart of the nation, but also a state with a heart."[7] Promoters encouraged farmers to donate part of their crop to purchase shares, which would be used to buy rice, medical supplies, and other necessities for the overseas refugee population.

The Governor's Office coordinated Iowa SHARES, a non-profit corporation with tax exemption. The program's bipartisan and ecumenical board of director included Ray, Quinn, and other prominent Iowans. Religious figures rallied to promote SHARES; early leaders included Rabbi Jay Goldberg and the Rev. Fred Strickland. Iowa Public Television media personality Mary Jane Odell and Michael Gartner, President and Editor of the *Des Moines Register* and *Tribune*, were also closely involved, helping the Governor's Office launch Iowa SHARES with a well-orchestrated publicity campaign. Odell described how she would talk about the program to people in elevators and to anyone who would listen. She told her fellow members of the board of directors, "If you need me, I am on somebody's telephone."[8] Early fundraising strategically connected Iowa SHARES to the spirit of charity during 1979's holiday season. The Governor's Office declared the week right before Christmas to be an official Iowa SHARES week. Echoing the emotional impact of refugee misery that had commanded Governor Ray's attention, the *Des Moines Register* published articles dramatically detailing the plight of the Cambodians. The paper printed vivid images of starving children, next to a coupon that readers could mail in to make an Iowa SHARES donation, with a bountiful Thanksgiving food basket pictured on it. Other state newspapers also promoted the program and to gain more publicity, Quinn sent dozens of letters to other major newspapers throughout the U.S.

Over their seventeen-month-long fundraising campaign, program officials spent $5,606 on advertising. Mounting extra publicity through Iowa's radio and television stations, Governor Ray joined Odell to record four public service announcements, ranging from ten to sixty seconds long. In the middle of her emotional plea for funds, Odell crumpled up her script and fought back tears as she said, "I just want to talk to you for a minute about the starvation and disease of the Cambodian refugees. Lot of hunger and starvation around the world and at home too. But the situation of the Cambodians is so desperate so immediate...."⁹

On November 21, 1979, Odell hosted a special Iowa Public Television program, titled *Cambodia: What Iowans Need to Know.* On this show, Governor Ray, his wife Billie, and Kenneth Quinn spoke about witnessing refugees die of starvation. Viewers saw emotionally-moving photographs that Ray had taken, documenting the camps' terrible conditions. IPTV followed up by screening several other programs focused on the issue, such as World's *Cambodia: A Nation Is Dying* and *Don't Forget the Khmer.*

Quinn made lists of hundreds of names of Iowans whom he hoped to mobilize to promote SHARES. His office fielded hundreds of inquiries and suggestions, quickly responding to letters from citizens such as Scott Larsen, student council president of the Washington School in Council Bluffs.¹⁰ The campaign immediately drew responses from Iowa's young people, who often came up with ingenious methods for raising money. Nine-year-old Eric Sharp got an advance on his Christmas money and then wrote Governor Ray: "Please take my Christmas money of $50 and send it to the Cambodians. I think they deserve a Christmas too."¹¹ Angie King's third grade class at King Elementary took out a loan from First Federal Bank to buy and sell popcorn balls. Youngsters Dan VandeLune, Rob Tompkins, Ryan Tompkins, and Travis Spurgeon of West Des Moines raised money by going door to door. One sixth-grade class at Malcolm Price Laboratory School raised money through a candy sale, while Beaverdale's Holy Trinity School sponsored a Mardi Gras parade and food sale. Students in the Aquin School system held an eleven mile walkathon from Garryowen to Cascade. In February 1980, instead of exchanging Valentines, fifth and sixth graders at Washington Elementary in Mason City gave money to SHARES. The ten person youth group team at Altoona Christian Church fasted for twenty-two hours to raise funds.

College-age Iowans also mobilized, following Quinn's call for cash-strapped students to have "one less beer, one less movie, or one less meal" and donate the savings to SHARES. At the University of Northern Iowa, students in the Kappa Delta Pi Honorary Society for Education raised money. Cornell College students could buy special cafeteria meals that included a one-dollar contribution to SHARES. At Cornell's student and faculty Christmas dinner, "symbolic empty [collection] bowls" sat at the dinner tables.¹² David Kalianov, an engineering student at Iowa State University, composed and recorded a song titled "Child of Cambodia," then donated the copyright to make that music the theme for Iowa SHARES.

Community organizations and companies also got involved; one group advertised the chance for families to take photographs of their children with Santa Claus for a dollar each, donating all the proceeds. The Des Moines Judo Club held a special tournament at the YMCA, sending the admissions fees to Iowa SHARES. Employees at Weitz Brothers Construction Company forfeited their usual Christmas bonus of ham or a fruit basket in order to help. Individual Iowans also responded. After seeing a PBS special on Cambodia, Therese Koch of Boone felt guilty for buying an electric frying pan. She returned it and donated the funds to SHARES. The Wilson family of Des Moines felt compelled to donate despite their own struggles with age, cancer, and heart failure. They apologized: "We are not too flush but feel we must help this much."[13]

The overall success of Iowa SHARES stunned even the most optimistic members of the board. In its first week of existence, the program raised $25,102. By the fourteenth of December 1979, $204,724 had been raised. Between the time the campaign opened on November 23, 1979, through its conclusion on April 30, 1981, SHARES raised $554,789, more than quadruple the total of $115,500 that Ray had initially called for. Iowa SHARES board members voted on how to spend these funds, sending the aid to the Cambodians through private relief agencies such as Catholic Relief Services, UNICEF, American Refugee Services, and the World Food Program.[14] Iowa medical professionals like Dr. Harlo Hove and RN Debra Tate volunteered their services and worked in refugee camps in Thailand, supported by Iowa SHARES funds.

Individual Iowans chose to donate to SHARES for a variety of reasons, emotional, personal, and political. Many felt compelled to donate after being bombarded with powerful and sad images from newspapers, radio, and television. In their letters to the Governor's Office, people constantly referred to the PBS films *Cambodia: A Nation Is Dying*, *Cambodia: What Iowans Need to Know*, and *Don't Forget the Khmer*. A couple requested tapes or transcripts of the IPTV interview with Governor Ray, to show to others for raising more money. Edna Spencer of Chariton wrote, "The pictures and reports are heartbreaking." Kathie Horney felt guilty for having a huge meal before seeing Cambodian refugee pictures in the paper. Referring to her own four-month and seven-year-old children, Horney wrote, "I cannot imagine what they would look like if they were starving."[15] Some Iowans gave in honor of others; when First Lady Rosalyn Carter visited Clinton, Iowa, Catholic grade school students there donated to SHARES in her name. For the grandchildren of the deceased Herman VanOort, SHARES meant a way to honor their grandfather by donating

Khmer refugees seek medical treatment at a field hospital, Thailand, 1979. A desire to help Cambodians such as these prompted Iowan Debra Tate to volunteer as an Iowa SHARES nurse. Tate experienced medical problems while working at Khao I Dang. She had a tumor removed from her breast, an emergency appendectomy, and a bout of pneumonia during her service. Despite the setbacks, the twenty-five-year old informed Ray and Quinn, "This is still the most rewarding work I have ever done and am enjoying my life immensely" (courtesy Robert Ray).

in his name, and a way of cheering up their grandmother, his widow, when Kenneth Quinn's thank you note from the Governor's Office arrived shortly afterward. While some givers preferred to remain anonymous, Iowa's newspapers recognized others by printing long lists of names.

Many Iowans supported SHARES because they had participated in the earlier refugee resettlement of Indochinese. Through her church, Newburg resident Norma Weaver had helped sponsor a Cambodian family, helping them adjust to Iowa life and driving them to doctor's visits. In donating to SHARES, Weaver recognized how much the starving Cambodians she saw on PBS specials looked so much like the family she had come to adore. William Rosenfeld, a doctor in Mason City, volunteered to serve on Iowa medical teams sent by SHARES to aid Cambodian refugees in Thailand, citing his earlier experience working at the Khao-I-Dang refugee camp in that very country. As a medical student and doctor, Rosenfeld had read in textbooks about exotic diseases, but to encounter them in real life shocked him, "In four days, I saw more acute medicine than I will ever see again." He continued: "People had malaria, dysentery with dehydration to the point of shock and coma, large tropical ulcers crawling with maggots, meningococcal meningitis, polio, measles, severe pneumonia, and draining abscesses from Potts disease of the spine. Most of them had worms or other intestinal parasites." Rosenfeld had treated sixty to seventy patients daily, at a camp housing over 130,000 refugees. He recalled seeing a young boy who stayed with an older woman through her death, then just sat there: "He didn't cry; he didn't do anything. He just sat there. He had no one else...." Other children "would enact atrocities done under Pol Pot's regime," Rosenfeld wrote: "A child would act like an old woman being led with a rope to a pit. Another child would hit her over the head with a stick, and she'd fall into the pit. That's the way they executed people.... The children would tie another child to a tree and pretend they were cutting out the captive's gall bladder and drinking the bile from it, another thing they recalled that the troops did." Yet Rosenfeld also appreciated the refugees' resilience, how they laughed and played pranks on one another even under extreme hardships, Observing how much such people felt happy simply to be alive had changed his outlook on life, Rosenfeld wrote, showing him how little material goods and superficial pleasures mattered.[16]

A number of Iowans supported the cause out of religious belief. For some Jews, SHARES represented a means to fulfill the post–Holocaust pledge, "never again." Synagogues joined in fundraising, while five Iowa rabbis wrote an open letter to the Jewish community, citing the Torah's dictum, "Do not stand by idly while your fellow human being's blood is spilled." Their message continued: "The reality of Cambodia, in all its tragedy, assaults us daily. As Jews who are survivors of the Holocaust, be it fact or in memory, we recall the silence and the indifference of the world during those days. We vowed that it would never happen again. Today, it is time for us to redeem that vow."[17]

All along, Iowa's governor explicitly portrayed refugee aid as a religious obligation. In his St. Louis speech to the General Assembly of the

Christian Church, Ray declared, "Christianity and Christian love know
no boundaries. They don't stop at state lines or national borders. They are
universal." He quoted the bible's account of Christ's declaration: "Lord,
when did we see you hungry, thirsty, tired, sick, in prison.... In as much
as you did unto the least of these, you did it unto me."[18] Across Iowa, min-
isters and other religious leaders wrote sermons addressing the Cambodian crisis and publicized SHARES in church bulletins. Churchgoers
collected contributions by fasting, holding silent auctions, and tithing. St.
Johns High School in Independence announced a "pilgrimage" in which
their self-proclaimed "Holy Strollers" would walk eighty miles from Independence to Guttenberg, Iowa, to raise awareness of the Christian mission
to help others and raise donations. Other religiously-motivated donors
connected SHARES with an anti-abortion political stance. Theodore Pederson linked SHARES' lifesaving measures in Cambodia with the need to
save the lives of unborn children. He compared the U.S. oil crisis to the
abortion issue, asking, if Americans cared so much about conservation of
energy, why not conserve life?

From the start, the governor's office also structured Iowa SHARES
as a distinctively Iowan civic engagement, and comments by many donors
reflected that appeal to state pride. 1979's record harvest size showed off
Iowa's agricultural power, at the same times that residents saw newspaper
photographs and television images of people elsewhere starving to death.
One columnist with the *Des Moines Register* emphasized Iowa's opportunity, as one of the "leading farm states," to feed not just the Midwest, but
ideally the needy around the world. California resident Harvey Glasser
declared that the campaign helped to "restore" his joy in his Iowa roots.
Glasser wrote to Ray that the push for Cambodian aid "certainly breaks
all stereotypes of Midwestern provincialism to find this wonderful spirit
of international consciousness and sensitivity to the plight that these suffering people is not only shared but responded to by your generous contributors to Iowa Shares."[19]

Others contributed to SHARES to demonstrate support for Governor
Ray himself, who had enjoyed strong popularity since his initial election
in 1968. Donor John Murray commented, "It is not my nature to write letters to political leaders. I am compelled to do so, however, by your activities on behalf of the hapless refugees.... Never have I been more proud
of the conduct of any representative of my interests in the world."
Seventeen-year-old Fort Dodge resident Tom Yetmar echoed that praise,
writing, "In a time when everything is up in the air such as inflation,
energy, Iran, and the election you still have the time to go to Cambodia,

and see for your self the suffering. You really amaze me as a strong leader of the state of Iowa. I'm really happy to live in Iowa, I would like to thank you and your administration for making this a state to be proud of."[20]

Noting the international political context of the refugee disaster, other contributors supported SHARES as a way to extend America's Cold War fight against Soviet influence. Former intelligence officer Hugh Stafford of Tri State Toro Company worried that the Cambodian government might take advantage of the crisis to send spies and communist agents to infiltrate refugee camps and destabilize the government of Thailand. Writing to Quinn, Stafford recommended that SHARES should send aid directly to Thailand, as a "breadbasket" and a crucial Cold War ally. He feared that any funds going through Cambodia's communist government would ultimately backfire "to the detriment of our allies." West Des Moines resident Jerry Johnson wanted to extend the scope of Iowa SHARES to fight communist aggression even more widely, referring to America's grain embargo against the Soviet Union after its 1979 invasion of Afghanistan. Donations to non-profit organizations like SHARES should be set up to flood grain into places where the Soviets encroached, Johnson suggested. Such food purchases would help Iowa farmers while also weakening Soviet power and promoting America's global reputation after its post–Vietnam War slump.[21]

It was that international political dimension of relief that proved most controversial. Despite the heart-rending images, widespread publicity, and community support for refugee aid, a non-negligible number of Iowans opposed SHARES for a multitude of reasons. The most passionate backers of a Cold War hard-line objected that the program channeled funds to support Cambodians whose communist government took directives from the Vietnamese communists who had just inflicted humiliating defeat on the United States. Lawrence Adams of Ottumwa mailed in his SHARES coupon with a bold zero written in the donation line, writing angrily, "Not one penney to Cambodia or Gov. Ray am I going to give you. If we had won that war in southeast asia and kept the Communists out they wouldn't have that trouble now. I am a world war ii veteran and 65 years of age." Critics like Adams blamed wartime Cambodians for helping smuggle provisions and troops along the Ho Chi Minh Trail, so these critics felt that Americans had no obligation to help deal with the consequences. Similarly, Ella Brown complained to the Governor's Office, "We have been reading for years that UNICEF MONEY GOES TO THE COMMUNISTS. With Vietnam a communist takeover, wont the same thing happen??? In Cambodia. Will your Governor be in for a possible embarrassment??? I hope not."[22]

Other critics, both within Iowa and nationwide, worried about American food and medicine falling into the hands of the Vietnamese communists. Widespread rumors reported that Vietnamese trucks were hauling Cambodian refugee supplies into Vietnam. To counter such rumors, representatives from the group Church World Services issued public statements. Since poorly-built Cambodian roads became impassable during the wet season, they noted, cargo had to be trucked northeast through Vietnam before reaching refugee camps. Far from blocking aid, they said, the Vietnamese had opened up the Mekong River and local airports to speed up special shipments. Skepticism persisted; a December 1979 letter printed in the *Algona Upper Des Moines Newspaper* maintained that the funds donated to SHARES had never reached Cambodian refugees. Through the media, Kenneth Quinn flatly denied such charges; he pointed out that since the Iowa SHARES program had just started and had not yet actually distributed any money, it was therefore impossible for its relief to have fallen into the wrong hands. Other Iowa citizens ignored or discounted such disturbing rumors, counting on what one called the "squeaky clean" record of Governor Ray to trust that their donations got to the right place.[23]

Even as some critics worried that Iowa SHARES might end up bolstering communism, observers on the other side of the political spectrum feared that aid might unnecessarily prolong the Cold War. Writing to the governor's office, members of the Consortium on International Peace and Reconciliation (CIPAR) stressed that paranoia about communism should not trump humanitarian considerations. CIPAR chairperson Chester Guinn criticized SHARES for focusing relief efforts on Cambodians in Thailand, a non-communist state, while overlooking greater need within Cambodia itself. CIPAR questioned whether Quinn's past political involvement with the State Department and U.S. military forces in Vietnam had biased his ideas about the allocation of funds. They warned that misguided relief that only provided funds to refugees fleeing to Thailand risked destabilizing Cambodia and worsening tension between the Soviet Union and Vietnam alliance versus the China and Cambodia alliance.[24]

Ironically, Governor Ray's appeal to state pride and agricultural abundance in promoting Iowa SHARES wound up alienating and even aggravating some Iowans. A farm woman from New English, Iowa, Mrs. Harmon Rose, felt "disgusted" with fundraising and media appeals for implying that all Iowa farmers were prosperous and therefore obliged to donate. She noted that 1979's record crop hardly made up for the bad year prior and the uncertainties of the next. After seeing a SHARES commercial featuring a farm family, she wrote to Governor Ray: "Why don't you show the labor man receiving his large paycheck and then flash the picture of the starving Cam. People? Why is it only the grain harvest? Let's show equal responsibility! I am a farm wife, work hard, last year [1978] we had nearly no crop."[25] Rose wanted the campaign to emphasize that everyone should pitch in, not just farmers.

The largest group of opponents criticized SHARES for diverting funds from domestic needs. One Iowan wrote that SHARES "disturbed" him because "there are too many people in Iowa as well as the rest of the United States who will go hungry possibly starve or freeze to death this winter because they have to make the choice between food or warmth."[26] Others criticized Ray for focusing too much attention on issues thousands of miles away from Iowa. Asserting that charity must begin at home, these critics pointed to local difficulties connected to the energy crisis, inflation, and growing unemployment. One suggested that relief money could be put to better use by building a para-transit system for Iowa's elderly and disabled.

Other skeptics feared that the SHARES initiative might bring more refugees to Iowa, something the governor had already promoted. According to a September 1979 *Des Moines Register* poll, more than half of all Iowans opposed the additional resettlement of refugees in the state. By decade's end, the state economy had taken a downturn, and some worried that the newcomers took jobs from Americans and imposed additional burdens on the welfare system. On December 4, 1979, the conservative syndicated columnist Paul Harvey, a Midwesterner himself, wrote an article printed in forums such as the *Clinton Herald Newspaper* that denounced what he called refugees' "parasitism" and "welfare–Cadillac" lifestyle. Harvey wrote that the Indochinese "buy and sell their teenage daughters; they skin and eat dogs and cats; they ravage our fishing grounds.... Transporting them here is cruel to them and a rude affront to our own jobless." He cautioned readers not to get suckered into donating to relief efforts by the emotionalized appeals pushed by bleeding-hearts, preachers, and fundraisers.[27]

Such hostility to refugee resettlement spilled over into the Iowa SHARES campaign. One anonymous person mailed to the Governor a revised donation coupon; on the line, "Yes, I'd Like to Share," the person crossed out "Share" and penciled in "Ship everyone back." Underneath, this person wrote, "Name: Mrs. Refugee. Address: Trying to Keep Alive." Finally, the correspondent crossed out, "Send your check or money order to" and replaced it with "Those men go back to their country and fight for it instead of coming her and live off of us for nothing." Another Iowan wrote, "These people don't belong in our country.... We don't need more people.... Maybe they have by their own actions and complacency permitted these situations to happen...."[28]

Still more criticism of the Iowa program came from outside, even from Ray's fellow governors. After reading Quinn's publicity promoting Iowa SHARES, Governor William Janklow of South Dakota responded that he felt it to be improper for any governor to engage in private fundraising. "I wholeheartedly endorse the efforts being made by private agencies and certain federal agencies to accommodate immigrants," Janklow wrote to Ray, but added, "Despite my personal feelings of compassion, I honestly believe it would be improper for a state government to initiate a private fundraising effort. There are many private charity organizations in South Dakota. We cooperate with them in proclaiming weeks in their honor and helping them with publicity. However, we do not actively promote one charity more than any other."[29] Janklow interpreted SHARES to be at the least a misuse and at the worst an abuse of the Governor's power. For Janklow, a governor's creation and promotion of one charity over others led to conflicts of interest; it diverted a governor from attending to the issues the people had elected their governor to solve and infringed upon private charities' domain.

The political dimensions of the SHARES program inspired deep reactions, both pro and con, from Iowans, but the ultimate purpose, of course, was humanitarian. The money raised in the November 23, 1979, thru April 30, 1981, campaign accomplished a number of immediate results. It meant rehabilitating three rural hospital dispensaries in the Kandal Province. It meant the creation of two rural orphanages in Svey Rieng and Prey Veng. A special nine-truck Christmas convoy carried rice, mosquito nets, sleeping mats, and medicine to the neediest populations. American donations helped purchase K-MIX-2, a concentrated nutrition source that brought people back from the brink of starvation. Iowa funded, organized, and sent two medical teams to Southeast Asia, each comprised of a doctor and several nurses, who treated refugees for months.

For refugees who had arrived in Iowa earlier, such efforts had especially deep meaning. At a SHARES benefit in Farley, Iowa, people gave gifts to the Ban family, to make their first Christmas in America special. The relief project meant hope for Sothira Pan, a young fifth grader in North Dakota, who hoped his family back in Cambodia might benefit from it.[30]

For some Iowans, the SHARES campaign seemingly offered a way to help themselves, the U.S., and the world begin to heal the wounds of the Vietnam War and Watergate debacle. Some Americans felt guilty for the secret bombings of Cambodia, and even public officials like Kenneth Quinn felt the stigma of being associated with the U.S. government. Prior to the turbulent Vietnam era, Quinn had believed that "the White House was always the symbol of all that was right and good of our country. The presidents were all noble people to be emulated." But during the Watergate scandal, Quinn realized how much ordinary citizens felt betrayed by their officials. He recalled that when he used a White House identification card at a Washington, D.C., store, the clerk snapped, "That's nothing to be proud of."[31]

Such negative attitudes toward government had spread from D.C. to Iowa, as seen in the attitude of Iowa State University student David Kalianov. After reading William Shawcross's book *Sideshow: Kissinger, Nixon and the Destruction of Cambodia,* Kalianov felt profoundly affected by that recent history. He later remembered, "It was my personal intro-duction to the notion that what we believe to be true, as told to us by the powers that be, may not be truth at all…. I could not help but ponder what the children of Cambodia must think of us. And after reading *Sideshow,* I did not know what to think of us either."[32] That dismay came through in the first verse of the theme song for SHARES, "Child of Cam-bodia," that Kalianov wrote:

> Child of Cambodia, what do you think when you think of U.S.?
> Oh Child of Cambodia, do you see compassion, or the reach of love?
> For we live in a way, that sometimes,
> Blinds our eyes, from the painful cries,
> Of a people that live in a world much less than ours…

While appalled by the role of the United States in first creating misery in Cambodia, then in being deaf to the "painful cries" of the Cambodians, Kalianov did not believe that Americans were bad at heart. When the Governor's Office launched Iowa SHARES, Kalianov stated that, "It gave me a renewed sense of us."[33] The final verse of his song stressed the promise represented by Iowans' "giving" and "helping":

> Child of Cambodia, what do you think when you think of us?
> Oh Child of Cambodia, help us to remember we were made for love,
> It is in giving, that we receive,
> And by helping you, make it through,
> These painful times in your world much less than ours…

In seeking to alleviate the suffering of refugees thousands of miles away, Governor Ray's leadership served to preserve faith in government for at least some Iowans during tumultuous times. Quinn's work with SHARES renewed his own self-image as a public official: "I felt so proud to be a part of Iowa and Iowa government and Governor Ray's administration because of our work on refugees...."[34] The campaign could not end all controversy or uncertainty about how the United States could act in a world still torn by Cold War suspicions, and it fed into and even fanned some mistrust of foreigners and relief programs. But for other citizens of Iowa, Ray's relief campaign allowed Republicans and Democrats, hawks and doves, Christians and Jews, young and old, rich and poor, to rally behind a singular humanitarian cause. By healing Cambodian refugees through their participation in Iowa SHARES, some Iowans hoped to find a way to heal themselves.

7

The Littlest Victims

"Them that knows nothing fears nothing."
Proverb as quoted[1]

For Robert Ray and Colleen Shearer, a successful refugee resettlement program meant placing adults into the workforce. Nevertheless, no history of Southeast Asian refugees can be complete without addressing the experiences of those too young to work. The history of children has only recently been addressed in academic circles. Historians have long considered children as passive onlookers to the historical dramas acted out by adults.[2] Even if the historian has studied youngsters, researching youths has been fraught with difficulties and for good reason. Parents and institutional review boards have needed to protect the young from any harm that may have resulted from research projects; studying the history of refugee youths has been especially delicate given their traumatic experiences. For this reason, many histories of childhood have relied on the testimonials of adults who have reflected back on their younger days. Oral histories have provided a valuable glimpse into the lives of youngsters, and they are used in the chapter that follows. However, these and all other oral histories have their shortcomings. Memories fade, become jumbled and or lost as years from childhood pass. In addition to oral histories, this study of refugee youth has been built from essays written by English Second Language students in the Des Moines public school system beginning in 1980.

In their school essays, many of Des Moines' refugees recounted ideal childhoods being shattered by communist takeovers in Vietnam, Laos, and Cambodia. Iowa's refugee youths singled out communists for wrenching them from their studies and forcing them to work. Under communist rule, many of the youngsters witnessed horrible events. Some students wrote about the last time they saw their fathers alive before execution. Fear of losing a father often compelled the families of these children to flee. While escaping communism, youths saw fellow evacuees drown in the Mekong River and South China Sea. Students expressed mixed emotions when explaining their personal journeys to Iowa. For every happy reunion, a painful separation seemed to occur in their unstable world. They left behind homes, relatives, favorite pets, and best friends. At refugee camps throughout Southeast Asia, the youngsters made powerful new friendships with those in similar circumstances only to leave behind these newfound friends during the resettlement process. When they arrived in Des Moines, Iowa, they focused once more on fitting in and building new friendships.

In addition to examining the traumas suffered by refugee minors, this chapter complicates the scholarly community's usual portrayal of young refugees as "those who are the most vulnerable and deeply affected by war and social disruption."[3] Studying refugee youths yields important information because they experienced refugee life in ways different from adults. Insulated by their naiveté, many young refugees proved incapable of fully comprehending the trauma that had enveloped their families. This led youths to interpret events around them in ways unique from adults, and this continued as the youngsters began to explore their new surroundings in the United States. In both size and degree of suffering, young refugees were the littlest victims.

Cam Quang, an ethnic Chinese from a suburb of Saigon, remembered his picturesque childhood being disrupted by the communists. He came of age in the town of Cholon, which had a bustling marketplace full of vendors selling sticky rice, wonton soup, chow mein and many other items. Cam enjoyed watching bicyclists and motorcyclists race and perform tricks. By the time Cam reached ten years of age, the communists had seized power and life changed for the worse. The communists even treated young people poorly. He wrote:

> What happened in Vietnam when it changed to Communism was horrible. One of the first things that they did was to change the money. Everyone ended up with equal money. It made no difference how hard your family had worked and saved in the past, most people lost their money. They made you go to meetings to learn about the communist system. They made you fear for your family if you didn't go to the meetings. Sometimes at meetings if you were a young person, they forced you into the army. Also, if you were a young person with long hair walking on the street, the government people would take you and put you in the army.[4]

Cam emphasized the economic repercussions of communism because his family had much to lose when the new regime came to power. Cam's father had made a career out of making soy, bean, and hot pepper sauces along with preservatives for the Saigon marketplace. When the communists obtained firmer control over the South, the ethnic Chinese community suffered the greatest because of their heavy involvement in South Vietnam's business sector.

Ky Tu, also an ethnic Chinese from South Vietnam, enjoyed his childhood until the political situation changed. Ky fondly remembered celebrating the New Year in his home country. Adults gave children money, fireworks lit up the sky for two nights, and everyone dressed in new cloths. Ky wrote about one New Year when his aunt took him and his sister downtown. When the three returned home after the celebration, Ky and his aunt realized that his sister had lost one of her shoes, and both laughed at his sister's expense. When Ky turned six years of age, the communists seized power and ruined life in Vietnam. He explained, "We would have stayed there if it hadn't been for the Communists. No one liked them." Continuing on, Ky emphasized the communists' mistreatment of children: "They ordered young people to work in fields and all of the people suffered because of them. People who worked in fields had to stay there all day. They worked from dawn until dusk. Some became ill but the communists didn't care."[5] Both Cam Quang and Ky Tu's families made the decision to flee communism, and the two youths joined the growing ranks of boat people.

Mek Baccam, a Tai Dam living in Laos, learned about the Pathet Lao's seizure of power over the radio. He explained his family's flight: "We had to leave Laos because we didn't like the communists, and we were afraid of them, and they weren't good; we were afraid that there was going to be fight between Laos and the Laos communists." Some of the Tai Dam in Laos had reason to fear the new regime. Many had fought alongside the French against the communists in Vietnam. After the 1954 Battle of Dien Bien Phu, North Vietnam fell to the communists, and a group of Tai Dam fled to Laos. Because of their experiences in North Vietnam, the Tai Dam understood communist rule more so than their Lao cousins. For this reason, many Tai Dam escaped to Thailand in May of 1975, months before the capital of Vientiane fell to the Pathet Lao. Mek Baccam explained what would happen under the new regime: new laws, conscription, and prison camps. He wrote, "I didn't like that they were going to make a new law. Like, if you weren't in the Laos army, then they would arrest you and send you to another state to teach you how the new law is or how the communists do, and they want you to forget your old laws."[6]

In contrast to the Tai Dam who feared communist reprisals and left for Thailand, the Lao prepared for an easy peace; this difference in expectations appeared in the recollections of Lao youths. Orathay Fongdara resented King Savang Vatthana and other leaders for naively believing the false promises of the Pathet Lao. He wrote, "I don't know why the King of Laos let the Communists come in the country.... All the leaders of Laos believed in the Communists. They were going to be friends." Unfortunately, thousands of these leaders paid dearly for their naïveté. They languished in reeducation camps for many years. Many Lao, including King Savang Vatthana, died during their imprisonment. Orathay noted the communists' method for creating new leaders. They advised college students to demonstrate, and they promised these students leadership positions in the new government. These strikes prompted Orathay's family to leave Laos. Similar to the leaders in Orathay's narrative, Boonleng Keongam remembered being duped by the promises of the communists. They told him, "We bring you the new life; better than before and we have great power." The communists vowed to "make the Laotian people and poor people feel happy." Boonleng told the reader that these good times never came under communist rule. He explained, "Everything began to decline, the roads were destroyed and never restored. The city was destroyed and declined. People under the communists' control did not have enough food to eat. Some factories stopped working and education was never promoted. Students studied only a few hours a day."[7]

As a ten-year-old girl from southwest Cambodia, Sovouthy Tith refused to believe communist propaganda from the start. Her father rose to the rank of Lt. Colonel before he died in the war against the infamous Khmer Rouge. Sovouthy noted, "Even if he didn't earn much money for the family, I still loved him because he was a nationalist." In April of 1975, students had time off from school, but escalating warfare prevented them from enjoying their vacation. Guns went off throughout the night, and by the seventeenth, Sovouthy and others listened to a radio broadcast emanating from the capital of Phnom Penh; the communists announced that they had seized power and were nationalists. Souvothy remembered that fateful moment: "I didn't believe them, not even a single word. I had never felt so worried or upset as I was at that time because I knew what was going to happen. I walked away from the group of people, my mind going back to the death of my father. I thought if I were older, I would not let my father down this way at all. No one got a good night's sleep on that night; some cried and some asked God for help."[8]

Iowa's refugee youths connected the deterioration of life under communist rule with being removed from school and being forced to work. Two days after Sovouthy heard the radio announcement, the Khmer Rouge demanded all students in the seventh grade and up appear at a meeting; fear for her life compelled the young girl to attend. At the gathering, the Khmer Rouge informed the schoolchildren that they would not be able to continue their studies. The communists told Sovouthy and other students, "We can't eat paper instead of food to survive, so we have to work on the farm." Puzzled pupils looked at one another, but they refused to protest out of fear. Upon hearing this bad news, Sovouthy recalled, "I almost cried, but I tried to hold back and pretended to look at the pool with fish swimming slowly in the shadow of the trees. I did want to drag my bicycle and ride away, but I could not; I just didn't listen to them anymore." Nib Thongchine, a twelve-year-old girl when Laos became communist, also connected the unfairness of communism with children having to work without pay: "My country deteriorated and became an indigent country. People got poorer and poorer until there was no food to eat, no clothes to wear.... Everything changed rapidly such as living, wandering to visit each other, education and other things. The communists compelled people to work for them. If they did not do what they said, they punished or killed them like animals. I was one of them. I worked for the Communists. But, we did not get anything from them." Phoeun Chey, a Cambodian from Battambang, noted how only cows, water buffalo, and elephants pulled carts in Cambodia before the Khmer Rouge. Afterwards, humans pulled carts. According to Phoeun, "Sometimes, the Khmer Rouge rode on the wagons and you had to pull them too, and if you went too slow, they hit you with a piece of wood to make you pull faster." He also explained the specific work duties of youths: "The young children, aged eight through sixteen, had to go to work, too. Their job was to pick up little pieces of wood that were on the water. They worked from 6:00 a.m. to 6:30 p.m. Then they came home for dinner time. Work like that was not easy because if you rested you got killed."[9]

Like Sovouthy Tith, many of Des Moines' refugee authors wrote about losing their fathers in the struggle against communism. Cher Vang's father had been killed fighting the communists in 1969. Pao Lee, also a Hmong, lamented the loss of a father at the hands of Vietnamese soldiers in 1972. To make matters worse, the family never recovered father's body to perform the proper last rites. Monyra Chau remembered her father fighting all over Cambodia before he died when she was eight. Born in Cambodia in 1972, Veasna Ham also lost his father at a young age. He wrote, "My mother said that my father was a soldier and that he was killed. I never saw my father. I wonder what he was like."[10]

In her essay, Saran Chau narrated her father's tragic last days. Before being a soldier, Saran's father had been employed as a doctor. Because of his work connections, he had an opportunity to leave Cambodia for America, but he refused to turn his back on his homeland. Saran envied her father's patriotism. She recalled how her father dreamt of being shot in the shoulder. This dream came true, but her father survived. Ultimately, the Khmer Rouge learned that Saran's father fought against them. The young author explained what happened as a result: "One day some soldiers who were Cambodian, but who were secretly working for the Communists, came to my house and told my father that he was to go with them to a governmental office to receive another stripe (his fourth) for his uniform. These men were lying, but we did not know it at this time. My father went with them and we never saw him again. Only later, when these same soldiers returned to our house and stole our furniture and made us leave, did we realize they had lied. Then we knew for sure that my father had been killed." Saran wrote about her family's most cherished possession. After the Khmer Rouge evicted her family from their home, a cousin snuck into the house and found a photograph of Saran's father. The cousin wrapped the photo in plastic and buried it. Though damaged by dirt and water, the photograph came with Saran to Des Moines, Iowa.[11]

Even if their fathers had not died at the hands of the communists, childhood fears of losing their fathers appeared in the writings of Des Moines' Southeast Asian students. Bounsong Manivanh's father worked for the king of Laos during the day, and he tended to the family farm in the evenings. In 1977, a man summoned her father to a meeting with the king. On this same day, the fifteen-year-old Bounsong had to take her final exams for that semester. She remembered those worrisome times: "After the test, we were asking my mom why my dad didn't come home to eat lunch with us and she said he had not come home from the meeting yet. In the late afternoon on that day, my parents' old friend came to my mom and told her he saw them take my dad and some other people in a car and they drove away. We never knew where he went. We tried and tried so many times to find out where he was but nobody knew." During her father's three-month absence, Bounsong described the communists' seizure of her family's apartment, many possessions, and her mother's struggle to keep the family farm. Pathana Luvan, a ten-year-old from Laos, feared losing her father as well. At school, she overheard students talking about how the communists were "taking the leaders or people that [are] smart away from their family. Then I got worried about my father because he was a mayor. My mom got worried too; we didn't know when they would get him."[12] One day Pathana's elder sister visited the family. This sister worked for an American, and she warned that the family must leave Laos as soon as possible or else their father would be captured. Fear of losing male heads of households often prompted departures from their homelands. The route to Iowa was often an arduous one.

Des Moines' refugee youths recounted their harrowing escapes to nations of first asylum. Fue Yang's father worried his children might be drafted into Vietnam's ever-growing Army. Prior to leaving Laos, Fue's elder brother just managed to evade being drafted. This close call resulted in the Hmong family's decision to seek asylum in Thailand. For Fue, his journey to freedom seemed surreal, "When we went to Thailand it was not easy and I don't mind talking about it, but when it was real it was not fun at all, and when I talk about it, it's just like a story." Fue marched for seven days through the jungles of Laos to reach Thailand. For three of those days, heavy rains slowed their pace. The mud seemed impassable. With each step, Fue feared being discovered by Vietnamese soldiers. He explained, "Every time we thought in our hearts that something might go wrong. We couldn't even let the children cry. If the children cried, the Vietnamese soldiers would hear and they would shoot us. They couldn't say a word." Fue remembered being in tears and doubting his ability to continue the hard journey to Thailand. He wrote, "I was very weak and I hardly had the strength to walk. My father said I had to get up to eat and I said I didn't want to get up. I was tired and all I wanted to do was just sleep and I didn't feel like eating. I was sick about one week…. I think that God helped me and God gave me the strength so I could walk."[13]

Reaching the Mekong River and crossing into Thailand did not bring Fue's group of about forty-eight Hmong immediate relief. While traveling in four boats across the Mekong, the Thai sank the boat Fue's brother rode. Watching from the riverbank, Fue feared for his brother's life, but he knew how to swim and was not among the eight who drowned. After reaching the Thai side, the Hmong stayed in lodging provided by the Thai. That first night in Thailand, the same individuals who sank their boat returned to the Hmong's quarters and robbed the newcomers. The small lodging could not fit Fue's family, so they slept outside and avoided being robbed. Fue remembered the group's sadness, "In the morning, everybody came to us and everybody was crying. Some of the people were crying because the day before they had lost part of their family by drowning…. My best friend was in one of the boats with his family. His mother and sister drowned when the Thai sank the boat."[14] Fue's father advised the Hmong to fight the next time the Thai tried to rob them. When the group first arrived at their camp, these bandits returned and grabbed Fue's father. Heeding his father's advice, fellow Hmong pulled out their knives and drove their attackers away.

Vay Ho demonstrated an in depth knowledge of the boat people trade and its many tragedies. On two separate occasions, his father and mother had been caught attempting to escape communist Vietnam. Vay wrote about his parents' suffering while imprisoned: "My father was punished by being struck with strong sticks. He was sickened several times in a month.... They both had not enough food to eat, no blanket kept them warm, [they] took a shower once every two weeks." While taking food to father, Vay noticed "a lot of prisoners looked with hungry eyes." Retaliation would have occurred if his father had not shared the food. After an entire month, Vay's elder brother found a Mrs. Su who bribed officials and secured his parents' release from prison. A short time thereafter, Mrs. Su organized a plan for the family to leave South Vietnam. Demonstrating the duplicitous world of the boat people trade, Mrs. Su could not be trusted enough to orchestrate the family's exit from Vietnam even after she had obtained the release of Vay's parents. The family reasoned that Mrs. Su's bribe to prison officials seemed low, and she had been talking too much in public. Instead, the family waited until a safer plan presented itself six months later. All the while, Vay's family worried the government might search their home and find their valuables. The family pretended to farm while hiding their gold in the field. Ultimately, the family received government permission to leave Vietnam by boat.[15]

Vay Ho faced a grueling ordeal as a young boat person. His mere twenty-yard boat contained 210 individuals. After several attempts, the boat finally departed for Malaysia. The loaded down craft traveled sluggishly on the sea. At landfall in Malaysia, passengers became elated and jumped into the water with a "big freedom smile." However, one of the swimmers immediately realized the water's true depth. The boat's captain tried to pull the craft closer to shore. Vay vividly explained what happened next:

> Suddenly, the crest of the wave which was more than four stories high slammed against our boat. Children started to cry. The second crest of the wave raised and dropped the boat to the sea shore from about three stories high. The boat crashed, the salt water sank the boat. The next few waves pushed the boat closer and closer to the shore and pushed some people far away from the shore because they couldn't hang on to the boat or they were afraid the boat would flip over so they jumped

out of the boat. Some Malaysians helped to bring the children floating on the water to shore. Some swam out far away and tried to save people who were pulled out by the crest of the waves.[16]

Some drowned and one person's body could not be recovered. The hungry group had arrived in Malaysia and discovered that the Malaysians only traded food for gold, money, and watches.

Phoeun Chey, a Cambodian born in 1972, recalled his family's climactic flight to Thailand. One day, the seven-year-old's family and a group of others had been ordered to dig a large hole. The Khmer Rouge often demanded people dig their own graves before shooting their victims. He described his terrifying exit from Cambodia during the Vietnamese invasion: "My family and another family had finished digging a large hole. We were sitting in front of the hole waiting to be shot. The Khmer Rouge pointed the guns at us. One of the Khmer Rouge asked why we were still in Cambodia. My cousin said we couldn't get out. The Khmer Rouge said we could go if we would get out of there immediately. There was a reason why the Khmer Rouge did not want to shoot us then. If the South Vietnamese soldiers had heard the shooting, they would have come to fight the Khmer Rouge."[17] The Khmer Rouge advised the group to find sanctuary by traveling west. Fearing a trap, Phoeun's family went in the opposite direction. His family lived in constant fear of being discovered and killed by the communists until they escaped through the jungle to reach Thailand.

Whether arriving to nations of first asylum as "boat people" or "land people," some of Iowa's refugee children spoke about their difficulties in refugee camps throughout Asia. Boonleng Keongam lived at Ban Tong Camp with about sixteen thousand others. He worked for the Thai government from dawn until dusk. Soldiers watched over his every move. By 10:00 p.m., refugees had to be in their shelters with the lights off. Even with this strict curfew, robberies and murders took place. Boonleng summarized life in Ban Tong as follows, "We lived under poor conditions, unhappy and without freedom." For the author, refugee camp life did not improve much in the Philippines either. Boonleng went hungry while frequent outbreaks of fever and diarrhea wracked the refugees. Hoover School District classmates Sovouthy Tith and Khanny Um also described the hardships of camp life. At Khao I Dang, Tith felt powerless because refugees could not complain about their mistreatment. The Thai feared communist infiltration and worried western nations such as the United States might leave them the burden of caring for refugees like Khanny Um. Khanny described the Thais' cruel treatment of Cambodians:

Cambodian people died because of Thai soldiers, who were very cruel. They killed a lot of Cambodian people when the Cambodian people escaped to Thailand. They would take the Cambodian people to the mountain and when they got to the top, the Thai soldiers would make the Cambodian people go down the other side of the mountain. The Thai soldiers knew that there were a lot of bombs on that side of the mountain…. The Thai soldiers forced the Cambodian people to go down the side of the mountain so that the bombs will blow them up.[18]

Khanny also stayed at Khao I Dang. She described life there as boring. People did next to nothing while hoping to be accepted to the United States. While at their respective camps, refugees had time to reflect on being separated from loved ones.

In their narratives, Des Moines' refugee youths emphasized the pain caused by separation from family, friends, and pets. For some of Iowa's Cambodian youths, this separation from family occurred as a direct result of Khmer Rouge policy. The Khmer Rouge demanded loyalty to the state alone. Adults seeking to become members of the Santebal secret police force had to answer thirty-two questions about their relatives. The communists demanded adults inform on any family members with potential disloyalties to the regime, even children. The last of the questions asked, "Do your children have influence, power, or interaction of any kind with you?" In contrast, the Khmer Rouge viewed the young as the purest creatures to mold in their image. After the very young finished breast feeding, the Khmer Rouge separated children from their parents and placed them in communal barracks to be raised by adults loyal to the revolution. At the age of six, Chea Seng remembered the communists taking him away from his mother. He wrote, "I had to become part of the brigade of the children. I didn't go to work in the field with the adults because I was so small, but they told me to wash the dishes, clean the yard, and cut the grass. I ate lunch at 2:30 p.m. I had a meal only one time a day…. Every morning I got up at 6:00 a.m. and went to work."[19] In the barracks, Chea slept on the floor and shared a blanket with other children. Inevitably, the boy awoke coverless and cold in the middle of the night.

Using propaganda and the threat of force, the Khmer Rouge hoped to transform youths into soldiers, policemen, executioners, and spies loyal only to the state, but nine-year-old Khanny Um's narrative highlighted the Khmer Rouge's failure to break the strong ties of familial love. Some Cambodian youths learned a communist song that aimed to weaken their ties to their families. One portion of the song went as follows:

> You depend on your grandparents,
> But they are far away

> You depend on your mother
> But your mother is at home
> You depend on your elder sister,
> But she has married a [Lon Nol] soldier
> You depend on the rich people,
> But the rich people oppress the poor people.

Like Chea, Khanny Um had to live with other children in a communal building away from her parents. The communists might have permitted families to visit one another for a mere three days out of a month. Missing her parents prompted Khanny to defy the Khmer Rouge. She explained: "I was unhappy when I was taken away, because I missed my parents so much. One day, I missed my parents so much that I ran to my house to see them without permission from my leader. I knew that they would not let me go to see my parents if I asked for permission. I was lucky when I went to see my parents, but I got into trouble when I came back to my place. There were two watchgirls who followed me when I was walking back. I thought I was going to die that time because those girls almost shot me. They suddenly changed their mind."[20] After the Vietnamese invaded Cambodia in 1979, families attempted to regroup, and thousands fled to Thailand.

Even as refugee families regrouped and reached asylum in camps throughout Asia, they inevitably left behind loved ones. Boonleng Keongam wrote about the sorry state of some refugees at the Philippines Refugee Processing Center: "Some people were very sad, homesick. They thought about their children, their wife or their husband, whom they had left behind. Some of them killed or hung themselves." He left behind a brother, sisters, and many nieces and nephews. Ky Tu made it to safety in Iowa with a father, sister, and two brothers. However, Ky left behind a mother, grandmother, aunt, and youngest brother. Ky wrote, "I have lived here about six and one half years. The four people that I named before are not here yet. I miss them very, very much.... We're hoping they'll come this year. We have been separated more than seven years."[21]

Even if a family made it to safety together, they faced breakup during the resettlement process. Siamphone Xayavong escaped Laos and lived in Thailand with grandparents. Eventually, his grandparents were accepted for resettlement in Texas: a mixed blessing for the family. The young author wrote a heart rendering recollection of being separated from his grandmother: "When my grandmother and her family were able to leave for Texas, I cried a lot. I didn't want them to move so I started to pull my grandmother and I would cry very loudly. That was when I was about four or five. My grandmother tried to leave but I wouldn't let go of her. Finally, my mom pulled me away. Then I started to cry even louder. I didn't want my grandmother to move away. After they left, my family and I lived alone. Sometimes I was happy and sometimes I thought about my grandparents. I was sad whenever I saw a plane fly across the sky. I thought about my grandparents."[22] On the whole, young Tai Dam did not have to endure as much separation because Governor Robert Ray had decided to resettle them as a group. However, all Southeast Asian refugee children had been separated from relatives during resettlement, including the Tai Dam.

No group of young refugees left behind more loved ones than unaccompanied minors. These individuals may or may not have been orphaned, and this complicated any adoption process. The state of Iowa took guardianship over these individuals and then transferred this guardianship to the Iowa Department of Social Services. These unaccompanied minors then entered the state's foster care system. For unaccompanied minors like Cam Quang, adjusting to life in Iowa without family proved difficult. Cam had four older sisters and three brothers in his family of ten. He survived being a boat person, but he still missed his relatives. He finished his ESL essay with a somber sentence, "Everyone in my family is still in Vietnam, except me."[23]

In oral histories and in their student essays, Iowa's refugee youths lamented being torn from the company of good friends during their journeys to America. Parents advised their children to keep their exit plans secret. This might have prevented a family's escape plot from being discovered by the communists, but it also prevented children from saying goodbye to dear friends. As a five-year-old, Me Duong remembered a mixture of emotions when leaving Laos: "I was very excited and overjoyed but I was unhappy to leave my friends. We couldn't say anything to our friends about our moving."[24]

At displaced persons camps, Iowa's refugee youths formed powerful bonds with those in similar circumstances only to see these bonds broken during resettlement. Theun Deo from Laos stated the importance of good friends to a young person's wellbeing in camp. He wrote, "Friends in refugee camp, they usually have a gang. If you don't have friends they like to bother you all the time." Some lucky youths reunited with pals from their hometowns while in nations of first asylum. Pathana Luvan became overjoyed when she learned her Laotian friend had escaped to Thailand. She wrote, "I visited her all the time so we could talk about school, friends and our village. I asked her how Laos was when I was away.... I felt really happy because I see my friend once again." In addition to old pals, Iowa's refugee youths formed new relationships while in camp. Sivilay Phabmixay described how the refugee experience disrupted friendships: "I had many friends in the camp, they are good friends good persons to be friends with…. I lived in the camp about a year and a half. I felt bad and sad to leave my friends. I just left my friends from Laos, and then I had to leave my friends I just knew in camp. That was the worst feeling I ever had, sad and it made me cry." In her narrative, Pathana Luvan described the mixed emotions refugees felt after learning that they had been accepted to America. She wrote, "I felt happy and sad because I had to abandon my house, my things and all of my friends once again, and the happy part was I just wanted to see what it was like in America."[25]

In addition to friends, Des Moines' refugee youngsters wrote about missing their animals. By the late 1970s, more Indochinese refugees came from agricultural backgrounds than had the first 130,000 arrivals to America. Farm children grew up surrounded by animals. Veasna Ham wrote, "I am glad I was born on a farm. There were lots of things to see and do." Interacting with farm animals represented one of those many things to do. Laotian Oubonh Phanthavong lived on a farm that produced rice. The Phanthavong family owned chickens, ducks, cows, and water buffalo. When he tired of walking home from the field, Ounbonh remembered riding on the backs of water buffalo. As a Buddhist, Khanny Um learned to treat animals kindly while growing up in Monkolbarei, Cambodia. Folks from her hometown enjoyed feeding pigs and chickens, and they lived with the company of many other animals.[26]

Whether or not they farmed, nearly all of these children had favorite pets that could not come with them. The Vietnamese communists forced Amkha Xam out of Laos in a hurry. The youngster only managed to grab two outfits, but leaving behind clothing did not hurt as badly as leaving behind a furry friend. Amkha stated, "I wanted to take my dog with me but I couldn't." Similarly, Mek Baccam "felt sad to leave behind my house, garden and all my animals." Oune Be wrote about his dog's premonition that something was amiss just prior to the author's exit from Laos. He explained, "At 3:00 o'clock I was coming back home and I saw my dog. He was just standing and not running to me, and I looked at him. He was looking strange. Later at 4:45 I was going up to the house to pack my clothes to take with me, and he just ran to me, gave me a kiss and ran away. After I was going to leave my house, I went to my brother's house and told my brother to take good care of him."[27]

Sovane Bethi's essay best represented the blurred line between separation and reunion, and the emotional roller coaster endured by Iowa's refugee youths. Sovane fled Laos for Thailand accompanied by her parents and a brother, but the youngster felt sorrow because the trip to freedom meant separating from her big brother, dog, home, and bicycle. At a refugee camp in Thailand, Sovane reunited with many cousins and developed strong friendships with new playmates. Upon learning about being accepted to America, Sovane expressed the mixed emotions so common in the disrupted life of refugee youngsters. The author explained: "I found out I was going to leave the camp by seeing our name in front of the office in the camp. I felt happy and sad. I felt happy because when I get to America, I get to see my sister and her family. I hadn't seen her for a long, long time. I thought, I get to see my sister and how beautiful the United States is. I felt sad because when I left the camp, I would miss my good friends in the camp, and I think I will never come back to see my friends. All my friends had to go the other way, and I will never ever see my good friends again. That makes me sad."[28] These powerful friendships helped refugee youths endure difficult times, and they are important for understanding an alternative narrative about the resiliency of refugee youths.

An odd segue appeared in Siamphone Xayavong's retelling of life as a four-year-old child refugee. His family had just escaped the communists in Laos, who "were killing all of the innocent people." Eventually, the Xayavongs reached Thailand and built a shelter. Siamphone wrote: "We built a tall fence and a gate to go outside. We built it because we didn't want any robbers and killers to get into our house. We didn't have any lock on the door. That was why we built a fence and a door with a stick to keep the door locked. We had fun. When it was raining we would climb the mountain and play. The mountains were very high. Then we got some mud and we made things like statues out of it."[29] Siamphone's narrative, like many of the other refugee essayists, contained an odd mixture of prescience and ignorance. This ignorance resulted from their youthful naiveté and parents' conscious attempts to shield children from the problems at hand. Siamphone's mother, pregnant with her fourth child, probably had different feelings about her life as a refugee in Thailand. Siamphone's remembrance of refugee camp life as "fun" was not unique. In their essays and oral histories about their younger days, many of Iowa's Indochinese refugees described having pleasant times at refugee camps. The following argument does not deny that young refugees suffered. This suffering has already been explained in detail above. However, to dismiss their accounts because of their youth would be a greater disservice than to propose that the young were the most resilient group of refugees.

Somkong Vong, a seven-year-old Tai Dam, remembered her family's flight from Vientiane, Laos, in ways different than her parents. Her father translated Morse code for an aeronautical company and her mother performed housekeeping for a U.S. family. As the communists continued to make gains into Laos, Somkong's parents fled because their connections to the United States placed their lives in jeopardy. They feared for their safety, and they made the difficult decision to leave behind a land they had called home for many years. Conversely, Somkong had only a faint memory of leaving the capital for her grandparents' place in Laos. She recalled, "I had no idea what was happening.... I do not remember packing my cloths. I think my mom did all those things." Somkong's parents arranged for transportation from her grandparents' home to Thailand. In contrast to the adults, the child failed to comprehend the seriousness of the moment. Somkong compared her carefree mental state to that of her distressed parents as the family finally left Laos for Thailand, "They showed emotions. When somebody came to pick us up in a big truck we were all riding in the back of the truck, and I just noticed my mom was crying. I didn't know why."[30]

The brazenness and ignorance of youth often shielded refugees from the realities of refugee life; this brazenness and ignorance appeared in many of the Des Moines students' ESL essays. In 1975, Somaly Chak escaped from the murderous Pol Pot regime earlier than most others, but the early evacuees still faced a difficult journey to Thailand. On the way, Somaly explained how her group caught, plied with alcohol, and then killed several Khmer Rouge soldiers. Barefooted people went without food, drink, and sleep during the two day ordeal. Little children and babies cried during this trip to Thailand, but not big nine-year-old Somaly. The author boasted, "When I walked at night, I wasn't even scared of anything." Crossing the Mekong River, people drowned and others were shot. Five-year-old Me Duong crossed the river at night, but the author incorrectly believed their family had crossed a lake into Thailand. However, Me Duong feared the boat might hit a rock and or be tipped over in comparison to the carefree youths in Phouthasone "Larry" Khounxay's account. Larry's family paid a person to smuggle them into Thailand. While navigating the dangerous Mekong River, Larry's younger sister and little cousin erupted in laughter. Initially, the young children failed to comprehend the seriousness of the moment. Larry's mother frantically tried to quiet the children by covering their mouths with her hands. In the midst of the commotion, the boat suddenly tipped and ejected everyone into the water. The family nearly drowned and lost most of their valuables in the accident.[31]

The ignorance of youth also appeared in Vay Ho's essay about boat people. Vay's family had made preparations to leave Vietnam from Ray Gia Bay. The police did a four hour roll call for the 210 passengers. Unfortunately, the many passengers loaded down the twenty-yard boat, and the water's depths prevented the group from embarking. The people had to wait four more days before another chance to leave communist Vietnam presented itself. During their next attempt, the vessel's water pump broke, and the boat filled with water. People tried to eject the water until a police boat arrived four hours later. The police demanded the group return to shore once again. The boat sat for another five days while being repaired. Adults sold clothing, watches, and gold to buy food and have the boat fixed. They had already paid exit fees and bribes many times over in their attempts to exit Vietnam. On the third attempt, Vay contrasted the reactions of knowledgeable parents and ignorant youths. The student wrote, "When the boat came, all the children were happy, but not their parents. Their parents were afraid it might happen again and they would have to return to sell clothes, watches and gold or something else would happen."[32]

Tai Dam oral histories have demonstrated that youths also interpreted life in refugee camps differently than adults. Youngsters stayed at the same camp at the same time as their parents. However, adults hated life in Nong Khai, Thailand, while the youngsters enjoyed their stay. After the Tai Dam had arrived in Thailand in May of 1975, over 1,200 had to be trucked to a Buddhist temple near Nong Khai. This temple and the surrounding grounds served as the Tai Dam's refugee camp. Houng Baccam, an adult political leader, had a horrible time at the refugee camp. He feared communist infiltration, and he participated in an around the clock watch. Would his family be broken up during the resettlement process? Would the Tai Dam find asylum as an entire group or be scattered across the globe? Where would the Tai Dam go next? These questions led to worry-filled nights for Houng and the other adults. Houng remembered that frustrating time: "Sometimes at night in Nong Khai, I would be talking with my wife and I'd feel as if I wanted to beat my fists against my chest. It was terrible." Thuong Lo, a former soldier for the French and Lao armies, did not arrive at Nong Khai until four years after Houng Baccam. He too had an awful experience there. Thuong worried other Tai Dam might kill him.[33] Tai Dam had family and political rivalries that they brought with them to camp. Some charged others with being allied to the communists back in Laos.

From the very start of refugee life for the Tai Dam, children had more positive memories than their parents. Houng Baccam described untroubled youths' behavior on the truck ride to Nong Khai: "The children thought it was a picnic at first." Their carefree mentality continued throughout their stay at camp. Somkong Vong and Mike Rasavanh resided at Nong Khai as youngsters during the same time as Houng, but they remembered refugee life there differently. Adults feared staying near the Buddhist funerary complex; the ancestor worshipping Tai Dam believed the power of returning spirits could make one ill. In contrast, Somkong Vong had a pleasant time. She used tombstones as her makeshift sliding boards. Playing jump rope, stick and rubber band games, Somkong described life at Nong Khai as "pretty relaxed. Actually, to me, it was pretty fun. I got to run around a new place, meet new people, and play with new friends." Mike Rasavanh spoke about similar memories of camp life. He stated, "As kids, it was fun. Many other kids were running around playing. We did not even think of how worried our parents must have been." In comparison to Thuong who feared for his life while at Nong Khai, his twelve-year-old daughter Dara Rasavanh recalled life at this very same camp as being "very fun" and "festive."[34]

In their oral histories, some of the Tai Dam appeared to feel guilty for remembering life in camp with fondness. As adults, they have become more aware of their parents' suffering, and some may have reinterpreted their life in camp in more somber tones. Nonetheless, their memories of fun times at refugee camps have been corroborated by the essays written by refugee students in the Des Moines public school system. While at his camp, Mek Baccam stated, "I did nothing—just had fun with my many friends." Pathana Luvan acknowledged her camp was "very dangerous because there were killing, stealing, and gambling," but in that very same paragraph, she stated, "In the camp I made a lot of new friends and it was fun."[35]

Refugee youths put their imaginations to use while in the camps. They played old games like soccer and invented new ones with their limited resources. In contrast to what might have been a gloomy environment for adults, refugee camps represented new terrains to be explored by youths. Phonesamay Fongdara's narrative best illustrated how youngsters put their imaginations to work in the refugee camps. The author described daily life the Philippines Refugee Processing Center: "We had a lot of fun there. I learned how to swim in a stream. During the daytime I usually went into the woods and hunted or looked for fruit for my little brother. There once was an earthquake but it didn't affect us. I liked playing in the sand with my friends. In the woods, I liked to climb and chop trees and

An adult shields a malnourished Khmer child from the sun, Thailand, 1979. At refugee camps such as Sa Kaeo, children were especially vulnerable to malnutrition and disease. At more stable refugee camps, youths proved remarkably resilient. Their own naiveté and loving adults shielded youngsters from fully understanding the gravity of the situation. In their autobiographies, many Des Moines school students fondly remembered life in the refugee camps (courtesy Robert Ray).

branches. I made a lot of friends in the Philippines.... My brother loved to make and fly kites.... We played a lot of games and it was the happiest time in my life." At Larry Khounxay's second refugee camp, the rhythm of play dictated his daily routine. In the early morning, he ran to his parents and asked for money to buy rice noodles from a vendor. By 10:00

a.m., he sprinted with friends to a local lake and dug for clay. Then, Larry and playmates began sculpting whatever their imaginations dictated. By the afternoon, Larry and friends bought ice cream and played numerous games. In the evenings, jokes and scary stories proliferated around a bon fire. Young teenagers also enjoyed camp life more so than adults. They flirted with new love interests, and they enjoyed moonlit walks together.[36]

Youthful ignorance and protective parents shielded many refugee youths from the full rigors of being a refugee. By the time Vilayvanh Senephansiri penned her essay, she had become aware of her parents' conscious effort to shield youths from refugee life. The author explained, "My parents had a hard time to decide to leave my country. My parents did not tell us because they thought we were not old enough. Maybe they would tell us later. On the last day, my parents just told us we had to go." The innocence and ignorance of childhood even existed in the killing fields of Cambodia. In 1976 when Chea Seng was just five years of age, his sister died, but he failed to comprehend what happened. The young author remembered, "My mother cried a lot. I asked her, why are you crying, mother?" Ignorance might also have shielded very young refugees from what otherwise would have been painful family separations. During Chea's last days under the Khmer Rouge, he recalled an awkward meeting with a sobbing woman; the child did not know the identity of this person. That was the first time Chea remembered meeting his grandmother.[37]

In addition to being protected by ignorance, the young have always been more ready to explore new terrains than the old. Leaving home was hardest on the elderly who had invested their entire lives in their homelands. Vilayvanh Senephansiri realized the decision to leave home most affected adults, especially the elderly. She wrote, "My grandmother lived in the country. We tried to get her to come with us, but she said no. She had a hard time to move to a new place. She wants to live and enjoy the only place where she was born and lived all her life. My parents had a hard time too."[38] When families arrived at refugee camps, the young adapted faster than the old. At these camps throughout Asia, the adults worried and the children played.

According to historian Tara Zahra, refugee youths have not always been "quintessential victims of war." In her monograph *The Lost Children: Reconstructing Europe's Families after World War II*, Zahra traced the development of psychology and its application to refugee children. Initially, relief workers worried about the physical well-being of children. For example, Herbert Hoover's World War I era American Relief Administration focused on the caloric intake of European children. Youths had to finish their meals in front of relief workers out of fear they would smuggle foodstuffs home to their parents. This attention to physical well-being appeared in the League of Nations' 1924 Declaration of the Rights of the Child: "The child that is hungry must be fed; the child that is sick must be nursed; the child that is backward must be helped; the delinquent child must be reclaimed; the orphan and the waif must be sheltered and succored." In the World War II era, psychologists such as Anna Freud and John Bowlsby called attention to the psychological well-being of children. They pioneered theories such as "separation anxiety" and "maternal deprivation." This greater emphasis on the psychological well-being of children informed the United Nations' 1959 Declaration of the Rights of the Child: "The child, for the full and harmonious development of his personality, needs love and understanding.... He shall, wherever possible, grow up in the care and under the responsibility of his parents, and, in any case, in an atmosphere of affection and of moral material security; a child of tender years shall not, save in exceptional circumstances, be separated from his mother."[39]

The emergence of child psychology has resulted in studies of refugee children being dominated by pathology. In their research, child psychologists often generalize and apply universal principles to children. For example, Bruno Bettelheim compared child victims of neglect to child victims of the Nazis. Similarly, Ernst Papanek wrote, "One may compare the child victims of war with any children anywhere who have suffered from family disruption or are orphans. The same mechanism responsible in both cases for the disturbance of psychological and spiritual health."[40] Psychologists have made important contributions, but more research on child refugees needs to be done by historians who may provide a greater understanding of the backgrounds of these youths. In reading their short autobiographies and listening to their oral histories, Iowa's refugee children do not always appear to be the "quintessential victims of war." Rather, they were the littlest victims. These youths' greater better ability to adapt to the ever-changing life of a refugee continued in Iowa.

8

Children as
Cultural Go Betweens

Des Moines' Indochinese schoolchildren had great expectations for life in America. Several, including Pa Mao, could not sleep because of the excitement. During a layover in Hong Kong, Pa explained, "Sleeping in the hotel on a bed, I should have slept well, as I didn't have much sleep the night before, but I couldn't sleep because my mind was thinking about the United States, and how beautiful it was." Throughout her stay at a refugee camp, Pathana Luvan remembered watching orientation films about all of the states. She noted, "When they talked about Iowa I didn't understand what they said. I saw lots of snow and many cornfields."[1] Despite immigration officials' attempts to orientate Indochinese to future life in America, Des Moines' young refugees still wrote about information overload during their first days in the United States. They learned about America only by experiencing it, but refugee youths' first impressions of the United States were as much about remembering as encountering. With their limited memories of home, the youngsters often focused on the physical dissimilarities between the United States and their homelands. They emphasized differences in the land, the people, and schools.

Youths experienced refugee life in ways different from their parents. Ignorance and naiveté insulated youngsters from comprehending the severity of their situations in Southeast Asia. The experiences of adults and children also diverged throughout the resettlement process in Iowa. Refugee youths and adults lived in different arenas in Iowa. Youngsters did not immediately enter the workforce; they tried to make sense of life in public schools. Mainly due to their schooling, Indochinese youths adapted to their new surroundings more quickly than their elders. This

170

quick adaptation brought with it both rewards and punishments. In Iowa, refugee adults became the ones who needed help understanding "American" culture, and refugee youths served as their guides.

Many Indochinese children first flew on an airplane during their trips to the United States. The confusion began immediately for Pao Lee. The Hmong student remembered, "When we arrived at the airport, one of the Americans took us to the door that went into the airplane, but we didn't realize that we were in the airplane because it just seemed like a long hallway." Mek Baccam felt elation while riding an airplane for the first time. However, this joy turned to worry when the plane climbed in elevation. Mek wrote, "When the airplane flew too high, I felt scared and my ears couldn't hear anything." Veasna Ham also felt uneasy during flight, and he refused a meal because he did not know how to eat American food. Other Indochinese refugees in Iowa had strong food-related memories of their first flights to the United States. Siamphone Xayavong had a mixed encounter with American foodstuffs. He wrote, "The pilot gave me an apple and I didn't know what it was because I had never had a big apple before. So I started to taste it. It was good and juicy. Then they gave me a piece of chicken but I didn't know how to eat it. When we made chicken in Laos, we made it differently. When I saw the crust I didn't want to eat it. It was strange."[2]

After landing in the United States, the students wrote about information overload. They surveyed their surroundings and compared them to their homelands. Theun Deo described California's lights, motels, and foods. He recalled, "I feel great when I get off the plane and I seen a lot of new things.... All stuff I never test." Oune Be also stopped over in California. The author tried to find words to describe the beauty of the Golden Gate Bridge. In addition to its sheer size, the student had been impressed by the basic function of the bridge. He wrote, "That is a long bridge, and the first time I ever saw a road that has one on the bottom and one on the top of each other." At the Des Moines International Airport, Savy Chhith marveled at the elevator and escalator, "things that I never seen before." Vay Ho, a student interested in becoming a mechanical engineer, enjoyed living in the United States because of its modern technology. In Vay's composition, the author noticed the pop, candy, and newspaper machines.[3]

When Des Moines' ESL students remembered their native land, they focused on physical differences. The younger children only held faint memories of home. For example, Oubonh Phanthavong remembered only the fun associated with a couple of Lao holidays. Oubonh recalled participating in water fights and seeing fireworks competitions, but he did not understand the cultural significance of these events nor their specific names. The student admitted, "There were many more holidays that I forgot about. All of these holidays were very important to us." Although some students struggled to remember the meanings of holidays and religious ceremonies, they still had retained a concrete knowledge of their homes and the physical appearance of their native lands. The Indochinese, particularly the Laotians, came from a mountainous region. Over 90 percent of Laos rests at 600 feet in elevation or higher.[4] The Luang Prabang Mountain range towers in the North of Laos while the Annamite range straddles the nation's eastern border with Vietnam. Whether they lived atop, on the sides, or in their shadows, nearly all Laotians lived with the mountains.

Unsurprisingly, mountains have figured prominently in Laotian folklore. For example, the legend of Phu Si explained the origin of the mountain in front of the royal palace at Luang Prabang. One day, Queen Sida, the wife of King Rama, prepared for mealtime in the royal palace. The Queen wanted to eat tiger ear mushrooms, but in the northern Lao language, these were called monkey ear mushrooms. Queen Sida demanded her aid Hanuman, the flying monkey, travel to Oudomxay Mountain to find her mushrooms. Hanuman flew to the mountain and returned with a basketful. Queen Sida rejected this kind of mushroom and ordered Hanuman to fetch some others, but she did not want to offend her monkey aide by specifically requesting monkey ear mushrooms. Hanuman then soared off and brought back some more mushrooms from Oudomxay Mountain, but the Queen refused them. Several more times the monkey returned with mushrooms not to the Queen's liking. Hanuman flew off one last time and picked up the entire top of Oudoxmay Mountain and plopped it right in front of the royal palace. Hanuman stated, "There you are, Your Majesty! What you want MUST be here somewhere. Just pick whatever you like!" This folktale explained the origin of the mountain in front of the royal palace, Phu Sida or Phu Si for short. It also described the process by which Oudoxmay Mountain obtained its flattened peak; the pointed top had been transplanted by Hanuman to Luang Prabang.[5]

No wonder the motif of mountains appeared in Des Moines refugee students' essays and illustrations. They distinguished their new homes in the plains from their old homes near the mountains. Bounsong Manivanh of Luang Prabang, Laos, described her homeland as follows: "My country is very small and very beautiful. It has a lot of mountains." Vilayvanh Senephansiri of Sayabury, Laos, also associated the mountains with home: "When I got up, I would see a sunrise from the high Phouzan Mountains."

Nib Thongchine described Laos as a beautiful land abundant with nature. She advised the reader to find in Vientiane "a high step, look far away from the city, you will see the beautiful mountains growing with many kinds of plants."[6]

Many student authors drew their homes foregrounding farmland with mountainous landscapes in the background. A student artist described one such drawing: "Rice fields in moonlight. Stalks of gold gleam in stillness. The night to remember." One student's illustration had been inspired by a dream about their birthplace. The author described their illustration of home: "One morn I woke up. Sun was sitting on mountain. I thought of my house." A fellow student illustrator realized that they could only travel home in their dreams. The youth commented on the mountain drawing, "I like scenery of the mountains of my country before, but now that is not true anymore. It's just a dream." Another young refugee illustrator noted, "They were very nice mountains, green with animals. I love my country." Many students missed the mountains, and it drove some to homesickness. One author captioned their drawing of mountains with the phrase, "When the sun shines on Green mountain like my country, I love to go back."[7]

Many of Iowa's late 1970s and early 1980s Indochinese refugees came from agricultural and rural backgrounds. In their essays and sketches, these students compared their old homelands to their new environment in Des Moines. Cher Vang drew a picture of a farmstead. Above the sketch, he wrote, "My house was a farm. Rice and corn are in the house. Do you have a farm?" Khanny Um compared life in rural Cambodia to life in the city of Des Moines. She noted, "People in Mongkolbarei liked living far away from each other, not like in America where the people live close to each other." Laotian Phonesamay Fongdara described a rural upbringing too, "There was nobody living near us because we lived in a forest." Pao Lee also made the rural to urban comparison. Pao wrote, "Life in my country was very different from this country, because we didn't live in a big city. We lived in a camp or group—several houses together in a special place." Oubonh Phanthavong grew up on a farm in Kene Thao, Laos. In contrast to Des Moines, a city with a 1980 population of over 191,000, Kene Thao was a small town of just one thousand. Oubonh also noted technological differences; his hometown lacked radio and TV stations. Boonleng Keongam came of age in rural Northern Laos. For this student, entering America seemed like being "reborn." The author related the Americanization process to transitioning from his rural Laotian background to an urban American one. For his future plans, Boonleng commented, "If it is possible, I would like to change from my old life to a new lifestyle, change to be an American citizen and try to be an urban planner program student to provide for the future growth and the renewal of urban communities."[8]

Des Moines' Indochinese school students also held firm memories of their actual homes, and they compared them to their homes in Iowa. Sovane Bethi preferred the privacy of her family's new apartment as compared to the quarters in the crowded and noisy refugee camp. Students noticed their old homes had been made from different materials. Me Duong's home in Laos had been built from sticks and straw. The author's father and uncle used ropes for construction because the family could not afford nails. Pao Lee described how the Hmong constructed their homes out of bamboo and trees. These homes only lasted for two or three years before a new one needed to be built. Cam Quang, from the urban Saigon area, contrasted his old home from American homes. He explained, "Our houses do not have basements and usually have a balcony on the second floor. It is common to have two houses joined together with a wall in between them. This is because in Vietnam there are so many people and we lack space."[9]

Students noted not only physical differences between their old and new homes, but also focused on the household items inside. Homes in Iowa contained many odd machines, especially in the kitchen. From a cousin, Pao Lee learned how to use the stove and washing machine. Pao caught on faster than mother, "We tried very hard to help my mom to use the stove and other things, too." Many of the students obtained a familiarity with electricity only after living in Iowa. One author drew a candle which illuminated a book. On the left page, the student drew their home with fencing, a tree, and the shining sun. On the right page, the student drew a starry night with mountains towering over farmland below. Above the drawing read, "When the sun is going down all the city lights go on, in my country where I was born they don't have electric light all the dark night I use the candle for study." Cambodian Saroeum Loeurng expressed an initial fear of this unfamiliar technology. She stated, "My sponsor took us to see our new house. I didn't know how to turn the light on. I was afraid that it might shock me. Then I learned how to use everything in my house."[10]

In addition to encountering a new land and new household goods, Des Moines' refugee youths also sized up their new American neighbors. Pathana Luvan noticed her family represented the only Asians on the plane ride to Iowa. Most of the people in her new country would not be Asian-looking like her. Saroeum Loeurng emphasized the physical appearance of Americans. The author stated, "When I got to America, I saw so many people with different colors of hair. The first time I saw American people, I thought they looked very strange." Many students commented on the sheer size of Americans. Kham Sackpraseuth wrote, "I think the American people are very tall, nobody is short like me." Some students envisioned America as a land of milk and honey. Vilayvanh Senephansiri had learned that the United States had the most wealth in the world. This led her to incorrectly believe that all Americans were wealthy and owned their own vehicle. Senephansiri reasoned, "People never seemed to be out walking and nobody rode the buses, everybody drove." Theun Deo formed negative opinions of Americans because they took advantage of Asians in the United States. He angrily declared, "I do like America, but I don't like American people. They like mistreat my people. If in my country I do like they did to us, you think they [would] like…. I don't think so. Some family had robs or plunder. If they live in my country, I'll kill them all who had ever plunder my people."[11] Part of Theun's negative opinion of Americans originated from negative interactions with peers at school.

Studying Iowa's refugee youths has value because these youths largely encountered America in the public schools whereas their parents did so in the workplace. As an adult Tai Dam, Em Quang labored in an old age home in Story City, Iowa. One of the residents had lost a son in Vietnam and took out her frustrations on Em. On the fourth of July, the resident mocked Em stating "Happy Vietnam Day" or "Why are you here when my son died in Vietnam?" Em often came home from work in tears. Em's husband also faced difficulties adjusting to a new job in Iowa. He found himself unable to work after being hit by a drunk driver during the family's first years in the United States. Som Baccam compared her parents' adjustment process with her own: "I didn't experience it as awful as my parents did. I knew that they were unhappy, but me, I was just going to school. What did I know? What responsibility did I have?" What refugee youths did know was school. Nearly all had been students in Southeast Asia. Monyra Chau of Battambang, Cambodia, even interpreted refugee life to being a school student. Each of the five camps she lived at compared to being in a grade at school. She had to pass through each camp in order to graduate to America.[12] In their ESL essays, students wrote at length about their transition to life in Iowa's schools.

Many of Des Moines' ESL students agreed with Khanny Um that "American school was very very different" from their old schools. Sovou - thy Tith outlined the differences between Cambodian and American schools. In Cambodia, students wore uniforms with white tops and blue bottoms. Sovouthy understood schools did this to mask the social class of its pupils, but students at her Des Moines school did not have uniforms. Cambodian students had to take the same classes from first through twelfth grade whereas Des Moines students had a choice of electives. In addition to Sundays, Sovouthy's school had off Thursdays instead of Saturdays. Southeast Asia's climate also demanded school days and semesters start at different times than the schools in Des Moines. In Southeast Asia, students had long breaks during the middle of the day because of the heat. They enjoyed extended lunches before going back to school in the afternoon. Boonleng Keongam explained that schools in Laos closed from October through December so children could help out on the family farm during the rainy season.[13]

Several of Des Moines' Southeast Asian students noted that their old schools lacked resources but not competitiveness. Sovouthy Tith's American school had far more resources than her Cambodian school. For example, Cambodians studied mostly without the help of libraries and books. Without libraries and books, Tith and other classmates had relied on lecture notes. American teachers permitted students to turn in assignments if absent, but Cambodian students did not have a chance to makeup schoolwork, even a final exam. Tith and other Indochinese students wrote of the competitive nature of their old schools. They noted the importance of class rank and how only grades of A and B were acceptable to pass each grade. Khanny Um observed that Iowa's students talked a lot more during class. She reasoned students in Cambodia had been quieter because teachers used corporal punishment.[14]

Most Des Moines refugee students preferred their Iowa teachers because their new teachers did not hit them. If students had an unkempt appearance or misbehaved in the classroom, the teachers back home struck them. Veasna Ham's dislike of school in Southeast Asia stemmed from an instructor's use of corporal punishment. Veasna explained: "When I was five years old, I went to school. The teacher was mean. Every day when school started she looked at our fingernails. She hit our hands hard with a stick. It was not a very big stick. One Monday morning after having been in school two or three weeks, I told my mother that I was going to school. I started walking but then I hid behind some bushes. When my mother went back in to the apartment, I walked to my friends' house to play marbles with them. Every day I skipped school." Saroeum Loeurng also wrote about teachers hitting students, and she compared them to Des Moines' teachers: "I am so happy to be in America because the teachers help me learn about a lot of things, and they are all very nice to me."

Because language barriers often stymied early friendships between the Indochinese schoolchildren and their American classmates, young refugees often formed quick and intense bonds with teachers. Cher Vang explained, "My first friends in America were just the teachers." Somkong Vong remembered her third grade teacher, Ken Miller, looking after her. He packed her lunches for school events and other retired teachers provided one on one English language help.[15] Hoover High School ESL instructor Simone Soria understood her students' plight as well as anyone. She too had been a child refugee. Her Jewish family split up and went into hiding in Nazi Europe. Dedicated teachers such as Soria helped the newcomers adjust to life in the Des Moines public school system.

Des Moines Indochinese students recounted fear of starting new schools without friends and English language skills. Say Lo described a tense start to the second grade in America, "It was terrible, but I got through it." Orathay Fongdara recalled being somewhat intimidated while first attending middle school on the south side of Des Moines. He explained, "I felt nervous about school, the American students were tall and big." With the language barrier, Oune Be felt out of place at North Pines Jr. High School. Even when the nice kids wanted to become friends, he experienced discomfort: "I didn't know how to talk to them, and I just felt like this was their school." Cher Vang's first involvement with school of any kind took place in Iowa. He explained the obstacles with an emphasis on learning English, "I didn't know anything in the classrooms, and I didn't know what the teacher talked about.... I don't know how to talk all the American words, and when I talk some words, it doesn't naje sebse [sic]."[16]

Though scholars of Indochinese refugee resettlement have described the inversion process for adults in the workforce, they have failed to address this change in status for refugee students in the public school system. While parents might have dropped from working professionals to menial laborers in the United States, their children witnessed a decline in their confidence at school both intellectually and socially. Phouvong Senephansiri had difficulty learning the English language, and the student incorrectly associated English-speaking ability with intelligence. Phouvong had lost confidence in her intellectual abilities in America because of the language barrier. The student wrote, "If I could change anything, I would like to be an intelligent student, speak English very well...." Sivilay Phabmixay expressed similar frustrations. Sivilay had the intellectual ability to solve problems, but could not always comprehend the tasks being asked by the teacher. She recalled, "I went to class and teacher told me to do this ... but I didn't understand and I did know what to do. I just sat there." Des Moines' young refugees also illustrated their difficulties adjusting to the English language and school in Iowa. One student drew an image of an Asian boy with arms crossed in frustration with the caption, "It was hard for me to understand how to do it. Soon it'll be better." The new language barrier also caused some normally outgoing students to become reserved in Iowa. Some schoolchildren refused to speak because they feared making a mistake. Others stayed silent to avoid being taunted by their classmates. Theun Deo explained his transformation: "I felt in an American school very very different than my school in Laos.... I am like mute boy."[17]

While their parents often witnessed a decline in wages, students new to America often endured a decline in popularity. Many Des Moines refugee students wrote about being taunted. Vay Ho noted, "I still have trouble with customs, language, and people who make fun of me. But I have to let it go. I think they will understand more about me or other refugees if they were in my situation." Orathay Fongdara handled the taunts as best as possible. He explained, "Students sometime made fun of me, but I didn't care, they just talked and yelled, they didn't hurt me." In contrast to Vay and Orathay, Theun Deo had a more troublesome time adjusting to life in Iowa and the bullying of classmates. At first, Theun wore long hair, disobeyed his parents, cursed at others, and enjoyed fighting Americans. The author spoke of progress in correcting his past misbehavior. Theun offered a half promise to stop fighting, but if students kept bothering him, he warned, "I can't stop or promise on this answer." Theun drew a self-portrait that addressed his inability to fit in with American peers. He placed himself on a river bank with a heavy head in hand while looking towards a setting sun. Beneath the drawing the author wrote a homesick poem:

> My country is not beautiful
> No one cares, But I do
> Because I belong there.

Cambodian student Heng Ngan commented on the difficulties of being Asian in the Des Moines public schools during the 1980s. He recalled constant teasing, "I got it from both sides: black and white." Classmates called him "gook" and "chink" among many other things. This past and present racism has made Heng feel like a perpetual foreigner. After three decades of living in the United States, he self-identifies as Cambodian, not Cambodian American.[18]

Like their parents, many Indochinese students first interacted with African Americans in the United States. Thuen Deo never saw a black person in Southeast Asia; he had only heard of their existence. Some students like Cher Vang feared this unknown group of people. He wrote, "When I first saw the American black people, I felt scared." Of course most of the youths' interactions with African Americans occurred in schools across the state. According to Heng, the black kids at his school "seemed to be the big bully. I just tried to stay away from them." Mike Rasavanh remembered black students testing their Asian classmates during his time at a Des Moines junior high school. He explained, "A couple of them in junior high school wanted to see if we knew karate." Kham Sackpraseuth held negative opinions of black people. In his essay, the author compared blacks unfavorably to his fellow Laotians. He declared, "I saw on TV my countrymen. They are a good people, no bad people and no black people. I never saw black people before like the people here; and another thing, they can't live together, that's what I think."[19]

Because of initial fears of Americans and the language barrier, Indochinese children often bonded with classmates from similar ethnic backgrounds. In 1975, Governor Robert Ray had his state program resettle the Tai Dam as a group because it made logistical sense from an employment perspective. The state had to find employment for only one cultural and linguistic group. If a single Tai Dam spoke English, this person could have served as an interpreter for all Tai Dam coworkers. Ray's cluster resettlement had other positive influences as well. The Tai Dam enjoyed being together in the same state with most of them living in the Des Moines area. Over time, the Iowa Refugee Service Center started to resettle other Southeast Asians across the state, but Des Moines still contained the largest refugee population. This concentration in the Des Moines area also benefitted refugee schoolchildren. Amkha Xam of Laos wrote about having difficulty adjusting to life on a farm in rural Lamona, Iowa. He described Lamona's inhabitants as "good people," but Amkha lacked playmates. He explained, "Lamona, Iowa, has a small school, about 300 students. In the school I was so bored and I didn't have a friend and it is hard to learn." In May of 1983, Amkha moved to the capital and made friends. In addition to being near other Indochinese, Des Moines had grocers who sold Southeast Asian foodstuffs. Shopping at Des Moines' Thai market comforted Pathana Luvan during her first days in Iowa. She stated, "When we got there I was surprised because everything we eat was there. I never thought about it."[20]

Students wrote about meeting best friends in the Des Moines public schools, and these best friends were often from Southeast Asian backgrounds. Peer support helped these students adapt to life in Des Moines. In their classrooms, they found other students who looked like them and who had experienced similar upheavals in Indochina. Theun Deo fought with American classmates, but he formed a strong bond with Chey Leo Van. Being outnumbered by oversized American classmates intimidated some of the refugee students, but Orathay Fongdara noted, "I was not really nervous because I had a lot of friends in the school. They showed me the way to go, and helped when I had trouble." For Sivilay Phabmixay, language hindered early friendships with Americans. Sivilay stated, "I felt bad because I didn't know every [sic] much English. Some Americans talked to me but I couldn't answer them, I couldn't understand, because I didn't know how to speak English." Sivilay made mistakes often because of the language barrier. In this context, having fellow Lao speakers in ESL helped the author. Sivilay most enjoyed ESL class in Des Moines partially because she had peer support. She wrote, "I asked my friends and they told me what to do." Phouvong Senephansiri wrote about language barriers hindering new friendships with Americans too. She explained, "It seemed to me that it is difficult to make American friends, because we speak different languages, however, I will keep on trying until I know how to speak English better." Several students wished to change the language used in America from English to their native tongue. Kham Sackpraseuth stated, "If I could change anything, I would change my study of English to my language. It would be easier for me to talk to everybody and to make friends with Americans, and it would be easier to study."[21]

Although some Southeast Asian schoolchildren enjoyed peer support from fellow refugees, rivalries still existed between different ethnic groups in the Des Moines public schools. While coming of age, one student's Lao father advised her to marry any man of her choice so long as that man was not Vietnamese. Some Tai Dam, Lao, and Cambodians viewed Vietnam as the aggressor that brought communism into their homelands and forced their families to flee. These negative opinions of the Vietnamese existed among schoolchildren as well. Donechanh Southammavong recalled rivalries between students of Southeast Asian descent. She stated, "We were fighting with them but I am not quite sure why? It was a group of us who were Tai Dam who were fighting with the Vietnamese people. I really did not know why. I don't know if it just derived from what our parents would say.... It was really interesting because it was Tai Dam versus Vietnamese."[22]

One Vietnamese student in Iowa found himself in the middle of a political battle between Adel-Desoto High School Principal Stanley Norenberg and the Iowa Department of Social Services. Tuan Le came to Iowa as an unaccompanied minor in October of 1980. By 1981, foster service for the seventeen-year-old had changed, and Lutheran Social Services prepared to place Tuan with Arthur and Rita Keller of Adel, Iowa. However, Principal Norenberg refused to enroll Tuan at Adel-Desoto. Social worker Stephen Gross quoted Principal Norenberg as saying, "We don't want that Vietnamese kid in this school." In a testy conversation, Gross reminded Norenberg that he had no legal right to block any student's enrollment. According to Gross, Norenberg replied that he understood that rule but he could "certainly put a lot of pressure on a kid who's already under a lot of pressure." Barbara Cook of Lutheran Social Services suggested that Principal Norenberg twisted the words of an Urbandale High School counselor to make it appear as though Tuan Le had been a troublemaker at his old school. Norenberg also contacted the potential foster family and told the Kellers he did not want the student attending his school. The Kellers had other children enrolled in the district and did not want to cause an uproar, so they backed out of being Tuan Le's foster parents.[23] The Iowa Department of Social Services demanded the Adel-Desoto School Board counsel principal Norenberg for his actions.

Principal Norenberg rejected Tuan's enrollment because he believed the student should be placed in a district with an adequate ESL program. Norenberg argued that Adel-Desoto lacked the resources to properly educate Tuan, and he wanted Social Services to place the teenager in North High School. Part of this political debate arose from the costs of instructing refugee children. Ian Binnie of the Des Moines School Board noted Iowa school districts would need millions of dollars to educate the 1,500 additional refugees Ray had agreed to resettle in January of 1979. That same year, Robert Benton, the State Superintendent of Public Instruction, estimated the cost of educating one illiterate refugee student to be roughly $5,000: three times the cost of educating a regular student. Superintendent Benton wanted the state legislature to appropriate funding for language instruction to understaffed and underfunded school districts.[24]

With financial concerns in mind, some residents of the district rallied behind their principal. Mrs. Edna Burns supported Norenberg in her letter to Governor Ray. Mrs. Burns cited Adel-Desoto's budget constraints. In her opinion, admitting one student who would have demanded extra time and money unfairly hindered the education of many other students. Mrs. Burns had ten citizens sign her letter of support for the principal. Of course Mrs. Burns' opinion cannot be divorced from the refugee resettlement program in general. Burns argued that Iowa must not accept refugees when so many domestic problems existed at home. Tax dollars could be better spent on needy Iowans instead of resettling and educating refugees. She declared, "I would gratefully contribute to, aid and help, of my own desire, a number of needy causes, and SEND THE AID TO THE HOME COUNTRY OF THOSE INVOLVED." Because of the controversy, Social Services never placed Tuan in Adel-Desoto. When Tuan's caseworker Maggie King informed him of the change in plans, she noted that the teenager "seemed a little upset and I don't blame him. I'm sure this is all very confusing to him when I told him I had a placement and now I've had to change all the planning the last minute."[25]

Few refugee youths found themselves in the middle of political battles like Tuan Le, but most did find themselves in the middle of a cultural battle. The young refugees who had been born in Southeast Asia but matured in the United States have been referred to as generation 1.5.[26] These youngsters resembled Atlas, but they had to carry the weight of two worlds on their shoulders. Indochinese students came of age in two worlds, but they never felt totally comfortable in either one. Generation 1.5 had at least some knowledge of life from the old country, and they somewhat identified with their parents. As children in Southeast Asia, they had learned their native language and culture, and their parents had instilled in them traditional values such as respect for elders. However, as youths from Indochina matured in the United States, they learned the English language and Americanized faster and more fully than their elders. Over time, parents worried their children had lost touch with their traditional cultures and had become too "American." While parents may have chastised them for being too "American," generation 1.5 often found themselves being rejected by their American peers. Living in predominantly white Iowa, some youths developed negative self-images. They wanted to fit in but feared the way they looked prohibited them from ever doing so. Trapped in between two cultures, generation 1.5 found themselves in the awkward position of helping their elders navigate American culture. In the process of serving as cultural mediators, some youngsters gained confidence and leadership skills. As generation 1.5 reached adulthood and started families of their own, they have continued to be the middle men who try to balance the traditional cultures of their elders with the Americanized culture of their own children.

In Iowa, children often learned the English language faster than their elders, and this required them to serve as translators between their parents and the American community. For Monyra Chau, this process began immediately. The Chau family arrived in Pittsburgh, Pennsylvania, without any sponsor there to show them the way home. Luckily, a priest recognized the family's distress. As the clearest speaker of English, Chau did her best to explain the situation to the priest who then contacted the proper officials. As a child, Somkong Vong had participated in an "adopt a grandparent" program at the First Church of the Open Bible in Des Moines, Iowa. This adopted grandparent had sponsored refugees, and she often needed Somkong to be an interpreter. The child found herself translating important medical information between doctors and their Indochinese patients.[27]

Young refugees interpreting for their parents could upset the balance of power within the family. Youths had been taught to revere their elders, but children who knew English became empowered. One old ruse has been described many times over. School officials sent home letters reprimanding Indochinese students for poor grades and or behavior. Parents asked their child to read them the letter. The youth lied by telling their parents that the school had sent home a letter praising the student's success in the classroom. Acting as a cultural-go-between empowered Dara Rasavanh as a thirteen-year-old. She described herself as a "tour guide" for her Tai Dam family in America. She continued, "I became a leader in my family. My parents listened to me, and they would have me translate for them.... I was forced to mature quickly."[28] Serving as cultural mediators brought refugee youths into meaningful contact with adults outside of the teacher student relationship.

While interpreting for adults might have instilled youths with confidence, it also placed them in difficult circumstances at times. Somphong Baccam's father worked as a custodian at Iowa State University, and he carpooled to work. People in the carpool complained that his traditional foodstuffs smelled bad, and they did not want him riding with them any longer. Acting as an interpreter, Som told the driver that her father had agreed to eat only American food while riding to work. The driver relented and let her father stay in the carpool. Shortly thereafter, the driver called back to complain. They told Som that her father had body odor and would no longer be able to ride with the group. Relaying this information to the head of household placed the daughter in an uncomfortable situation.[29]

As Indochinese youths learned about American culture faster than their parents, they yearned to be like Americans. Surrounded by Caucasian classmates in Iowa, some Southeast Asian youngsters had poor self-images. Boonsao Keongam had many American friends, but he still felt different. He concluded his ESL essay by stating, "If I could change anything,

I would change my name and all of my body to be different or to be a movie star like James Bond." Some recent scholarship has suggested that gender differences may have influenced the adjustment process of immigrants in America. Traditionally, the image of the Asian male has not been as positive as the female. In American popular culture, Asian males had been feminized and associated with being quirky characters. In comparison, Asian females have had the more positive china doll stereotype. Because of these American attitudes about Asian males and females, parents seeking to adopt a Vietnamese girl during the final days of the Vietnam War faced extended waiting periods while paperwork to adopt a boy started immediately.[30]

Though the image of the Asian female might have been more positive in American popular culture, some Asian female school students also had identity issues in Iowa. Somphong Baccam recounted her double life during adolescence: "I grew up in two different worlds. At home, I had to be this Tai Dam girl. When I went out, I wanted to be this American person because I didn't want to be left out. I hated the way I looked. I wanted to look American. I dressed American because I wanted to have what they had. When I came home, I knew that I was poor.... It was really tough. There were days that I cried and thought why did I have to go through this? Why can't I have a simple life?" Tensions often arose between daughters and parents over the American style of dating. In Laos, a boy interested in dating a girl traveled to the girl's home in a group. Parents had the ability to supervise young couples. In America, dating boys meant daughters traveled away from the home and the watchful eyes of their parents.[31]

Indochinese parents and their Americanized children sometimes found themselves at odds over dating and marrying outside of their ethnic group. Generational tensions over interethnic marriage figured prominently in the old Hmong folktale, "The Little Mouse Girl Who Did Not Want to Marry Her Own Kind." In the story retold by elder Vamouachee Xiong, the little mouse girl did not find her fellow mice to be attractive, and she wanted to marry another type of animal against the wishes of her parents. The little mouse girl then went to ask for God's permission to marry outside of her kind. God advised the little mouse girl, "You have to marry your own kind of animal." God then told the little mouse girl to seek the powerful Sun's counsel because the Sun illuminated all of God's creations. The Sun also advised the little mouse girl to marry her own kind, but the Sun told the little mouse girl to visit the Cloud who had the power to block the Sun's rays. The Cloud advised the little mouse girl to marry another mouse, but the Cloud told the little mouse girl to visit the Wind who had the power to blow the Cloud away. The Wind also rebuked the little mouse girl's wishes to marry outside of her own kind, but the Wind told the little mouse girl to visit the powerful Mountain because the Mountain stood firm against the power of the Wind.

At this final stop, the little mouse girl learned the moral of the story. She conversed with the Mountain: "I asked my mother and father, I asked God, I asked the Sun, I asked the Cloud, and I asked the Wind. The Wind says that you are the most powerful on Earth, so I have a question for you. I do not want to marry my own kind. What do you say?" The Mountain then replied to the little mouse girl, "You see, I am the Mountain. I stand here and the Wind never blows me away. But any little mouse can come to the Mountain and make holes all over me to make a home here. I cannot tell the mouse to stop. The mouse is a little one, but the mouse is very smart and very hardworking. You need to go back and marry a mouse." Through this folktale, Hmong elders like Vamouachee Xiong impressed upon their children the importance of marrying fellow Hmong. Xiong believed that marriage outside of the Hmong culture most often resulted in sadness. Xiong's children had followed his advice by dating fellow Hmong. However, they have been Americanized and have interpreted the story differently than their father. The "same kind" of mate may also refer to abstract qualities such as values and goals.[32]

Coming of age in Iowa, some Tai Dam women challenged the traditional patriarchy which has revered men. Even if men treated their wives poorly, Tai Dam females encouraged women to stay with their husbands. Donechanh Southammavong experienced cultural conflict between her generation and older females over these gender roles. At meal time, her Tai Dam aunts reprimanded her, "Get food for your husband! Why are you eating first? Why don't you serve your husband more?" Don responded, "He has two feet, two hands. He can get it himself." Don and her Lao husband have their own bathrooms, and she refused to clean his mess. Don's behavior earned her the angst of her Tai Dam female relatives who feel as if she does not take care of her husband like a Tai Dam woman should. Don found her female relatives' advice to be somewhat hypocritical, "My aunts sound resentful about always having to serve their husbands, but they want their children to serve their husbands."[33]

As children born in Southeast Asia have matured and started families of their own, they have continued to be pressed between two cultures: that of their children and that of their parents. Growing up, Somkong Vong's parents impressed upon her the importance of taking care of her elders as they aged. In contrast, Somkong has taught her children to take care of themselves instead of worrying about her wellbeing. Grandparents have reprimanded their children for allowing grandchildren to become too Americanized. For example, some Tai Dam have argued that their grandchildren lack respect for elders. In the old country, Tai Dam used titles for those with important positions, and Tai Dam addressed all elders with the respectful titles of "uncle" or "aunt."[34] This practice has ended in Iowa. Worse yet, according to Tai Dam culture, Southeast Asian American youths have spoken vulgar language to their parents, something seen as being American.

As generation 1.5 began families of their own, they have had to cater to the demands of their born and raised American offspring. They have chosen to let their children participate in numerous activities and attend a myriad of after school events. Thomas Baccam, a father of two, has described what life has been like for parents born in Southeast Asia but who came of age and began their own families in Iowa. He explained being trapped in the middle: "I have to be flexible to my dad, the culture, the elder generation and I have to be flexible to my daughter. They cannot be flexible to me because they were born in this country.... I am the one who is in the middle. It is very difficult."[35]

The first generation of youths born in Southeast Asia at times quarreled with their parents over cultural differences, but early on, both parents and children understood the important concept of freedom. As youngsters in the 1970s and 1980s, Southeast Asian refugees in Iowa remembered the physical characteristics of their homeland with the greatest detail, and they compared their homelands with their new environment in Iowa. Abstract concepts such as Buddhism infrequently appeared in their ESL essays, but the students spoke about the important concept of freedom.

Students old enough to recall life before the communists seized power compared the new regime unfavorably to the past one. Nib Thongchine noted how life changed under communist rule in Laos. The teenager wrote, "Before the communists, I was feeling vivacious. But I felt doleful, and famished under that rule with absolute power; a dictator like an animal. I am hopeful never to be under such atrocious rule by communists ever again in my life." Some students accepted their hardships as the necessary price to pay for liberty. In an insightful poem, Vay Ho, a boat person refugee, lamented the loss of freedom under communist rule in Vietnam. The student wrote about the corrupt government of his homeland:

Oh! Freedom, freedom
The wishes of my grandfather.
Is he still wishing?

Even boats didn't like
They ran away communist
No doubt about me

First, Cold War began.
Later, became a hot war.
It became so hot, so hot...

My homeland was lost.
Made from my blood, and my tears
Cowards took it, why?

Vietnamese government works.
Money does the talking.[36]

Once in Iowa, Indochinese students contrasted their newfound freedom with their experiences under communist rule. In a few sentences, Say Lo compared his life in Iowa to the old country. Laos had two seasons whereas Iowa had four. Laotians were mostly poor whereas Americans had wealth. Laotians worked on farms while Americans worked in factories. Most importantly, he recognized that "America is a free country, not like Laos because Laos is not a free country.... Since the communists took over my country, Laos cannot be free." Before reaching the age of twenty, Viseth Tith had experienced life under several governments. He described these governments in terms of degrees of freedom. According to Viseth, no freedom existed under the Khmer Rouge. During their reign of terror, Cambodians did not even dream of freedom. After the Vietnamese invaded in 1979 and placed Heng Samrin into power, Cambodians "got some more freedom than under the first communists," but not enough. In Iowa, Viseth found the best type of government: a republic.[37]

Some of Iowa's refugee youths wanted to return home, but they recognized their homelands lacked liberty. Even with all of the suffering, Pathana Luvan still loved her native land, "No matter what terrible thing we had been through." She expressed her homesickness in a poem:

Goodbye, my village
It was nice to live in such
A beautiful place.

I was born in the
country, I was raised with the
sun, flowers are my friends.

> I kiss my friends goodbye
> it is hard to see them cry
> worries in their eyes.
>
> There is no place like home.
> Home's where I was born and raised.
> It's still there, lonely,

However, students understood that going back home had become unrealistic. Sivilay Phabmixay believed the communists would kill her family if they ever returned to Laos. Living in the United States brought Sivilay the taste of freedom and self-confidence. She wrote, "I am a new person. I am free to go anywhere and I can stand by myself."[38] In the future, Sivilay planned to become a businesswoman or member of the armed forces to fight for liberty.

Viseth Tith yearned to export his newfound freedom to Cambodia; if Cambodia turned into a republic, he could return home. Likewise, Monyra Chau wanted Cambodia to become a free country so she could visit relatives left behind. Pa Mao went one step further than Viseth and Monyra. Pa wrote, "I am very happy because I have freedom.... If I could change anything, I would change all the communist countries to be democratic. I hate the communist countries because I have known it for four years in my country, Cambodia. Now we hope we never have it again. WE HAVE FREEDOM!"[39]

Adjusting to life in the United States, Iowa's Indochinese youths did not always agree with their parents. Encountering American culture often led to disputes over clothing, curfew, courtship, child-rearing, and a host of other issues. However, experiencing and appreciating newfound freedom in America brought refugee children and their parents closer together. In Iowa, these youths and their parents both believed in the American dream. Through study and hard work, they believed the younger generation could achieve great things in the United States.[40] After all, ensuring a good future for their children had been the main reason why parents made the difficult decision to leave home in the first place. Some refugee youths like Vay Ho had been aware of their parents' sacrifice for some time. He wrote, "I learned a lot from the voyage to the United States, and how the United States government compares to the Vietnamese government.... I believe my parents spent all their money and courage just to buy freedom in the United States for their children. My father at age sixty never gave up on his dream to come to the United States. My parents are the greatest people, who [are] the first generation to bring their family to the powerful country."[41]

9

Robert Ray and
the Indochinese Refugees

Robert Ray influenced Indochinese refugee resettlement and relief more so than any other governor in the United States. In 1975, he established his own refugee program to help the Tai Dam resettle in Iowa. To aid the boat people, the Governor made the executive decision to increase the Iowa Refugee Service Center's intake by an additional 1,500. In doing so, Ray became one of the earliest elected officials to publicly support increased assistance to the boat people. Because of his influence over refugee matters, Ray was one of just two U.S. governors invited to attend the Special United Nations Conference on Refugees in Geneva, Switzerland. At the 1979 conference, Ray urged senior political officials from several nations to admit greater numbers of Indochinese. Around this same time, Ray began lobbying federal authorities to pass what became the Refugee Act of 1980. Consequently, Ray became the first governor to influence federal refugee law by pushing for a longer period of federal reimbursement to states for refugee resettlement costs. Ray's work on behalf of refugees helped some Iowans heal from the wounds of a controversial war. Many Iowans beamed with pride at the humanitarianism of their governor and their state. Of all the actions he took while in office, Ray's work with Indochinese refugees remains his greatest and most enduring legacy.

After the Vietnam War, Ray decided to launch his own refugee resettlement program. He obtained an exemption to relocate the Tai Dam as a large group under the classification of their ethnic rivals: the Vietnamese. Ray needed the exemption because federal resettlement policy forbade bringing large groups to any one locale; officials feared that relocating refugees as clusters would overwhelm the resources of local communities and states as the Cubans had done in Dade County, Florida.[1] The Tai Dam needed to be resettled as "Vietnamese" because the Indochinese Migration and Assistance Act of 1975 only allocated funding for Vietnamese and Cambodians to come to the United States. Ray brought the Tai Dam to Iowa because of humanitarian considerations, and he wanted to help his friend President Gerald Ford. Additionally, Ray sought greater control over the refugee resettlement process in his state. The federal government decided which and how many refugees to admit. Afterwards, private voluntary agencies resettled refugees in states. This entire process occurred with no input from the nation's governors. The VOLAGS' tendency to place refugees on welfare upset Ray the most. He vowed to oversee a work-first state resettlement agency infused with his fiscal conservative ideals.

When admitting refugees to Iowa, Ray faced fewer political obstacles than the president did when admitting refugees to the United States. Before the Refugee Act of 1980, U.S. presidents used the attorney general's parole power to designate and resettle certain groups as refugees. However, the president had to wrestle funding from Congress to help the newcomers' transition to life in America. For the initial resettlement of Indochinese, President Ford asked for 507 million dollars. As the House of Representatives mulled over his request, two Iowa Democrats sought to revise the President's proposal. Michael Blouin suggested a ceiling of 407 million dollars, and Berkley Bedell wanted Ford to provide monthly updates on the refugee program to the House Judiciary and Senate Foreign Relations Committees. Ultimately, HR-6894 cleared the Senate only after the President's suggested ceiling had been reduced by $102 million.[2]

In contrast to President Ford, Ray made the executive decision to establish his own resettlement agency without consulting the legislature. Ray's decision to resettle the Tai Dam mimicked the parole power of the federal government; he basically paroled the paroled. However, Ray did not have to wrangle with Iowa's state legislature because the federal government funded his refugee program. From the State Department, the Governor's Task Force received $500 per refugee resettled, and Congress allocated federal reimbursement to each state for refugees drawing cash and medical assistance. Federal funding permitted Ray to keep the legislature uninvolved in refugee affairs in Iowa.

Ray's creation and control over the Iowa Refugee Service Center represented a continuation in the shift in power from the state legislature to the executive. Under the governorship of Harold Hughes (1963–1969), the legislature granted the executive greater power of appointment. In the past, a board or commission of citizens oversaw the appointment and supervision of department heads. Some of these department heads served longer terms than the governor, and they reported to a board of three people independent from the executive. Experienced legislators had difficulty relinquishing their power of patronage, but newer representatives disliked having their time consumed by appointing and confirming staff.[3]

Under Ray, the power of appointment, the consolidation of state agencies, and the move from two to four year executive terms enhanced the power of the Governor's Office. David Oman, Ray's Executive Assistant, recalled the Governor made 500 to 600 appointments per year, and that Ray had roughly 2,000 appointees serving at any given time. During Ray's fourteen consecutive years in office, he had appointed every board and commission member at least once: some of them several times over. As the head of state chosen by the voting public, Ray argued that he should have control over directors and commissioners. He stated, "I knew it was not good management to have the legislature deprive the governor the power of appointment of the directors who run the agencies of government. They couldn't very well hold me responsible, as they should be able to, if I couldn't control those appointments." Ray had been elected to his fourth term in 1975, and this was his first of two four year terms. The Governor's longevity in office also manifested itself in the makeup of the judicial branch. During Ray's tenure, eight of the nine acting Iowa State Supreme Court justices and 90 percent of district court judges had been appointed by him.[4]

Ray unilaterally created his own resettlement agency without consulting with the state legislature. He appointed Colleen Shearer, the director of Job Service of Iowa, to oversee his refugee program. In the past, Job Service had been run by three individuals. By the Ray years, a single director appointed by and responsible to the governor ran this agency. From 1975 until Ray left office in 1982, Shearer served as the head of Job Service and the Iowa Refugee Service Center. Shearer anticipated managing the Governor's refugee initiative for a mere two years. As time passed, she felt uneasy as to how the IRSC had been created by the Governor. Five years after Ray started his resettlement program, Shearer expressed her concerns about the legitimacy of the IRSC. She confided in Ray, "I am reminded of the old saying, 'there's no such thing as being a little bit pregnant,' because in some ways the refugee center has been in this uncomfortable situation for five years, and is still experiencing labor pains. I refer to the fact that it is a state agency and yet it is *not* a state agency, having been created neither legally nor officially."[5] A lawyer from Job Service advised Shearer that the IRSC was a de facto agency. As a result, Shearer had some "sleepless nights" fearing someone might challenge its legitimacy. She wanted to know if the IRSC should remain an offshoot of Job Service or become a standalone agency. Shearer believed the permanency of refugee and immigrant admissions to America would require all states to respond by establishing permanent agencies; these state agencies would have to be funded by state legislatures. She hoped to find stronger legal footing for the IRSC before that day arrived.

Federal officials recognized the influence Ray had over refugee matters, and they allied with him to resettle refugees. Scholars such as Gil Leoscher and Robert Scanlan have addressed the importance of mid-level Foreign Service officers' advocating for an open door policy during the boat people crisis. Shepard Lowman, Lionel Rosenblatt, Hank Cushing, and others had served in Vietnam and fell in love with the people. In the final days before the collapse of Saigon, Lowman helped evacuate hundreds of Vietnamese before he too departed with the mayor of Saigon on April 29, 1975. Taking an unofficial leave, Rosenblatt paid his own way to Vietnam in order to arrange the departure of former allies. Cushing led a barge full of refugees along the Mekong River before being rescued by the U.S. Navy. During the war years, these men formed strong personal bonds with the Vietnamese. All three had experienced the evacuation themselves. They carried with them a deep sense of guilt because they knew many former allies had been abandoned. This sense of guilt compelled the "Saigon cowboys" to lobby their superior Richard Holbrooke to increase refugee admissions. Holbrooke, the Assistant Secretary of State for East Asian and Pacific Affairs, in turn advised President Carter to use the parole authority to resettle greater numbers of boat people.[6]

The relationship between the Saigon cowboys and the President was mimicked by Kenneth Quinn and Governor Ray at the state level. Quinn fit the profile of many other Foreign Service officers. After serving in Vietnam for seven years, he developed a deep emotional attachment to the people. Like Lowman, he married a Vietnamese woman. Quinn witnessed personal human suffering firsthand during his service in Vietnam; his brother-in-law died in the struggle against communism. Like the Saigon cowboys, Quinn carried a sense of guilt for abandoning former allies. The former resident of Dubuque, Iowa, had many contacts in federal government, and he used Governor Ray's power to promote refugee resettlement and relief in Iowa and beyond.

Quinn's role in advocating for resettlement can be witnessed in the Governor's January 1979 decision to admit an additional 1,500 Indochinese. According to the Iowa Public Television documentary *A Promise Called Iowa*, the Governor made the executive decision after witnessing Ed Bradley's special report on *60 Minutes*. However, Quinn had been pushing for greater numbers of refugees to be resettled in Iowa well before Bradley's report aired. On December 4, 1978, Quinn and Shearer attended a State Department meeting where they learned of the escalating boat people crisis. The refugee flow had increased tenfold from 1,500 to 15,000 persons fleeing per month. President Carter agreed to accept 60,000 Indochinese from that December through the first four months of 1979. With this knowledge, Quinn advised Ray: "There appears to be no real effort in the states at generating public support for additional resettlement. We therefore believe that a considerable opportunity exists for Iowa to once again provide leadership to the nation in a humanities endeavor. We believe Iowa could resettle an additional 1,500 refugees through an Indochina Refugee Center.... We would propose that you undertake an effort to rally support among the other Republican Governors, and the public at large through mailgrams and a 'guest editorial' to be submitted to selected newspapers." Quinn's contact, Deputy Assistant Secretary of State Frank Sieverts, agreed that the 1,500 refugees to Iowa could be Hmong. Quinn and Shearer believed the Hmong to be the most compatible with the Tai Dam, and working with a single ethnic group would be easier than with several.[7]

In addition to the number of Indochinese to be brought to Iowa, Quinn made several other recommendations for the Governor. First, he advised Ray to write President Carter informing him of Iowa's decision to admit more Indochinese. Second, he asked Ray to approve a mailgram to be sent to every U.S. governor. This mailgram would urge each governor to accept more refugees. Next, Quinn wanted Ray to approve a list of civic and religious leaders who would support the effort. Last, Quinn suggested the Governor release a pro-resettlement letter to media outlets in the hopes of garnering widespread support for this cause.

Shearer agreed with Quinn's recommendations. She realized any decision by Ray to resettle additional Indochinese would be controversial. Shearer forecasted the United States would increase its refugee intake during the boat people crisis; allies like France, Australia, Canada, and others could not absorb the Indochinese on their own. Shearer reasoned greater numbers of refugees would be coming to Iowa and every other state whether Ray supported resettlement or not. Still, she realized it would be a bold stance for Ray to publicly support such a divisive issue. As a department head appointed by the Governor, she sought to protect Ray from

(Left to right) Kenneth Quinn, Robert Ray, and Colleen Shearer at the Tai Dam Freedom Festival in Des Moines, Iowa, 1978. Quinn, a Foreign Service officer, served as a mediator between federal and state government while serving as Ray's special aide. He played an important role in Iowa's refugee program during Ray's last term in office. In 2017 Quinn was serving as president of the World Food Prize Foundation (Houng Baccam).

criticism at all times. The busy governor needed good counsel on this matter. Shearer feared her and Quinn's advising Ray to accept more refugees might be walking him into a "no-win situation." Despite these concerns, Shearer believed admitting more Indochinese would be the right decision. She wrote Quinn, "There is some risk for him to go public.... But life really isn't worth anything without risks … and here is an opportunity for Governor Ray to create opinions, rather than react to them." Shearer compared the dangers of boat people resettlement with the state's initial worries about working with the Tai Dam. She continued, "We walked in despite our fear … and we must do so again in Iowa. How *can* we be made to pay a very big price when what we are doing is so *right!*"[8] At the urging of Quinn and Shearer, Ray had been considering doing something to ameliorate the boat people crisis for at least a month. Witnessing this human tragedy on the television screen compelled the Governor to take the advice of two of his most trusted aides. He agreed to accept 1,500 additional refugees to Iowa.

Subsequently, Ray followed all of Quinn's boat people recommendations, and this permitted the Foreign Service officer to use the Governor's influence to promote Indochinese resettlement. Ray reinforced President Carter's decision to resettle additional Indochinese. The Governor wrote the President, "Action is necessary to prevent further suffering and loss of life. We in Iowa want you to know of our concern about what we read and hear and of our willingness to support your recent decision to admit additional refugees into the United States." Ray then provided a brief history of Iowa's resettlement program, and disclosed his decision to admit an additional 1,500 refugees to "prevent the further loss of life and suffering by these innocent people."[9] U.S. presidents made refugee policy decisions independent of the nation's governors, but no president wanted fifty angry governors opposing resettlement. Having a powerful ally from the rival political party offer support must have reassured President Carter. The federal government needed state-level cooperation to resettle refugees.

In a moving letter to his forty-nine colleagues, Ray pleaded for the nation's governors to support additional resettlement. He began: "I am writing to let you know that you can have a direct effect on the saving of lives. I want to ask your help in relieving the suffering of the refugees fleeing Communist rule in Southeast Asia.... Unless we act, this tragic loss of life and human suffering will continue. I believe we have a humanitarian obligation to try to help alleviate this situation. I don't see how we can sit by while innocent people suffer and die. Immediate and positive action is necessary." Ray addressed how unemployment and budgetary issues might easily allow governors to ignore the disaster, but human lives hung in the balance. The governors needed to take action. He advised them to coordinate with their voluntary agencies to see how many more refugees they could admit to their respective states. Ray also asked his colleagues to write a letter in support of resettlement to President Carter. Ray closed his message by reminding each governor of America's immigrant heritage. He wrote, "Consider for a moment where we might be today if our forefathers had been denied entry to our shores. In good conscience we should not deny these refugees either. Helping them start new lives is the right thing to do. It is something we can do—together."[10]

Ray's request produced mixed responses. Governor Julian Carroll commended Ray's efforts on behalf of the Indochinese. However, Kentuckians had endured terrible floods, and the state could not admit more refugees. John Dalton of Virginia offered a lukewarm response. With nearly ten thousand refugees and another two thousand on the way, Virginia had one of the nation's higher Indochinese populations. Dalton offered his support for the program, but he fretted over whether or not the federal government would continue to reimburse states for the cost of resettlement. Several governors, such as Lee Dreyfus of Wisconsin, Richard Snelling of Vermont, Thomas Judge of Montana, and John Evans of Idaho, informed Ray they had taken measures to prepare for greater intake of refugees in their states. Governors Hugh Carey of New York, Richard Thornburg of Pennsylvania, and James Thompson of Illinois all offered to increase their refugee admissions at Ray's urging.[11]

Ray's work on behalf of the boat people had the most profound influence on Governor William Milliken of Michigan. In March of 1979, Milliken informed President Carter that the state of Michigan planned to directly resettle refugees. He wrote, "This program would be patterned after the highly successful program which Iowa is conducting and would draw upon the expertise which that state has gained.... I believe it is possible to do as Iowa has done and develop programs which do not impact on the economy or work hardships on the state and which reflect the humanitarian instincts that I think the people of Michigan have."[12]

Because of his prominent role in refugee affairs, Governor Ray received an invitation from Secretary of State Cyrus Vance to attend the Special United Nations Conference on Refugees in Geneva, Switzerland. Only two governors, Ray and Brendan Byrne of New Jersey, joined the U.S. delegation headed by Vice President Walter Mondale. Kenneth Quinn also attended. U.S. diplomatic actions to ameliorate the growing refugee crisis culminated at Geneva in July of 1979. *Refoulement*, the return of an asylum seeker to a land where they faced persecution, remained a major issue of concern for UN officials. Countries of first asylum—often poorer nations—resented having to support the newcomers while the affluent West resettled refugees at a slow pace; by July of 1979, a backlog of 350,000 displaced persons remained in camps throughout Southeast Asia. As the refugee flow continued, Southeast Asian nations refused asylum to refugees. They towed boat people back to sea and forced others to return to Cambodia at gunpoint.

The Indochinese refugee crisis affected Thailand as much as any other nation. The important U.S. ally against communism had received nearly a quarter of a million asylum seekers from 1975 into the summer of 1979. Although the Thai government warmly received some refugees such as the Tai Dam, they also turned away Vietnamese and Cambodians at times. In a Thai Ministry of the Interior publication, *The Unfair Burden: Our House Is Full!*, frustrated officials complained about the costs of caring for refugees. On the cover of the pamphlet, a traditional Thai-style home on poles has been flooded by Vietnamese coming by land and sea. The Undersecretary of the State for the Interior commented, "We are drowning in a humanitarian ocean." The author of the booklet described how refugees overwhelmed the financial and natural resources of Thailand. Impoverished Thai farmers resented the foreigners' exhaustion of natural resources and access to financial and medical support in refugee camps. Thai officials also feared infiltration by communist agents. The author firmly stated, "We want the displaced persons out of our country."[13]

At Geneva, Ray worked to increase the number of refugees other nations would receive. With greater admissions, nations of first asylum would not be as inclined to engage in *refoulement*. The Governor of Iowa held bilateral meetings with senior representatives from Germany, Spain, Brazil, and Venezuela. During these talks, Ray provided an overview of Iowa's renowned resettlement methods, and he urged representatives from these nations to receive more refugees. The Midwestern state's successful program so impressed the German representatives that they ultimately sent a delegation to Iowa to learn more. Ray also met with Foreign Minister Carlos Pastor of Argentina. The Governor suggested Argentina, a prosperous nation in South America, had the ability to resettle more Indochinese. He believed Argentina's agricultural background made it a good fit for the predominantly rural and agrarian lifestyle of the Southeast Asians. Ray also had a private meeting with Vietnam's Foreign Minister Phon Hien. During the discussion, the Foreign Minister reassured Ray that Vietnam would "take measures to erase the pressure on its citizens to leave the country."[14]

The highpoint of the UN conference occurred during a riveting speech by Walter Mondale. The Vice President started by referencing the failings of the international community during the rise of the Third Reich. At Evian, France, in 1938, thirty-two nations met to discuss the plight of the Jews. If every nation at the conference had accepted just 17,000, all of the Jews in Germany and Austria could have been saved. Instead, lamented Mondale, "the world failed the test of civilization" by turning their backs on those in need. Soon afterward, Hitler conceived his final solution to the Jewish question, and millions lost their lives. Mondale pleaded to other nations: "Let us not re-enact their error. Let us not be the heirs to their shame." The Vice President asked all nations to do their part to help the Indochinese.

Mondale notified the delegates that the United States had agreed to lead the way by doubling its refugee intake from 84,000 to 168,000. The

U.S. offered millions in financial support for an international refugee reset-tlement fund and the construction of a UN refugee processing center. Additionally, Mondale informed representatives that President Carter authorized the U.S. Navy to begin search and rescue missions in the South China Sea. The Vice President finished his presentation by referring back to the failings at Evian: "Our children will deal harshly with us if we fail.... Let us not be like the others. Let us renounce that legacy of shame. Let us reach beyond metaphor. Let us honor the moral principle we inherit. Let us do something meaningful—something profound—to stem this misery. We face a world problem. Let us fashion a world solution. History will not forgive us if we fail. History will not forget us if we succeed."[15]

Mondale's powerful speech represented a special moment in U.S. and international history, and Iowans played an important role in it. Quinn reflected: "Here I am with Governor Ray. First, I felt so very good that I was able to play this critical role and make Iowa a critical part of changing the [closed door] policy. Something we had not been able to do in Hol-brooke's office in the State Department in Washington. We were able to bring about a policy change because I was in Iowa and the power of a state—even a small state like Iowa—was able to have on issues like this. It was quite stunning.... I was just a mid-level Foreign Service officer. I could not have had that kind of impact in Washington that I had out here." Immediately following the presentation, Mondale earned a standing ova-tion from the delegates. Ray shook Mondale's hand and noted it was one of the proudest moments of his life. Afterward, the two men exchanged letters of thanks for their work at the conference. Mondale wrote, "Dear Bob, It was a pleasure to have your participation as part of the U.S. dele-gation to the refugee meeting in Geneva. We were extremely grateful at the results of the meeting which was in no small part due to efforts of individual members of the U.S. delegation such as yourself."[16]

The Indochinese crisis that climaxed at Geneva demonstrated the inadequacy of U.S. refugee law; America found itself repeatedly enacting emergency legislation as a result. For starters, U.S. law placed geographic and ideological limitations on who may enter the nation as a refugee. In contrast to the UN, the United States narrowly defined a "refugee" as one escaping communism or persecution in the Middle East. Throughout the 1970s, refugees entered America in one of two ways. First, Section 203(a) (7) of the Immigration and Nationality Act permitted the entry of 17,400 refugees per year. Second, Section 212 (d) (12) of the Immigration and Nationality Act granted the attorney general the power of parole. The president, secretary of state, and attorney general discussed which groups to parole. Then, they worked with members of the Senate and House Judiciary Committees to pass ad hoc legislation to fund resettlement. Because only 17,400 refugees were permitted entry per year, the president, through the attorney general, relied on the parole power far too often. In 1979 alone, more than 200,000 refugees, mostly Indochinese and Soviet Jews, entered the United States. Originally, the parole power had been intended for use on individuals, but the executive continued to parole large groups such as the Hungarians, Cubans, and Vietnamese.[17]

The Refugee Act of 1980 broadened the definition of a "refugee" to include any person who has or may face "persecution on account of race, religion, nationality, membership in a particular social group, or political opinion." The law also raised the annual admissions ceiling from 17,400 to 50,000. In emergency situations, the president had to consult with Congress and demonstrate extra admissions to be "justified by grave humanitarian concerns or in the national interest." By limiting the need to parole refugees, the Act shifted the balance of power over admissions from the executive to legislative branch.[18]

Congressional leaders such as Edward Kennedy, Elizabeth Holtzman, and Peter Rodino have been credited for their part in the passage of the Refugee Act of 1980, but Governor Ray's role in the final version of the law has been overlooked. According to Senator Kennedy's legislative history of the Act, federal reimbursement to the states represented the greatest source of contention between the House of Representatives and the Senate. The House bill (HR-2816) contained a four year reimbursement to states for refugees drawing cash and medical assistance under the Social Security Act. In contrast, the Senate bill (S-643) called for only two years of federal reimbursement.[19]

By lobbying for longer federal reimbursement, Ray played more of a role in the final outcome of the Refugee Act of 1980 than any other governor. In April of 1979, Chairman Peter Rodino invited Ray to testify before the Subcommittee on Immigration, Refugees, and International Law of the Judiciary Committee. Rodino valued the Governor's opinion because of his "personal attention to refugee resettlement" and the "leadership of the State of Iowa on this issue." On May 24, 1979, Ray urged House members to reject the Senate's shorter reimbursement period. He stated:

> One of the most important things we can now do is maintain a hospitable climate within the states for receiving the additional refugees which this bill would permit to enter the country. Increasing the financial burden that the states and local government must bear in this program could adversely affect that climate—particularly

in states which already have a disproportionate share of the refugees living within their borders.... Increases in highly visible local taxes, such as property taxes, perceived to be related in part or in whole to the refugee program could cause a significant reduction in the support the program has both within the general public and elected officials.[20]

Also on May 24, Ray met with Senator Kennedy to push for greater financial support to the states. Being an ardent public supporter of Indochinese resettlement, Ray had invested tremendous political capital. If the federal government limited funds, it opened the Governor up to even more political attacks. More importantly, fewer refugees would find asylum in America.

In addition to his testimony before the House, Ray used his influence to rally the support of the nation's governors. Ray held considerable political clout among his peers. During his time in office, Ray had chaired the Midwest Governors, Republican Governors, and National Governors Associations. In the midst of the boat people catastrophe, Ray asked his colleagues to increase their resettlement efforts; this put his peers on notice about the escalating problem. Shortly after he wrote, the NGA formed a Task Force on Indochina Refugees, and Ray served as chairman. At the NGA meeting in July of 1979, the Task Force informed the association of the continuing Indochinese calamity and the pending refugee legislation. Ray asked and was granted a special suspension of NGA rules to address refugee matters at the plenary session. Ultimately, the NGA unanimously adopted all four positions offered by Ray's Task Force. Three of those recommendations called for international cooperation to resettle more Indochinese. The fourth stated the governors' unified opposition to a two year limitation on full reimbursement to states for cash and medical assistance.[21] Ray wrote congressional leaders to inform them of the governors' unanimous position.

Ironically, eight years before the passage of the Refugee Act of 1980, Ray earned a reputation as a strong governor by fighting the federal government over reimbursement. In 1968, a Wisconsin Air Guard F-102 jet crashed into the home of Emma McCarville of Cresco, Iowa. Just a few months later, an Iowa Air National Guard jet destroyed Peter and Marie Tjernagel's house near Story City. Less than two months after the second accident, Marie's disabled husband passed away. For the next four years, the state of Iowa and the federal government bickered over who would compensate the families for their losses. In the meantime, McCarville, an eighty-three-year-old widow, resorted to living in a chicken coop. To force the federal government to pay for the damages, Ray described what hap-

Billie and Robert Ray at the U.S. Capitol in Washington, D.C., circa 1975. Ray had more influence over Indochinese refugee policy than any other U.S. governor. He created his own resettlement agency, demanded President Jimmy Carter and fellow governors take action to help the boat people, formed the Iowa SHARES program for Cambodian relief, and testified before members of Congress in support of the Refugee Act of 1980. Billie was a supporter of her husband's refugee advocacy. She also toured the refugee camps in Southeast Asia. As the Governor's term in office neared its end, Billie handed out certificates of recognition to the state's volunteer tutors of refugees (courtesy Robert Ray).

pened next: "As commander-in-chief, if I said so, they could not move a vehicle. I decided that was the only thing to do. I could write letters, I could threaten to sue, but who knew how long that would take.... So we grounded them. And I don't think there was a person out of 220 million Americans who thought you could ground the National Guard, least of all me."[22]

Ray's political activities with regards to the Refugee Act of 1980 closely paralleled his earlier grounding of the Iowa Air National Guard. Dollars and cents alone did not motivate Ray to push for the longer period of federal funding. He viewed this as a matter of principle. Like the National Guard, refugee resettlement represented a national mission. Therefore, the federal government must assist the states in resettling refugees. Ray sympathized with the governors of California and Texas because of the high concentration of Indochinese in those states. Why should a few states be required to bear a disproportionate burden of a national mission? Why should state governments bear the costs of resettlement when governors held little sway over federal refugee policy?[23]

Ray was the one governor who influenced the final outcome of the Refugee Act of 1980. Initially, Senator Kennedy supported the two year limitation of federal reimbursement to states; under this plan, the federal government would not reimburse the states for refugees already residing in the nation for two or more years. Eventually, Kennedy later backed a one year transition period for refugees who had been in the United States longer than two years. While speaking on the Senate floor, Kennedy referenced "the very powerful testimony by Governor Ray of Iowa" as influencing his change of position. Ultimately, the Refugee Act of 1980 provided three years of federal reimbursement to states and an eighteen month transition period for refugees who had resided in the United States three or more years. On February 25, 1980, Ray shared the good news with the NGA. He commented:

> I am delighted to report to you that our activities have produced positive results. Last week a House-Senate Conference Committee agreed to language providing for full federal reimbursement to the states for cash and medical assistance costs incurred by refugees for a period of three years after they arrive in the United States. There will also be a one and one-half year transition period to cover those refugees who have already been here three years. This final time frame provides almost twice as much financial coverage to the states as the bill originally considered by Congress. The changes we worked to achieve will result in savings of millions of dollars to states with significant refugee populations.

By lobbying for a longer period of federal funding to the states, Ray became the first governor to actively influence federal refugee policy. The day the legislation cleared Congress for approval by President Carter, Senator Kennedy wrote Ray, "I greatly valued receiving your counsel and knowing of your strong support for the bill. The Refugee Act of 1980 is the first major reform of the refugee provisions of American immigration law in nearly three decades, and it would never have been possible had it not been for the support of you and others."[24]

Ray's victory on the behalf of governors proved short-lived. As financial woes hit Iowa and the nation, federal funds for refugee aid dried up in the 1980s. In the late spring and summer of 1981, federal reimbursement checks came to states late or did not come at all. The federal funding problem created a panicked atmosphere among refugees and relief workers alike. State officials such as Victor Atiyeh, Governor of Oregon, had to deal with the fallout. In July of 1981, Oregon administrators notified refugees that their federal funding would not arrive for the month of August. In despair, Shue Long Vue, a Hmong head of household, hanged himself from a tree. The sixty-two-year-old possessed limited English-speaking skills, could not find work, and depended on federal assistance to support his wife and five children. Tragically, hours after the suicide, the federal government notified Oregon officials that funds would be made available for that August. Many in the Hmong community erroneously believed that Shue's suicide resulted in the restoration of the funds. Social workers heard rumors that more Hmong planned to "sacrifice themselves" if it ensured continual aid to their families.[25]

In response to the tragedy, Governor Atiyeh fired off an angry letter to President Ronald Reagan. He began, "The federal government must stop playing games with the Refugee Program!" Atiyeh described how the federal government dumped refugees onto the states and had failed to provide for them. Oregon's refugee population had an unemployment rate of 50 percent, and 70 percent of the 300 refugees resettled in Oregon each month could not read or write in their native language. Atiyeh finished his letter, "For six years Oregon has faithfully and effectively served as the fiscal agent of the federal government in this program. I sincerely hope that it is not your intention to abandon this motivated, trusting and needy population who are already in the U.S. while continuing a foreign policy that swells their strength by three hundred per day. I cannot pick up the pieces for you."[26]

As seen in the Atiyeh letter, state support for resettlement faltered when federal funding disappeared during President Reagan's first term. In a July 1981 meeting with the President, Ray pointed out that William Clinton, Governor of Arkansas, lost reelection in 1980 because of a lack of federal support for resettlement. In May of 1980, President Carter informed Clinton that Fort Chafee would house thousands of Cuban refugees; rumors circulated that most of these exiles were criminals or mentally ill. Unfortunately for Clinton, Carter did not provide federal funding or staff to oversee the 20,000 Cubans being held in northwest Arkansas. In late May, several hundred refugees forced their way out of Fort Chaffee. Without assistance from federal authorities, the state and local police forces brought these escapees into custody and returned them to Fort Chaffee. In June, refugees rioted and forced their way out of Fort Chaffee once more. In the aftermath, sixty-two individuals suffered injuries and five refugees were shot. During the gubernatorial election, challenger Frank White portrayed Clinton as being weak and unable to stand up to the President; the Cuban debacle propelled White to victory.[27]

To the dismay of Iowa's governor, Reagan shrank federal reimbursement from thirty-six to just eighteen months, handed control of the refugee program to Health and Human Services, and eliminated the position of the U.S. Coordinator for Refugee Affairs. Like Atiyeh, Ray sent a complaint to the White House: "We governors were supportive of the refugee program because of the stark humanities problems these people faced, and we came forward to assist the federal government in this endeavor. Changing the rules now, three years into the program when approximately one-half million refugees are in the United States, is totally unfair and, in my view, not in keeping with the President's commitment to deal fairly with the states."[28] Without federal support for refugee programs, governors faced political backlash or even being voted out of office during the 1982 elections. Ray and Shearer opposed HHS control over refugee matters. They believed this structure pushed the newcomers toward welfare. Governors enjoyed having the U.S. Coordinator as a contact who provided them current and accurate information on refugee affairs. Reagan's elimination of the U.S. Coordinator position allowed him to distance his administration from an increasingly controversial subject. The recent wave of Cubans and rising concern over illegal Mexican immigration alarmed some Americans. Many questioned if the latest asylum seekers truly faced persecution or were merely "economic migrants" seeking a better life in the United States.

In 1982, Ray's long tenure as governor came to a conclusion. He became the President and Chief Executive Officer of Life Investors, Inc. Republican Terry Branstad succeeded Ray in office. During Branstad's first term, the Indochinese crisis slowed, and the Iowa economy soured. Whereas Ray served as governor during the prosperous 1970s, Branstad took office on the eve of the "farm crisis." Farmers expanded their operations during the optimistic 1970s by taking on debt, but this economic boom ended in the 1980s. After the Soviets invaded Afghanistan, President Carter retaliated with a 1980 grain embargo. Unfortunately, this embargo led to a drop in farm profits at a time when many farmers owed creditors. Desperate farmers seeking to restructure loans encountered escalating interest rates. To reduce inflation, the Federal Reserve raised the interest rate to a record high of 21 percent in 1981. Over the course of the decade, roughly one in three Iowa farms failed, thirty-eight state banks closed, and manufacturers of farm equipment drastically reduced their workforces or closed plants altogether.[29] Consumed with trying to ease the farm crisis, Branstad did not involve himself in refugee affairs as did his predecessor.

Soon after Ray's exit from office, Colleen Shearer and Kenneth Quinn both left Iowa politics. Governor Branstad notified Shearer that she could no longer be the director of both Job Service of Iowa and the Iowa Refugee Service Center. She had to choose one agency to head. Richard Freeman of Job Service advised Shearer to continue working with refugees, something that had become her passion. However, Shearer felt underappreciated and resigned in protest. Shortly before her resignation, hints of being burned out appeared in Shearer's private correspondence with Kenneth Quinn. In the summer of 1981, Shearer read about another group of boat people suffering severe hardship. One man had to lay his pregnant wife to rest at sea. IRSC worker Tue Phan Quang pleaded for Shearer and Ray to do more despite the harder economic times. Shearer confided in Quinn:

> The knowledge of the continuing agony is ever present. I'm not even asking you for a suggestion as to how I might respond to Tue—I'm just saying, "Hey, Ken, share with me one more heart rending reminder of what we've been about these past few years." You've been on both fronts—there and here. Ken, have we—are we—fortunate or unfortunate to have been so involved in one of the world's greatest human tragedies? I opt for the former description, though I sometimes feel awed by the exposure and carry a constant underlying feeling of melancholy and sadness— something like a low-grade infection that never goes away. It's strange. Something that occupied no portion of my life six years ago has become my life.[30]

Shearer moved to Minnesota and worked in state government before retiring. Quinn soon left Iowa and finished his distinguished thirty-two-year career in the Foreign Service, rising to the position of U.S. Ambassador to Cambodia.

In Jon Bowermaster's *Governor: An Oral Biography of Robert D. Ray*, respondents reflected on Ray's legacy. Some pundits focused on Ray's modernization of government and strengthening the Governor's Office.

Others credited Ray for tax reform. Public schools needed additional funding, but farmers resented the escalating property taxes. Ray oversaw the creation of the school aid plan which shifted support for public education from property to income tax. Several others, including Ray himself, cited the Governor's progressive environmental policies. He supported the passage of a bottle bill that required a nickel deposit on cans and bottles. Ray wanted to clean up Iowa, and he wanted Iowans to be proud of their state.[31] Despite these important contributions, Ray's work with refugees proved to be his greatest and most enduring legacy.

Ray provided clean government and strong moral leadership in Iowa during a time when citizens increasingly mistrusted public officials; many Iowans overcame their sense of guilt about the Vietnam War by supporting the Governor's refugee programs. Quinn remembered being overcome with pride during a 1979 visit to a Tai Dam refugee camp in Nong Khai, Thailand. Entering the grounds, Quinn and company noticed a large banner of welcome. A group of refugees soon emerged, and they wanted to show the Governor their symbol of hope. Quinn recalled:

> I thought wow what could this be? Some carved statue or something they had carried out of Laos with them, some animist type thing? They took us into this little thatched way station and up on a thatched wall was posted the Iowa Department of Transportation highway map with some pins in it representing where families already lived. They said there is our symbol of hope. I thought here we are 12,000 miles from Iowa on the other side of the world and the shape of our state and the map of our state would be the symbol of hope.... That our state would be that symbol of hope captured more than anything else what Bob Ray had done. What his leadership meant and what our state involvement in refugees was all about.

All Iowans present were touched by this symbol. A sobbing Shearer promised the Tai Dam that Iowa would remove them from the camp.[32]

In the correspondence of supporters, plenty of Iowans shared sentiments similar to Quinn; the theme of Iowa pride appeared frequently. When Mary Gebhart read in the *Minneapolis Tribune* that Ray decided to admit 1,500 more refugees, the student at Saint Mary's College wrote the Governor from her school's library: "Reading the article, I was struck with a real sense of pride. I am glad to say that I am an Iowan who comes to Minnesota from a state where people care. I am so happy that one politician's heart has been moved by the sorry plight of the boat people." Gebhart signed her letter, "A proud Iowan." R.L. Playle of Des Moines enjoyed paying his 1978 state taxes. He explained why in his letter to Ray, "I felt proud that you and Iowa could help those who are unfortunate." Even Ray's political opponents confessed their newfound respect for their governor's humanitarian efforts. Joseph Sullivan had voted to remove Ray from political office each time the opportunity presented itself. He informed Ray, "Regardless of our political differences, I am very pleased with your initiative in welcoming refugees to our state. I have always been proud of this great state of Iowa, and I am happy that you took the lead and reached out to these people who have no home. It is a good example to all of us."[33] Those who had moved out of Iowa also communicated their pride in their native state.

Ray's efforts on the behalf of the Indochinese inspired many Iowans to involve themselves in the humanitarian endeavor. Herb Welander's wife had been prodding him to do more to help refugees. The Welanders had seen the boat people disaster unfold on television like so many others. Welander told Ray, "I was proud that our governor had done something about it.... I had done nothing about it and that is not right." Following Ray's lead, Welander inquired into sponsoring four refugees.[34] Though the Vietnam War polarized the nation, a considerable number of Iowans overcame the wounds of the conflict by participating in refugee resettlement and relief efforts. Ray and Shearer noted that the sponsors often benefitted from the experience more so than the refugees.

Many outside of Iowa took notice of Ray's efforts on behalf of the Indochinese as well. Letters of support poured in from across the nation. Americans compared their states and governors unfavorably to Iowa and Ray. Robert Friedman could not believe that his larger and more powerful state of New York had been outdone by small-time Iowa. He wrote Ray, "It would never have occurred to me that your state 'Middle America' would be involved in something like this. It is more than New York is doing. Maybe a key to foreign activities is to get other parts of the country, aside from New York, California, and Washington, D.C., involved with the world." James Blakely of Rhode Island had been advocating for the better treatment of refugees in his state. He believed Indochinese to be an economic asset because they worked jobs and lived in housing that nobody else wanted. According to Blakely, state officials' negligence resulted in refugees fleeing Rhode Island. When trying to redress the situation, Blakely had "ran into a stone wall, especially from the office of our Governor J. Joseph Garrahy." Blakely wanted Ray to lobby Rhode Island's governor to do more. He told Ray, "Only through your experience and support of the refugees will our officials recognize the vital role that Indochinese will play in the future economy of our state." When residents from other states praised Ray, proud Iowans boasted, "That's *our* Governor Ray."[35]

Ray's resettlement agency lasted for thirty-five years. Eventually, the state stopped resettling refugees due to funding and longstanding identity problems. Caseworkers estimated the cost of resettling one individual to be roughly $3,000 in 2010, but the State Department only granted $1,800 in funds. More importantly, Iowa had always been an anomaly of sorts. From 1975 until 2010, Iowa alone operated as a federally approved state resettlement agency. Save for Iowa, all voluntary agencies had been national in scope, held 501(c)(3) nonprofit status, and raised funds from the private sector. If the Bureau of Refugee Services asked for resettlement money from the general public, it would betray the self-sufficient ideals it had been founded upon. In 2010, the state stopped resettling refugees. Houng Baccam, a Tai Dam resettled by the Task Force in 1975, worked for the refugee center for nearly thirty-four years. Houng reflected on the state's decision: "I felt very sad because we view a resettlement agency as saving the life of people, and we do not do it anymore.... Each time you bring the people in you save their life and their family. You give a future for their children."[36]

Though Iowa stopped resettling refugees in 2010, it is hoped that the Iowa anomaly can be studied and emulated by other governors in future times of crisis. Ray's support created a soft landing for refugees in the state. Iowa's Indochinese population took comfort in knowing that their governor welcomed them. The Governor's Office served as a clearinghouse of information for all refugees, relief workers, and interested parties. State officials, through public speaking tours, informed the general public about the refugees' cultural background and need for help, and they tried to include Iowans in the humanitarian effort by demanding all newcomers have an individual sponsor. The state's refugee programs worked so well that Australian officials created a volunteer tutor program modeled after Iowa's. In 1979, Germany sent a delegation to study the IRSC's methods and implemented similar policies in their nation. Following Iowa's lead, Governor Richard Snelling launched Vermont SHARES to raise funds for Cambodians. Though short-lived, Idaho and Michigan established their own resettlement initiatives after seeking the counsel of IRSC officials.

Iowa's refugee programs proved good enough to emulate by its con-temporaries, and a state resettlement agency can serve as an alternative model for resettling refugees in future times of crisis. The likelihood of this happening is difficult to gauge. Ray had the courage to establish his Task Force to aid individuals from America's most controversial war. Future governors attempting to resettle refugees may not face as intense a political climate as the one encountered by Ray. However, these gover-nors may have to overcome the apathy of the general public. Arguments against having a state resettlement program have little merit. Many of those opposed to Iowa's program were affiliated with private voluntary agencies, and these VOLAGS feared competition for federal funding. Others disliked the IRSC because they disagreed with any operation overseen by government in general. In 1980, political scientists Naomi and Norman Zucker favorably reviewed the IRSC, and they concluded, "The clue to good refugee resettlement is not who does it, but how it is done."[37]

Indochinese refugees drastically altered the demographics of Iowa. In 1960, roughly 89 percent of Iowa's foreign born population came from Europe compared to the 2.8 percent who came from Asia. By 1990, only 33 percent of Iowa's foreign born population originated from Europe, and the state's Asian born population had risen to account for nearly 43 percent of all foreign born Iowans. In general, the number of Indochinese in the United States had been minimal before the Vietnam War, but many states still had considerable Asian populations. In comparison, Iowa had a 1960 Asian population of only 1,189. In two short years, Ray oversaw the resettlement of over 1,200 Tai Dam, which doubled the state's total 1960 Asian population. During Ray's time in office, the state resettled roughly 4,000 Indochinese while private voluntary agencies brought another 4,000. Therefore, refugees accounted for a substantial number of the 11,577 Asians in Iowa's 1980 census.[38]

Like all Indochinese refugees, the Tai Dam community has culturally enriched Iowa. At the Iowa State Fairgrounds, the beating of drums marks the beginning of the Tai Dam New Year. The drum beat awakens the spirits of deceased loved ones. Attendees enjoy a meal of sticky rice while listening to live music. Participants hold hands and raise and lower their arms in unison while performing a traditional circle dance. In addition to the New Year celebration, the community hosts an annual Freedom Festival. Tai Dam throughout the state convene to give thanks that they escaped communism and arrived in Iowa as a group. For this reason, the Tai Dam community still reveres Ray. Houng Baccam explained, "Robert Ray is a very super human being…. If we did not have him, I do not know what would have happened to the Tai Dam group." Khouang Luong, a spiritual leader, considers Ray to be a father to the entire Tai Dam community. He believes that in the future, the Tai Dam will venerate Ray as if he was one of their ancestors. Som Baccam, a Polk County Public Hospital Trustee, explained Ray's significance: "I love the man. Forever, he will be our savior. He is almost like our Abraham Lincoln…. He freed us." Minister Mike Rasavanh described the Governor as a "visionary man who saw the true potential of our people." Ray has always deflected praise for the Tai Dam's

Tai Dam women dancing at the New Year Festival, Des Moines, Iowa, 1999. Pictured from left to right are Vieng Baccam, Noi Baccam, Thuoi Baccam, Vieng
Phonvisay. Held at the Iowa State Fairgrounds, Tai Dam New Year is open to the
public. Gift giving, dancing, and the beating of the ancestral drum highlight the
festivities. Sticky rice and pork are provided. Ray's greatest legacy is the preservation of this group's culture in Iowa (Houng Baccam).

successful transition to Iowa. In 1979, he stated, "We must recognize the
refugees, themselves. They are the ones who must struggle to make the
adjustment. They are the ones who must work the long hours mostly at
entry level wages. They are the ones who must endure the difficulties that
all immigrants undergo. In the final analysis, our success is their success
and vice versa."[39]

The Tai Dam have sought to repay the governor and the state that
welcomed them by creating a cultural center on the Northside of Des
Moines. The former refugees purchased and beautified land previously
used by locals as a dumping ground. On the acreage, the group constructed
a Tai Village consisting of spirit houses and a community center modeled
after a home from the old country. The Tai Village aims to preserve and
share Tai Dam culture. In August of 2013, the Tai Dam officially opened
the Robert D. Ray Welcome Center. In the summer heat, the frail former
Governor waited in an air conditioned vehicle until the dedication ceremony. Unable to walk on his own and refusing a wheelchair, a couple of
individuals helped Ray to his seat. Members of the community were

Robert Ray speaking at the 25th Anniversary Tai Dam Freedom Festival, Iowa, 2000. Wing Cam is pictured to the left. After his governorship, Ray has remained active in the state's Asian American community. He has supported the Iowa Asian Alliance, attended Tai Dam Freedom Festivals, and recently performed the ribbon cutting at the Tai Village dedication ceremony in 2013 (Houng Baccam).

moved that Ray attended despite poor health, but he had seemingly always been there for the refugees. Thousands of Tai Dam attended the festivities. Community leader Dinh VanLo has described the Tai Village as continuing the spark of the Tai Dam people.

Before the Tai Dam arrived in Iowa, many of them mistakenly believed all Americans were white. Unfortunately, Americans have often applied this same generalization to the Midwest in general and Iowa in particular. The stereotyping of Iowa as all white farmers manifested itself at the 2016 Rose Bowl game between Stanford University and the University of Iowa. At halftime, the Stanford Band played the farmersonly.com theme song. While two band members dressed in a cow suit wandered through a corn maze, marchers formed the image of a farmer. After the performance, band director Edward Beaux tweeted, "Glad you liked our corn show, Iowa! Couldn't tell, was that booing or mooing?"

In reality, Iowa has a diverse population, and much of this diversity originated from refugee resettlement. As an example, Donechanh Southammavong recently celebrated three weddings in Iowa: Tai Dam, Lao, and American. Her maternal Tai Dam grandmother made Don's *sinh* complete with silver lockets. Don provided her Lao in-laws with gifts of clothing. In return, Don's husband gave her parents money, liquor, and jewelry to pay for the "breast milk" Don's parents had invested in raising their daughter. At her home, Don wore her hair in the traditional bun that signifies a woman's married status. Relatives made a bed and provided chicken and eggs, which symbolizes fertility. The ceremony concluded after watching the couple eat the food. Don also celebrated a traditional Lao-style wedding for her in-laws. In Laos, the groom and his relatives sing and consume alcohol in route to the bride's village. Don's husband dressed in traditional Lao clothing and carried a sword on his way to meet his bride for their wedding at a local fitness center.

Ironically, Tai Dam and Lao cultural heritage played the greatest role at her "American" wedding. Don's grandfather and grandmother-in-law had recently passed away. Don decided to hold the American ceremony at her residence because her Tai Dam relatives know the spirits of the dead may only travel to places they visited while alive. This backyard ceremony enabled the spirit of Don's deceased grandfather to attend. During the celebration, two deer jumped a fence and watched the proceedings. Don and her Buddhist husband believe that these deer were the reincarnated spirits of their deceased loved ones.[40] As the nearly ten thousand Tai Dam continue to celebrate cultural events at the Tai Village and across the state, Ray's legacy endures. Of all the arguments made in this work, one is indisputable. The state's refugee program has made Iowa a more interesting place.

Social history has shed light on the experiences of previously overlooked groups such as women, the working-class, and minorities, yet refugees remain an understudied group. Oral history will prove to be a useful tool for accessing the important experiences of refugees and discovering the full range of diversity in Iowa. In addition to the Indochinese, Bosnian, Sudanese, Iraqi, and Afghani stories await to be told. Like an ex–Iowa governor attending the Tai Dam's Freedom Festival in the American Midwest, their stories will also demonstrate the interconnectedness of Iowa, national, and international history.

Chapter Notes

Introduction

1. Linguistic works by William Gedney, Dorothy and Jay Fippinger, and John Hartmann. Iowa Tai Dam works by Sue Bell and Michael Whiteford, "Tai Dam Health Care Practices: Asian Refugee Women in Iowa," *Social Science Medicine* 24 (1987): 317–325; Stephen Zolvinski, "Continuity and Change in Family Systems of the Central Iowa Tai Dam" (master's thesis, Iowa State University, 1993); John Hartmann, "Computations on a Tai Dam Origin Myth," *Anthropological Linguistics* 23 (May 1981): 200.
2. Sends Help to Aid Refugees and End Starvation.
3. Robert Ray, "Address by Governor Robert D. Ray to the General Assembly of the Christian Church, St. Louis Missouri," 30 October 1979, Iowa SHARES 1: 4, Robert D. Ray Papers, State Historical Society of Iowa, Des Moines, IA.

Chapter 1

1. Hartmann, "Computations on a Tai Dam Origin Myth," 189–190.
2. Siang Bachti, "King Cobra: A Tai History Booklet," *Tai Studies Center* (2000): 6.
3. For the talking animals version, James Chamberlain, "The Black Tai Chronicle of Muang Mouay," *Mon Khmer Studies* 21 (1984): 37. For creation stories, Dang Nghiem Van, "The Flood Myth and the Origins of Ethnic Groups in Southeast Asia," 310. Wing Cam, "ThaiDam History," trans. Dinh VanLo (unpublished document, Nong Khai, Thailand, 1975), 3.
4. Wing Cam, "ThaiDam History," 3. Dang Nghiem Van, "An Outline of the Thai in Vietnam," *Vietnamese Studies* 32 (1972): 146.
5. Gerald Hickey, "The Social Systems of Northern Vietnam" (PhD dissertation, University of Chicago, 1959), 135–140.
6. Sumitr Pitiphat, "The Religion and Beliefs of the Black Tai, and a Note on the Study of Cultural Origins," *Journal of Siam Society* 68.1 (1980): 31–33.
7. Hickey, "Social Systems of Northern Vietnam," 145–150.
8. Mukdawijitra, "Ethnicity and Multilingualism," 126–139.
9. Sumitr Pitiphat, "The Religion and Beliefs of the Black Tai," 37–38; Wing Cam, "ThaiDam History," 7.
10. Pierre Brocheux and Daniel Hemery, *Indochina: An Ambiguous Colonization, 1858–1954* (Berkeley: University of California Press, 2011), 14.
11. *Ibid.*, 18–20.
12. Joann Schrock et al., *Minority Groups in North Vietnam* (Washington, D.C.: U.S. Department of the Army, 1972), 66–67.
13. Neth Rasavanh, interviewed by author, translated by Matsalyn Brown, 6 September 2014.
14. Nga Baccam, interviewed by author, translated by Matsalyn Brown, 6 September 2014.
15. Bao Lo Cam, interviewed by author, 25 May 2014.

16. Neth Rasavanh, interviewed by author, translated by Matsalyn Brown, 6 September 2014.

17. Nga Baccam, interviewed by author, translated by Matsalyn Brown, 6 September 2014; Houng Baccam, interviewed by author, 16 February 2014.

18. Nga Baccam, interviewed by author, translated by Matsalyn Brown, 6 September 2014.

19. Bao Lo Cam, interviewed by author, 25 May 2014.

20. Thuong Lo, interviewed by author, translated by Dinh VanLo, 20 June 2014. For minority diplomacy, see McAllister, "Mountain Minorities and the Viet Minh," 833.

21. Neth Rasavanh, interviewed by author, translated by Matsalyn Brown, 6 September 2014.

22. Em Quang, interviewed by author, translated by Som Baccam, 21 June 2014.

23. Houng Baccam, interviewed by author, 16 February 2014.

24. Wing Cam, interviewed by author, 8 August 2014.

25. Elyse Demaray and Melody Keim-Shenk, "Always Remembering the Motherland: Tai Dam Wedding Textiles and Dress," in *Wedding Dress Across Cultures* edited by Helen Foster and Donald Johnson (New York: Bloomsbury Academic, 2004) 198–200.

26. Timothy Castle, *At War in the Shadow of Vietnam: U.S. Military Aid to the Royal Lao Government 1955–1975* (New York: Columbia University Press, 1993), 106.

27. Hickey, "Social Systems of Northern Vietnam," 13. Schrock et al., *Minority Groups in North Vietnam* (Washington, D.C.: Department of the Army, 1972), 37.

28. Dang Nghiem Van, "Dien Bien Phu: Some Ethnohistorical Data," *Vietnamese Studies* 43 (1975): 8.

29. Dang Nghiem Van, "An Outline of the Thai in Vietnam," 157–166, 194.

30. Dang Nghiem Van, "Dien Bien Phu," 23.

31. Siang Bachti, "King Cobra," 22–24.

32. *Ibid.*, 29–36.

33. Wing Cam, "Thaidam Freedom Festival 2000," 2.

Chapter 2

1. Dau Truong, interviewed by author, 12 March 2011.

2. Arthur Crisfield to Ray, Resettlement 5: Governor's Task Force for Indochinese Refugees, 1976–1977, Ray Papers.

3. Grant Evans, "Apprentice Ethnographers: Vietnam and the Study of Lao Minorities," in *Laos: Culture and Society* ed. Grant Evans (Chiang Mai: Silkworm Books, 1999); Yukti Mukdawijitra, "Ethnicity and Multilingualism: The Case of the Ethnic Tai in the Vietnamese State" (unpublished dissertation, 2007), 247–257.

4. Gil Loescher and John Scanlan, *Calculated Kindness: Refugees and America's Half-Open Door: 1945–Present* (New York: Free Press, 1998); Julia Taft quoted in Jeremy Hein, *States and International Migrants: The Incorporation of Indochinese Refugees in the United States and France* (Boulder: Westview Press, 1993), 71–73. See HR 1975a for dispersal policy.

5. Ray in *A Promise Called Iowa*, dir. Iowa Public Television (PBS; 2007 DVD).

6. Gerald Ford to Ray, 11 July 1975, Resettlement 6: Program Files (Correspondence and Memos) 1975–1976, Ray Papers.

7. Ray quoted in Jon Bowermaster, *Governor: An Oral Biography of Robert D. Ray* (Ames: Iowa State University Press, 1987), 137, 161–163.

8. *Ibid.*, 64.

9. *Ibid.*, 134; Kristelle Miller, untitled article in *Iowa Alumni Review*, 23 (December 1969–October 1970): 8–9.

10. Wadena resident Gary Bond quoted by Rick Frederickson, "Wadena Rocks at 40," *Iowa Public Radio* 25 July 2010 http://iowapublicradio.org/post/wadena-rocks-40#stream/0.

11. Song featured in Ronald Takaki, *Strangers from a Different Shore: A History of Asian Americans* (Boston: Little, Brown, 1989), 121.

12. "Displaced Persons" and "Postwar Refugee Crisis and the Establishment of the State of Israel," *U.S. Holocaust Museum and Memorial,* updated 2013, http://www.ushmm.org/wlc/en/article.php?ModuleId=10005459

13. See Public Law 89–236-1965.

14. Loescher and Scanlan, *Calculated Kindness*, 55–56; Carl Bon Tempo, *Americans at the Gate: The United States and Refugees During the Cold War* (Princeton: Princeton University Press, 2008), 71.

15. Ray in Bowermaster, *Governor*, 133; Robert Ray, "House of Representatives Transcripts of Proceedings: Committee on the Judiciary Subcommittee on Immigration, Refugees, and International Law. Hearing on H.R. 2816 Refugee Legislation, Washington, D.C. May 24, 1979," 93, General 1: Refugee Act of 1979 Federal, Ray Papers.

16. Both above quotes in Ray, "Statement by Honorable Robert D. Ray before the Subcommittee U.S. House of Representatives," 24 May 1979, General 1: Refugee Act of 1979, Ray Papers.

17. Cam, "Thaidam Freedom Festival 2000."

18. Sai Kham, "The Autobiography of Chao Sai Kham, Governor of Xiang Khoang Province," in *The Last Century of Lao Royalty: A Documentary History*, translated by Grant Evans (Thailand: Silkworm Books, 2009), 260.

19. Quy Baccam letter from Nong Khai 7 July 1975, Resettlement 5: Governor's Task Force for Indochinese Refugees, Ray Papers; Wing Cam, "Thaidam Freedom Festival 2000."

20. Wing Cam, interviewed by author, 8 August 2014.

21. Cam, "Thaidam Freedom Festival 2000."

22. Houng Baccam, interviewed by author, 16 February 2014; Mike Rasavanh, interviewed by author, 15 May 2014.

23. Houng Baccam, interviewed by author, 16 February 2014; Martin Stuart-Fox, *A History of Modern Laos* (Cambridge University Press, 1997), Chapter 5.

24. Dara Rasavanh, interviewed by author, 15 May 2014.

25. Sanda and Peter Simms, *The Kingdoms of Laos*, 143–160; Cam, "Thaidam Freedom Festival 2000."

26. Dinh VanLo, interviewed by author, 10 April 2014; Houng Baccam, interviewed by author, 16 February 2014.

27. Somphong Baccam, interviewed by author, 24 April 2014.

28. Houng Baccam, interviewed by author, 16 February 2014; Quy Baccam letter from Nong Khai, 7 July 1975, Resettlement 5: Governor's Task Force, Ray Papers.

29. Dinh VanLo, interviewed by author, 10 April 2014.

30. Cam, "Thaidam Freedom Festival 2000."

31. Mike Rasavanh, interviewed by author, 15 May 2014.

32. The Non-ethnic Lao include the Tai Dam, Mien, Lao Theung in Jeremy Hein, *From Vietnam, Laos, and Cambodia: A Refugee Experience in the United States* (Twayne Publishing, 1995), 37 Table 3.1; Betsy Kennedy Statistics, 9 November 1976, Resettlement 5: Governor's Task Force for Indochinese Refugees, Ray Papers.

Chapter 3

1. Jack Spear, interviewed by author, 8 May 2014.

2. *Ibid.*

3. *Ibid.*

4. Richard Freeman, interviewed by author, 18 April 2014.

5. Tomas Muñoz, interviewed by author, 19 May 2014.

6. Jack Spear, interviewed by author, 8 May 2014.

7. "Poll shows refugees welcome in IA," *Des Moines Register,* 14 August 1975.

8. Colleen Shearer, Adventure 1975, circa December 1975, pg. 2, Resettlement 5: Governor's Task Force for Indochinese Refugees, 1976–1977, Ray Papers.

9. Shearer, Adventure 1975, pg. 1, circa December 1975, Resettlement 5: Governor's Task Force for Indochinese Refugees, 1976–1977, Ray Papers; Richard Freeman, interviewed by author, 18 April 2014.

10. Jack Spear, interviewed by author, 8 May 2014.

11. Tomas Muñoz, interviewed by author, 19 May 2014.

12. Ray in Bowermaster, *Governor*, 238.

13. Jack Spear, interviewed by author, 8 May 2014.

14. Colleen Shearer, Governor's Task Force for Indochinese Resettlement (reorganized) undated, Resettlement 7: Program Files (Correspondence and Memos) 1976, Ray Papers.

15. Shearer to Quinn, Part II Explanation of Statistics pg. 1, 8 April 1976, Resettlement 5: Governor's Task Force for Indochinese Refugees, 1976–1977, Ray Papers.
16. Shearer Memo to Dennis Nagel, 25 March 1976, Resettlement 6: Program Files (Correspondence + Memo) 1975–1976, Ray Papers; Lawrence Rout, "Haven for Boat People: Iowa Does So Well by Its Indochinese Refugees that it's Gaining a Reputation in Asian Camps," *Wall Street Journal*, 27 June 1979.
17. Somphong Baccam, interviewed by author, 24 April 2014.
18. Tomas Muñoz, interviewed by author, 19 May 2014.
19. HEW Refugee Assessment Task Force Unit, "Iowa Assessment Report," 9 April 1976, pg. 6–20, Resettlement 1: Adm Reports 1976–1982, Ray Papers.
20. Shearer to HEW Refugee Task Force Acting Director Lawrence McDonough, 23 April 1976, Resettlement 6: Program Files (Correspondence and Memos) 1975–1976, Ray Papers.
21. Gilbert Cranberg, "Iowa's Failure to Feed," *Des Moines Register*, 23 October 1976.
22. *Ibid.*, 7.
23. Dennis Nagel response to Janet Baker, 22 March 1976, Resettlement 6: Program Files (Correspondence and Memos) 1975–1976, Ray Papers.
24. Steven Walters, "Questions welfare for Viets in Iowa," *Des Moines Tribune*, 21 October 1976, Resettlement 1: Governor's Task Force for Indochinese Refugees, 1976–1977, Ray Papers.
25. Pastor Pham Van Hein et al. to Ray, 22 October 1976, Resettlement 5: Governor's Task Force for Indochinese Refugees, 1976–1977, Ray Papers; Mr. Khao Dang Pham of Vietnamese Association in Iowa to Ray, 23 October 1976, Resettlement 5: Governor's Task Force for Indochinese Refugees, 1976–1977, Ray Papers.
26. John Zeitler to Ray, 30 October 1976, Resettlement 5: Governor's Task Force for Indochinese Refugees, 1976–1977, Ray Papers; John Zeitler to Ray, 22 November 1976, Resettlement 5: Governor's Task Force for Indochinese Refugees, 1976–1977, Ray Papers; Mary Ann Pederson to Shearer, received 12 January 1977, Resettlement 5: Governor's Task Force for Indochinese Refugees, 1976–1977, Ray Papers.
27. Ray quoted in "Refugee aid dispute," *Cedar Rapids Gazette* Editorial Page, 12 November 1976.
28. Gail Paradise Kelly, *From Vietnam to America: A Chronicle of the Vietnamese Immigration to the United States* (Boulder: Westview Press, 1977), 177–179; For gender inversion, see Chapter 5 "Negotiating Cultures" in Sucheng Chan, *Survivors: Cambodian Refugees in the United States* (Champagne: University of Illinois Press, 2004).
29. William Johnson, interviewed by author, 8 January 2014; Phuong Baccam, interviewed by author, 23 February 2014.
30. Vinh Nguyen, interviewed by author, 2 July 2014.
31. Charlene Heggen, Monthly Update, 20 September 1979, pg. 3, Resettlement 7: Program Files (Correspondence + Memos) 1979, Ray Papers.
32. Richard Whitaker, IRSC News Release, 23 April 1982, Resettlement 5: Education-Volunteer Tutor Program+ Awards, Ray Papers.
33. Colleen Shearer, "Refugee Resettlement: Not Why, But How," 9 February 1980, pg. 37, Resettlement 1: Conferences/Meetings/Workshops-National Governors Assoc Testimony before Select Commission on Immigration and Refugee Policy, Ray Papers.
34. *Ibid.*, 2–16.
35. Shearer, "Testimony Submitted to the Select Commission on Immigration and Refugee Policy: Refugee Resettlement: Not Why, But How," 25 February 1980, Denver, Colorado, Resettlement 1: Conferences/Meetings/Workshops-National Governor's Assoc. Testimony before the Select Commission on Immigration and Refugee Policy, Denver, Colorado, 1980, Ray Papers.
36. Shearer to Ray, Monthly Update, 20 September 1979, pg. 20, Resettlement 7: Program Files (Correspondence + Memos) 1979, Ray Papers.

Chapter 4

1. Jeremy Hein, *Ethnic Origins: The Adaptation of Cambodian and Hmong Refugees in Four American Cities* (Russell Sage Foundation, 2006), 35.
2. Siang Bachti, interviewed by author, 3 February 2013.
3. *Ibid.*

4. Wing Cam, interviewed by author, 8 August 2014.
5. Kelly, *From Vietnam to America*, 48.
6. Arthur Crisfield to Robert Ray, summer 1975, Resettlement 5: Governor's Task Force for Indochinese Refugees, 1976–1977, Ray Papers.
7. Siang Bachti, interviewed by author, 3 February 2014; U.S. Department of Agriculture, "Iowa Farms: Number, Average Size, and Land in Farms," Department of Agriculture National Agricultural Statistics Services, 6.
8. Tomas Muñoz, interviewed by author, 19 May 2014.
9. Dinh VanLo, interviewed by author, 10 April 2014.
10. *Ibid.*
11. Siang Bachti, interviewed by author, 3 February 2014.
12. Colleen Shearer, Part I Statistics to Kenneth Quinn, 8 April 1976, Resettlement 1: Adm-Reports 1976–1982, Ray Papers; Marv Weidner to Kenneth Quinn, Report for Geneva Conference, 24 September 1980, Resettlement 1:Conferences Meetings Workshops UN Conference on Refugees Geneva Switzerland July 1979, Ray Papers
13. Hickey, "The Social Systems of Northern Vietnam," 156.
14. *Ibid.*, 157.
15. Houng Baccam in "Refugee Resettlement Hearing before the Committee on Immigration and Refugee Policy of the Committee on the Judiciary," U.S. Senate, 97th Congress, First Session, Des Moines, IA, October 9, 1981, pg. 103.
16. Richard Murphy, interviewed by author, 15 February 2014.
17. Shearer, "Testimony Submitted to the Select Commission on Immigration and Refugee Policy, Denver, Colorado," 25 February 1980, 44, Resettlement 1: Conferences/Meetings/Workshops-National Governors Assoc. Testimony before select Commission on Immigration and Refugee Policy, Denver, Colorado, 1980, Ray Papers.
18. "Unburdening Our Mothers' Backs: An Oral History Project," *Monsoon United Asian Women of Iowa* (2009), 6–7, 25.
19. *Ibid.*, 27–28.
20. Tai Dam Newsletter by Governor's Task Force for Indochinese Resettlement, 27 May 1976, 3–4, Resettlement 7: Program Files (Correspondence and Memos) 1976, Ray Papers.
21. Houng Baccam, interviewed by author, 16 February 2014; Khoaung Luong, interviewed by author, 22 March 2014
22. Nga Baccam, interviewed by author, translated by Matsalyn Brown, 6 September 2014; Neth Rasavanh, interviewed by author, translated by Matsalyn Brown, 6 September 2014.
23. Neth Rasavanh, interviewed by author, translated by Matsalyn Brown, 6 September 2014.
24. *Ibid.*
25. Siang Bachti, interviewed by author, 3 February 2014; Khouang Luong, interviewed by author, 22 March 2014.
26. Siang Bachti, interviewed by author, 3 February 2014.
27. Frank Wu, *Yellow: Race in America Beyond Black and White* (New York: Basic Books, 2003), 79.
28. Shearer to Quinn, Subject: Refugees, 19 December 1978, Resettlement 7: Program Files (Correspondence + Memos) 1978, Ray Papers; Jack Spear, interviewed by author, 8 May 2014.
29. Dara Rasavanh, interviewed by author, 15 May 2014; Khouang Luong, interviewed by author, 22 March 2014; Houng Baccam, interviewed by author, 16 February 2014.
30. Ruth Ginio, "French Officers, African Officers, and the Violent Image of African Colonial Soldiers," *Historical Reflections* 36.2 (2010): 60–70.
31. Shearer to Quinn, 19 December 1978, Subject: Refugees, 2, Resettlement 7: Program Files (Correspondence + Memos) 1978, Ray Papers.
32. P.B. LaFont, "Pratiques medicales des Thai Noirs du Laos de l'ouest," *Anthoropos* 54 (1959): 820; Bell and Whiteford, "Tai Dam Health Care Practices," 320–321. The ISU researchers suggested the Iowa Tai Dam's Americanization and withholding of supernatural beliefs may account for their different findings.
33. Khouang Luong, interviewed by author, 22 March 2014.
34. Phuong Baccam, interviewed by author, 23 February 2014; Dinh VanLo, interviewed by author, 10 April 2014.
35. Dara Rasavanh, interviewed by author, 15 May 2014.
36. Mike Rasavanh, interviewed by author, 15 May 2014.
37. Baccam in "Refugee Resettlement Hearing before the Committee on Immigration

and Refugee Policy of the Committee on the Judiciary," U.S. Senate, 97th Congress, First Session, Des Moines, IA, October 9, 1981, 100.

38. HEW Refugee Assessment Task Force Unit, "Iowa Assessment Report," 9 April 1976, 15–20, Resettlement 1: Adm Reports 1976–1982, Ray Papers.

Chapter 5

1. Loescher and Scanlan, *Calculated Kindness*, 105–112, 121.
2. Dau and Thuong Truong, interviewed by author, 12 March 2011.
3. Kiet Tran, interviewed by author, 15 May 2014.
4. Grant, *The Boat People*, 98, 104–5; Vinh Nguyen, interviewed by author, 2 July 2014.
5. *Ibid.*
6. Ben Kiernan, *The Pol Pot Regime: Race, Power, and Genocide in Cambodia Under the Khmer Rouge, 1975–1979* (New Haven: Yale University Press, 2008).
7. Stanley Karnow, *Vietnam: A History* (New York: Viking Press, 1983), 153.
8. State Department Report, Vietnam's Refugee Machine, 20 July 1979, 1–2, General 1: Refugee Reports-1980, Ray Papers.
9. Kiet Tran, interviewed by author, 15 May 2014.
10. State Department Report, Vietnam's Refugee Machine, 20 July 1979, 1–2, General 1: Refugee Reports-1980, Ray Papers; Vinh Nguyen, interviewed by author, 2 July 2014.
11. Kiet Tran, interviewed by author, 15 May 2014.
12. Vinh Nguyen, interviewed by author, 2 July 2014; R.J. Rummel, "Statistics of Vietnamese Democide," in *Statistics in Democide* (University of Hawaii, 1997); Elizabeth Becker, *When the War Was Over: The Voices of Cambodia's Revolution and Its People* (New York: Simon & Schuster, 1986).
13. Vinh Nguyen, interviewed by author, 2 July 2014; Kiet Tran, interviewed by author, 15 May 2014.
14. Robert Ray Press Release, 17 January 1979, Resettlement 6: Press Releases + Speeches Governor's Office Iowa Refugee Service Center, Ray Papers; Shearer to Quinn, Subject Refugees, 19 December 1978, Resettlement 7: Program Files (Correspondence + Memos 1978), Ray Papers.
15. Kenneth Quinn, interviewed by author, 11 April 2014; Shearer to Ray, 20 February 1980, Resettlement 7: Program Files (Correspondence + Memos) 1980 (Jan.-June), Ray Papers.
16. Poll info in *ibid.*
17. Mrs. Phyllis Hansen to Ray, 8 February 1979, Resettlement 3: February 1979 Correspondence, Ray Papers.
18. Ray Ford to Ray, received 15 February 1979, Resettlement 3: May 1979 Correspondence, Ray Papers; Bowermaster, "Chapter XVII: Kansas City," in *Governor*, 177–187; Alice Hemsted to Ray, 9 August 1979; Alan Bullock to Ray, 2 October 1979, Resettlement 4: December 1979 (3), Ray Papers.
19. Sherry Ricchiardi, "The Hidden Poor of Rural Iowa," *Des Moines Register*, circa 1979, Resettlement 4: December 1979 Correspondence (3), Ray Papers; Sherry Ricchiardi, "Iowa's poor: The search for a helping hand," *Des Moines Register*, 16 September 1979, Resettlement 4: January-February 1980 Correspondence, Ray Papers.
20. Mrs. Hugh McLean to Ray, circa late January 1979, Resettlement 3: February Correspondence, Ray Papers; Etta Sluter to Ray, 10 March 1979, Resettlement 3: March 1979 Correspondence, Ray Papers; Mrs. Estella Jones to Ray, 1 May 1979, Resettlement 3: May 1979 Correspondence, Ray Papers.
21. Mrs. Estella Jones to Ray, 1 May 1979, Resettlement 3: May 1979 Correspondence, Ray Papers; Vesta Rhea to Ray, 1 November 1979, Resettlement 4: December 1979 Correspondence, Ray Papers; Kathy Rees to Ray, 13 September 1979, Resettlement 3: Sept-October 1979 Correspondence, Ray Papers; Mrs. Hugh McLean to Ray, circa late January 1979, Resettlement 3: February Correspondence, Ray Papers; Mrs. George Hamilton to Ray, 16 October 1979, Resettlement 4: November 1979 Correspondence, Ray Papers; Mrs. Levi Jacobsen to Ray, 6 August 1979, Resettlement 3: August 1–15, Ray Papers.
22. Mrs. Pauline Wright to Ray, 30 April 1979, Resettlement 3: May 1979 Correspondence, Ray Papers; M.W. to Ray and Shearer, 26 March 1979, Resettlement 3: March 1979 Correspondence, Ray Papers; Forrest Warner to Ray, 9 July 1979, Resettlement 3: July 17–31, 1979, Correspondence, Ray Papers.

23. Anonymous from Moorland, Iowa, to Ray, 30 December 1979, Resettlement 4: January-February 1980 Correspondence, Ray Papers; S.A. Ruber to Ray, received 5 October 1979, Resettlement 3: Sept-October 1979 Correspondence, Ray Papers; Robert Jackson to Ray, 3 May 1979, Resettlement 3: May 1979 Correspondence, Ray Papers.

24. Derrick Davis to Ray, 6 March 1979, Resettlement 3: June 1979 Correspondence, Ray Papers; State of Iowa Refugee Resettlement Program Fiscal Year 1982, Resettlement 1: Adm Refugee Resettlement State Plans 1980–1982, Ray Papers.

25. Williams' quote in "Refugee Resettlement Hearing," 87, 95; Frank Wu, *Yellow*, 40; Mike McGraw, "Iowa Farm/Business: Iowa Refugee Plan Built Around Jobs," *Des Moines Register*, 17 June 1979, Resettlement 1: Conference Meetings Workshops National Governors Assoc Testimony Before Select Commission on Immigration and Refugee Policy, Denver, Colorado 1980, Ray Papers.

26. Frank Wu, *Yellow*, 66.

27. Williams quoted by Lawrence Rout in, "Haven for Boat People: Iowa Does So Well by Its Indochinese Refugees that it's Gaining a Reputation in Asian Camps," *Wall Street Journal*, 27 June 1979, and Williams in "Refugee Resettlement Hearing," 87, 95.

28. Allen Ashby, "Views and Reviews," 2, *Iowa Bystander*, 8 February 1979.

29. Edna Griffin Open Letter to President Carter in Letters to the Editor, *Iowa Bystander*, 13 January 1977, and Edna Griffin Open Letter to Lincoln Post no. 126 of the American Legion and Roy Leonard Rolles Post No. 5487, *Iowa Bystander*, 20 January 1977.

30. Black Persons By Poverty Status in 1969, 1979, 1989, and 1999 by State and Persons 65 Years and Over by Poverty Status 1969, 1979, 1989, and 1999 by State: U.S. Census Bureau.

31. Etta Sluter to Ray, 10 March 1979, Resettlement 3: March 1979 Correspondence, Ray Papers; Anonymous to Ray, received 16 April 1979, Resettlement 3: April 1979 Correspondence, Ray Papers; Ray Ford to Ray, 15 February 1979, Resettlement 3: May 1979 Correspondence, Ray Papers; Marvin Fawcett, "Letters from the Readers: Opposes bringing refugees to Iowa," Resettlement 3: February 1979 Correspondence, Ray Papers; Esther and James Merrill to Ray, received 2 April 1979, Resettlement 3: April 1979 Correspondence, Ray Papers.

32. Mrs. Anthony Riley to Quinn, circa August 1979, Resettlement 3: August 1979 Correspondence, Ray Papers; Marilyn Krueger to Ray, 1 May 1979, Resettlement 3: May 1979 Correspondence, Ray Papers; Gary Ohls to Ray, received 21 November 1979, Resettlement 4: December Correspondence, Ray Papers.

33. Alan Bullock to Ray, 26 May 1979, Resettlement 3: July 1–16 Correspondence, Ray Papers; Clifford Rushton to Ray, 20 June 1979, Resettlement 3: July 1–16 Correspondence, Ray Papers.

34. Mrs. Cletus LeBarge to Ray, 1 May 1979, Resettlement 3: May 1979 Correspondence, Ray Papers; Mrs. Cletus LeBarge response to Quinn, 11 July 1979, Resettlement 3: July 1–16, 1979, Ray Papers.

35. Mrs. Earl Griffin to Ray, 9 March 1979, Resettlement 3: July 1–16, 1979, Ray Papers; Gay Van DeBoe response to Quinn, 22 July 1980, Resettlement 4: May-August 1980 Correspondence, Ray Papers.

36. Ray in "House of Representatives Transcript of Proceedings Committee on the Judiciary: Subcommittee on Immigration, Refugees, and International Law Hearing on Refugee Legislation Washington, D.C. 24 May 1979," General 1: Refugee Act of 1979 (Federal), 94, Ray Papers.

37. Quinn response to Mrs. Joan Laverty, 19 February 1979, Resettlement 3: February 1979 Correspondence, Ray Papers; Quinn response to Howard Grobe, 19 March 1979, Resettlement 3: March 1979 Correspondence, Ray Papers; Quinn interviewed by author, 29 November 2011.

38. Quinn, interviewed by author, 22 March 2014; Gaylord Thayer to Ray, 19 January 1979, Resettlement 3: February 1979 Correspondence, Ray Papers.

39. Colleen Shearer, Some Historical Facts circa 1979, Resettlement 7: Program Files (Correspondence and Memos) 1978, Ray Papers.

Chapter 6

1. Reprinted from, "Iowa SHARES & the Cambodian Refugees," by Matthew Walsh, *Iowa Heritage Illustrated* 92 (Fall & Winter), 100–109. Used with permission of the publisher.

2. Teeda Butt Mam, "Worms from Our Skin," in *Children of Cambodia's Killing Fields: Memoirs by Survivors*, ed. Dith Pran and Kim DePaul (New Haven: Yale University Press, 1999), 13; Robert Ray, Press Release, 24 December 1979, Iowa SHARES 1:4, Ray Papers.

3. *Enemies of the People*, dir, Thet Sambath (2010; PBS POV, July 2011 DVD).

4. Monyra Chau, "South East Asia at Hoover High School," ed. Simone Soria (unpublished manuscript, Des Moines, Iowa, 1983), 7–12; Pa Mao, "South East Asia at Hoover High School," 37–45.

5. Robert Ray, "Address by Governor Robert D. Ray to the General Assembly of the Christian Church, St. Louis Missouri," 30 October 1979, Iowa SHARES 1:4, Ray Papers.

6. Brooklyn-Guernsey-Malcolm 4th Grade to Ray, Iowa SHARES 2:6, Ray Papers.

7. Robert Ray, press release to Iowans, 21 November 1979, Iowa SHARES 1:4, Ray Papers.

8. Mary Jane Odell, Communication from MJO to Whomever, 5 December 1979, Iowa SHARES 1:8, Ray Papers.

9. Mary Jane Odell, 60 second commercial ad, undated, Iowa SHARES 1:1, Ray Papers, for info about the reading, Kenneth Quinn, interviewed by author, 28 November 2011.

10. Scott Larsen to Ray, received 15 January 1980, Iowa SHARES 1:10, Ray Papers.

11. Eric Sharp to Ray, 18 November 1979, Iowa SHARES 1:2, Ray Papers.

12. Kenneth Quinn quoted by Kevin Knickrehm, "Send help to end starvation-SHARES," *UNI Northern Iowan* vol. 76 no. 25, 11 December 1979, Iowa SHARES 1:10, Ray Papers; Ann Dundon to SHARES, 10 December 1979, Iowa SHARES 1:7, Ray Papers.

13. Mr. and Mrs. Claburn Wilson to Iowa SHARES, 22 November 1979, Iowa SHARES 2:8, Ray Papers.

14. Iowa SHARES Statement of Cash Receipts and Disbursements, 23 November–30 April 1981, Iowa SHARES 1:7, Ray Papers. Total amount more than quadrupled if one barge full of grain at $2.20 amounted to $115,500.

15. Edna Spencer to Ray, 26 November, 1979, Iowa SHARES 2:2, Ray Papers; Kathie Horney to Ray, 26 November 1979, Iowa SHARES 2:4, Ray Papers.

16. William Rosenfeld, "Please Don't forget the Cambodians," PACEMAKER: University of Iowa Hospitals and Clinics Newsletter Vol. 7 No. 7, July 1980, Iowa SHARES 1:6, Ray Papers.

17. An Open Letter to the Jewish Community, 1979, Iowa SHARES 2:2, Ray Papers.

18. Robert Ray, Address by Governor to General Assembly of Christian Church, 30 October 1979, Iowa SHARES 1:4, Ray Papers.

19. *Des Moines Register*, "Iowa cares and Shares," 22 November 1979; Harvey Glasser to Ray, 20 February 1980, Iowa SHARES 1:6, Ray Papers.

20. Hugh Stafford to Quinn, 31 December 1979, Iowa SHARES 2:9, Ray Papers; John Murray to Ray, 30 October 1979, Iowa SHARES 2:6, Ray Papers; Tom Yetmar to Ray, 31 January 1980, Iowa SHARES 2:10, Ray Papers.

21. Jerry Johnson to Ray, 18 January 1980, Iowa SHARES 2:8, Ray Papers.

22. Lawrence Adams coupon sent to Iowa Shares, 1979, Iowa SHARES 2:2, Ray Papers; Ella Brown to Ray, 29 November 1979, Iowa SHARES 2:6, Ray Papers.

23. Rosemary Drake to SHARES, 5 December 1979, Iowa SHARES 2:7, Ray Papers.

24. Chester Guinn to SHARES Board of Directors, 19 December 1979; 14 January 1980, Iowa SHARES 1:3, 1:5, Ray Papers.

25. Mrs. Harmon Rose to Ray, 17 December 1979, Iowa SHARES 2:9, Ray Papers.

26. Mike Derbyshire to Ray, 26 December 1979, Iowa SHARES 2:9, Ray Papers.

27. Paul Harvey, "Import-anybody's group plays dangerous game," *Clinton Herald Newspaper*, 4 December 1979, Iowa SHARES 2:9, Ray Papers.

28. Anonymous SHARES coupon sent to Ray, circa November 1979, Iowa SHARES 2:2, Ray Papers; Anonymous to Governor's Office, 2 November 1979, Iowa SHARES 2:2, Ray Papers.

29. Governor William Janklow to Ray, 19 May 1980, Iowa SHARES 2:10, Ray Papers.

30. Sothira Pan to Ray, 10 December 1979, Iowa SHARES 2:8, Ray Papers.

31. Kenneth Quinn, interviewed by author, 29 November 2011.

32. David Kalianov, email to author, 3 November 2011.

33. *Ibid.*

34. Kenneth Quinn, interviewed by author, 29 November 2011.

Chapter 7

1. Chinese proverb quoted in Elliot West, *Growing up with the Country: Childhood on the Far Western Frontier* (Albuquerque: University of New Mexico Press, 1989), 10. West has applied a similar argument to frontier youths.
2. Steven Mintz, preface to *Huck's Raft: A History of American Childhood* (Harvard University Press, 2006).
3. James Freeman and Nguyen Dinh Huu, *Voices from the Camps: Vietnamese Children Seeking Asylum* (Seattle: University of Washington Press, 2003), xv.
4. Cam Quang, "South East Asia at Hoover High School," 52.
5. Ky Tu, "Memories of Asian Students," edited by Marilyn Ritz (unpublished manuscript, Des Moines, Iowa, 1986), 54.
6. Mek Baccam, "Our Journey to Freedom: Written by Students of Des Moines Technical School District" (unpublished manuscript, Des Moines, IA, 1980), 13.
7. Orathay Fongdara, "Our Journey to Freedom," 29; Boonleng Keongam, "South East Asia at Hoover High School," 16.
8. Sovouthy Tith, "South East Asia at Hoover High School," 88–89.
9. Sovouthy Tith and Nib Thongchine, "South East Asia at Hoover High School," 88–90, 81; Phoeun Chey, "Memories of Asian Students," 8–9.
10. Veasna Ham, "Memories of Asian Students," 17.
11. Saran Chau, "Memories of Asian Students," 3, 7.
12. Bounsong Manivanh, "South East Asia at Hoover High School," 31–32; Pathana Luvan, "Memories of Asian Students," 40.
13. Fue Yang, "Memories of Asian Students," 63–64.
14. *Ibid.*, 65.
15. Vay Ho, "Our Journey to Freedom," 54–55.
16. *Ibid.*, 57.
17. Phoeun Chey, "Memories of Asian Students," 9.
18. Boonleng Keongam and Khanny Um, "South East Asia at Hoover High School," 18, 111.
19. Ben Kiernan, *Children of Cambodia's Killing Fields: Memoirs by Survivors*, ed. Dith Pran and Kim DePaul (Yale University Press, 1999), XIV; Chea Seng, "Memories of Asian Students," 43.
20. Song quoted in *Children of Cambodia's Killing Fields*, XII; Khanny Um, "South East Asia at Hoover High School," 110.
21. Boonleng Keongam, South East Asia at Hoover High School," 18; Ky Tu, "Memories of Asian Students," 55–56.
22. Siamphone Xayavong, "Memories of Asian Students," 58.
23. Cam Quang, "South East Asia at Hoover High School," 55.
24. Me Duong, "Memories of Asian Students," 12.
25. Theun Deo, Pathana Luvan, & Sivilay Phabmixay, "Our Journey to Freedom," 3, 43–44, 17.
26. Veasna Ham & Ounbonh Phanthavong, "Memories of Asian Students," 17, 40; Khanny Um, "South East Asia at Hoover High School," 105.
27. Amkha Xam, Mek Baccam, & Oune Be, "Our Journey to Freedom," 35, 13, 24.
28. Sovane Bethi, in *ibid.*, 9.
29. Siamphone Xayavong, "Memories of Asian Students," 58.
30. Somkong Vong, interviewed author, 5 May 2014.
31. Somaly Chak, "South East Asia at Hoover High School," 5; Me Duong and Phouthasone "Larry" Khounxay, "Memories of Asian Students," 12, 20.
32. Vay Ho, "Our Journey to Freedom," 56.
33. Houng Baccam, interviewed by author, 16 February 2014; Houng Baccam quoted in Mary Hutchinson Tone, "Iowa's Human Adventure," (unpublished manuscript, 1980), Resettlement 4: May-August 1980 Correspondence, Ray Papers; Thuong Lo, interviewed by author, 20 June 2014.
34. Houng Baccam in Tone, "Iowa's Human Adventure"; Somkong Vong, interviewed by author, 5 May 2014; Mike Rasavanh, interviewed author, 15 May 2014; Dara Rasavanh, interviewed by author, 15 May 2014.
35. Mek Baccam & Pathana Luvan, "Our Journey to Freedom," 14, 42.

36. Phonesamay Fongdara & Larry Khounxay, "Memories of Asian Students," 15, 21; Phouvong Senephansiri, "South East Asian at Hoover High School," 65.

37. Vilayvanh Senephansiri, "South East Asia at Hoover High School," 71; Chea Seng, "Memories of Asian Students," 43.

38. Vilayvanh Senephansiri, "South East Asia at Hoover High School," 72.

39. Tara Zahra, *The Lost Children: Reconstructing Europe's Families after World War II* (Cambridge: Harvard University Press, 2011) 24, 64–65, 235–237.

40. *Ibid.*, 237.

Chapter 8

1. Pa Mao, "South East Asia at Hoover High School," 42; Pathana Luvan, "Our Journey to Freedom," 44.

2. Pao Lee, "Memories of Asian Students," 23; Mek Baccam, "Our Journey to Freedom," 14; Veasna Ham, "Memories of Asian Students," 19; Siamphone Xayavong, "Memories of Asian Students," 58.

3. Theun Deo, "Our Journey to Freedom," 4; Oune Be, "Our Journey to Freedom," 25; Say Chhith, "Our Journey to Freedom," 20; Vay Ho, "Our Journey to Freedom," 58–59.

4. Oubonh Phanthavong, "Memories of Asian Students," 41–42. Boun Bang Fai is a firework festival that occurs in the sixth month of the lunar year. The fireworks are used to send messages to the gods asking for rain; Meg Regina Rakow, *Laos and Laotians* (Honolulu: University of Hawaii, 1992), 4.

5. Wajuppa Tossa and Kongdeuane Nettavong, *Lao Folktales*, ed. Margaret Read MacDonald (London: Greenwood Publishing Group, 2008), 118–119.

6. Bounsong Manivanh, "South East Asia at Hoover High School," 29; Vilayvanh Senephansiri, "South East Asia at Hoover High School," 70; Nib Thongchine, "South East Asia at Hoover High School," 79.

7. "South East Asia at Hoover High School," 37; "South East Asia at Hoover High School," 50; "South East Asia at Hoover High School," 51; "South East Asia at Hoover High School," 61.

8. Cher Vang, "Our Journey to Freedom," 71; Khanny Um, "South East Asia at Hoover High School," 105; Phonesamay Fongdara, "Memories of Asian Students," 14; Pao Lee, "Memories of Asian Students,"22; Oubonh Phanthavong, "Memories of Asian Students," 40; Boonleng Keongam, "South East Asia at Hoover High School," 19.

9. Sovane Bethi, "Our Journey to Freedom," 9; Me Duong, "Memories of Asian Students," 11; Pao Lee, "Memories of Asian Students," 22; Cam Quang, "South East Asia at Hoover High School," 51.

10. Pao Lee, "Memories of Asian Students," 23–24; "Our Journey to Freedom," 63; Saroeum Loeurng, "Memories of Asian Students," 29.

11. Pathana Luvan, "Our Journey to Freedom," 46; Saroeum Loeurng, "Memories of Asian Students," 29; Kham Sackpraseuth, "South East Asia at Hoover High School," 60; Vilayvanh Senephansiri, "South East Asia at Hoover High School," 75; Theun Deo, "Our Journey to Freedom," 4.

12. Somphong Baccam, interviewed by author, 24 April 2014; Monyra Chau, "South East Asia at Hoover High School," 10.

13. Khanny Um, "South East Asia at Hoover High School," 106; Sovouthy Tith, "South East Asia at Hoover High School," 86–87; Viseth Tith and Boonleng Keongam, "South East Asia at Hoover High School," 15, 101.

14. Sovouthy Tith, "South East Asia at Hoover High School," 86–87; "Memories of Asian Students," 40; Khanny Um, "South East Asia at Hoover High School," 106.

15. Veasna Ham, "Memories of Asian Students," 18–19; Saroeum Loeurng, "Memories of Asian Students," 29; Cher Vang, "Our Journey to Freedom," 7; Somkong Vong, interviewed by author, 5 May 2014.

16. Say Lo, "Memories of Asian Students," 26; Orathay Fongdara, "Our Journey to Freedom," 32; Oune Be, "Our Journey to Freedom," 25; Cher Vang, "Our Journey to Freedom," 7.

17. Kelly, *From Vietnam to America*, 179; Phouvong Senephansiri, "South East Asia at Hoover High School," 68; Sivilay Phabmixay, "Our Journey to Freedom," 18; "Our Journey to Freedom," 23; Theun Deo, "Our Journey to Freedom," 4.

18. Vay Ho and Orathay Fongdara, "Our Journey to Freedom," 32, 59; Theun Deo, "Our

Journey to Freedom," 4; "Our Journey to Freedom," 34; Heng Ngan, interviewed by author, 16 December 2013.

19. Cher Vang, "Our Journey to Freedom," 6; Heng Ngan, interviewed by author, 16 December 2013; Mike Rasavanh, interviewed by author, 15 May 2014; Kham Sackpraseuth, "South East Asia at Hoover High School," 61.

20. For a recent study on the benefit of cluster resettlement on youths, Tom Luster et al. "The Lost Boys of the Sudan: Ambiguous Loss, Search for Family, and Reestablishing Relationships with Family Members," *Family Relations* 57 (2008): 444–456; Amkha Xam, "Our Journey to Freedom," 36; Pathana Luvan, "Our Journey to Freedom," 46.

21. Orathay Fongdara, "Our Journey to Freedom," 32; Sivilay Phabmixay, "Our Journey to Freedom," 18; Phouvong Senephansiri, "South East Asia at Hoover High School," 68; Kham Sackpraseuth, "South East Asia at Hoover High School," 61.

22. Donechanh Southammavong, interviewed by author, 2 May 2014.

23. Melinda Voss, "Adel school flap over Viet student," *Des Moines Tribune*, 28 August 1981.

24. Robert Benton, "Refugee education needs aid: Benton," Refugee Resettlement 3: May 1979 Correspondence, Ray Papers.

25. Edna Burns to Ray, 22 September 1981, Resettlement 8: Program Files (Correspondence + Memos) 1981 (July-Dec), Ray Papers; Maggie King, Tuan Le Case Notes Lutheran Social Services of Iowa, Resettlement 8: Program Files (Correspondence + Memos) 1981 (July-Dec), Ray Papers.

26. Sucheng Chan, *The Vietnamese American 1.5 Generation: Stories of War, Revolution, Flight and New Beginnings* (Philadelphia: Temple University Press, 2006).

27. Monyra Chau, "South East Asia at Hoover High School," 11; Somkong Vong, interviewed by author, 5 May 2014.

28. Siang Bachti, interviewed by author, 3 February 2014; Dara Rasavanh, interviewed by author, 15 May 2014.

29. Somphong Baccam, interviewed by author, 24 April 2014.

30. Boonsao Keongam, "South East Asia at Hoover High School," 27; Carola Suarez-Orazco et al., *Immigrant Children: Change, Adaptation, and Cultural Transformation*, ed. Susan Chuang and Robert Moreno (Lanham, Maryland: Rowman & Littlefield, 2011), 15; Patricia Palmer, interviewed by author, 22 March 2011.

31. Somphong Baccam, interviewed by author, 24 April 2014; Somkong Vong, interviewed by author, 5 May 2014.

32. Vamouachee Xiong, "The Little Mouse Girl Who Did Not Want to Marry Her Own Kind," interviewed by Karen Harper, 21 February 2005.

33. Donechanh Southammavong, interviewed by author, 2 May 2014.

34. Somkong Vong, interviewed by author, 5 May 2014; Phuong Baccam, interviewed by author, 23 February 2014.

35. Thomas Baccam, interviewed by author, 23 February 2014.

36. Nib Thongchine, "South East Asia at Hoover High School," 80; Vay Ho, "Our Journey to Freedom," 47.

37. Say Lo, "Memories of Asian Students," 26; Viseth Tith, "South East Asia at Hoover High School," 104.

38. Pathana Luvan, "Our Journey to Freedom," 46; "Our Journey to Freedom," 2; Sivilay Phabmixay, "Our Journey to Freedom," 18.

39. Monyra Chau and Viseth Tith, "South East Asia at Hoover High School," 11, 104; Pa Mao, "South East Asia at Hoover High School," 44.

40. For similar argument, Nathan Caplan et al., *The Boat People and Achievement in America: A Study of Family Life, Hard Work, and Cultural Values* (Ann Arbor: University of Michigan Press, 1989), 97, 145–148

41. Vay Ho, "Our Journey to Freedom," 59.

Chapter 9

1. Testimony of Ambassador L. Dean Brown, Director of the Interagency Task Force, Indochina Refugees: May 5, 1975. House of Representatives, Subcommittee on Immigration, Citizenship, and International Law Committee of the Judiciary, 9.

2. "Congress Approves Indochinese Aid," CQ Almanac 31st Edition (1975): 315–320, accessed March 5, 2014 http://library.cqpress.com/cqalmanac/document.php?id=cqal75-1214026.

3. Maurice Baringer in Bowermaster, *Governor*, 156.

4. David Oman, interviewed by author, 13 February 2015; David Oman, Ray, Dick Gilbert in Bowermaster, *Governor*, 155–159, 338.

5. Shearer memo to Ray, Subject Iowa Refugee Service Center, 4 November 1980, Resettlement 8: Program Files (Correspondence + Memos) 1980 (July)–1981 (June), Ray Papers.

6. Gil Loescher and Jon Scanlan, *Calculated Kindness*, 123.

7. Colleen Shearer, Victor Preisser, Ken Quinn, Memorandum For: Governor Ray Subject: Indochinese Refugees, 4 December 1978, Resettlement 7: Program Files (Correspondence + Memos), 1–2, Ray Papers. Ultimately, several different ethnic groups comprised the 1500 additional refugees admitted to Iowa.

8. Shearer to Quinn Subject: Refugees, 19 December 1978, Resettlement 7: Program Files (Correspondence + Memos) 1978, Ray Papers.

9. Ray to President Jimmy Carter, 17 January 1979, Resettlement 6: Press Releases + Speeches Governor's Office Iowa Refugee Service Center, Ray Papers.

10. Ray to governors, 22 January 1979, Resettlement 2: Correspondence-Letter to Editors 1979, Ray Papers.

11. "Statement by Honorable Robert D. Ray, Governor of Iowa, Before the Subcommittee on Immigration, Refugee and International Law of the Judiciary Committee of the House of Representatives, Washington, D.C., May 24, 1979," General 1: Refugee Act of 1979 (federal), 9, Ray Papers.

12. William Milliken to President Carter, 22 March 1979, Resettlement 8: Conferences Meetings Workshops UN Conference on Geneva Refugees Switzerland July 1979, Ray Papers.

13. Anonymous, *The Unfair Burden: Our House is Full! Displaced Persons from Indochina in Thailand*, Operation Centre for Displaced Persons Ministry of Interior of Thailand, circa 1979, General 3: Publications-Misc 1980–1982, 13–15, Ray Papers.

14. "Governor Ray Reports on UN Meeting on Indochinese Refugees," 23 July 1979, Resettlement 1: Conferences Meetings Workshops UN Conference on Geneva Refugees Switzerland July 1979, Ray Papers.

15. Walter Mondale, "Speech to the U.N. Conference on Indochinese Refugees: Office of the Vice President's Press Secretary," July 1979.

16. Kenneth Quinn, interviewed by author, 11 April 2014; Mondale to Ray, 8 September 1979, Resettlement 1: Conferences Meetings Workshops UN Conference on Geneva Refugees Switzerland July 1979, Ray Papers.

17. Cyrus Vance, "The Proposed Refugee Act of 1979-Meeting the Need for a Comprehensive Long-Term Policy on Refugees," 1–6, General 1: Refugee Act of 1979 (federal), Ray Papers.

18. Edward Kennedy, "The Refugee Act of 1980," *International Migration Review*, Vol. 15 No. 1/2, Refugees Today (Spring-Summer, 1981): 146.

19. *Ibid.*, 151.

20. Peter Rodino to Ray, 17 April 1979, General 1: Refugee Act of 1979 (federal), Ray Papers; "Statement by Honorable Robert D. Ray, Governor of Iowa, Before the Subcommittee on Immigration, Refugee and International Law of the Judiciary Committee of the House of Representatives, Washington, D.C., May 24, 1979," General 1: Refugee Act of 1979 (federal), 10–11, Ray Papers.

21. Robert Ray, William Milliken, Brendan Byrne, "Report and Policy Position Recommendations of the Task Force on Indochina Refugees National Governor's Association Committee on International Trade and Foreign Relations, Louisville, KY, July 9, 1979," 4, Resettlement 6: National Governors Association—Refugee Task Force, 1979–1981, Ray Papers.

22. Ray in Bowermaster, *Governor*, 109–110. With strong national support for Ray's decision, the federal government ultimately agreed to payout roughly $200,000 in damages.

23. "Statement by Honorable Robert D. Ray, Governor of Iowa, Before the Subcommittee on Immigration, Refugee and International Law of the Judiciary Committee of the House of Representatives, Washington, D.C., May 24, 1979," General 1: Refugee Act of 1979 (federal), 8–11, Ray Papers.

24. Kennedy in "Congressional Record Proceedings and Debates of the 96th Congress, First Session, Vol. 125 No. 112 6 September 1979," General 1: Refugee Act of 1979–80 (federal) Congressional Reports, Ray Papers; Ray, Milliken, Byrne Report on the NGA Task Force on

Indochinese Refugees, 25 February 1980, Resettlement 6: National Governors Association Refugee Task Force, 1979–1981, 3, Ray Papers; Ed Kennedy to Ray, 4 March 1980, General 1: Refugee Act of 1979 1980 federal, Ray Papers.

25. Julie Tripp, "Officials fear for other refugees in the wake of Suicide," *The Oregonian*, 2 August 1981.

26. Victor Atiyeh to Ronald Reagan, 10 August 1981, Resettlement 8: Program Files (Correspondence + Memos) 1981 (July-Dec.), Ray Papers.

27. "1980 Re-Election Bid," Clinton House Museum Fayetteville, Arkansas, accessed 6 March 2015 http://www.clintonhousemuseum.org/learn/clintons-timeline/112–1980-re-election-bid.

28. Robert Ray to Rich Williamson of Intergovernmental Relations Office, 18 February 1982, Resettlement 1: Adm Refugee Resettlement Program Budget Requests funding 1979–1982, Ray Papers.

29. *The Farm Crisis*, dir. by Laura Bower Burgmaier (Iowa Public Television, 2013).

30. Shearer memo to Quinn, 5 August 1981, Resettlement 8: Program Files (Correspondence + Memos) 1981-(July-Dec.), Ray Papers.

31. Bowermaster, *Governor*, 329–342.

32. Quinn, interviewed by author, 11 April 2014; Thuong Lo, interviewed by author, 20 June 2014.

33. Mary Gebhart to Ray, 24 January 1979, Resettlement 3: February 1979 Correspondence, Ray Papers; R.L. Playle to Ray, 30 April 1979, Resettlement 3: May 1979 Correspondence, Ray Papers; Joseph Sullivan to Ray, 30 April 1979, Resettlement 3: May 1979 Correspondence, Ray Papers.

34. Herb Welander to Ray, Resettlement 4: Correspondence (Pro) 1979 (Feb), Ray Papers.

35. Robert Friedman to Ray, 9 May 1979, Resettlement 3: May 1979 Correspondence, Ray Papers; James Blakely to Ray, 23 September 1979, Resettlement 3: Sept-October 1979, Ray Papers; Yechiel Eckstein to Ray, circa November 1979, Resettlement 4: November 1979 Correspondence, Ray Papers.

36. State resettlement program was named Governor's Task Force for Indochinese Resettlement, Iowa Refugee Service Center, and the Bureau of Refugee Services; Houng Baccam, interviewed by author, 16 February 2014.

37. Naomi and Michael Zucker, "The Voluntary Agencies and Refugee Resettlement in the U.S.," August 1980 draft, 45–46, Resettlement 9: Reference-Refugee Resettlement Programs and Techniques and Refugee Resettlement in the U.S., Ray Papers.

38. "Nativity, Citizenship, and Place of Birth for Iowa: 1950–2000" and "Asian and Native Hawaiian and Other Pacific Islander Groups in Iowa: 1850–2000" in State Library of Iowa, State Data Center Program http://www.iowadatacenter.org.

39. Houng Baccam, interviewed by author, 16 February 2014; Khouang Luong, interviewed by author, 22 March 2014; Somphong Baccam, interviewed by author, 24 April 2014; Mike Rasavanh, interviewed by author, 15 May 2014; "Statement by Honorable Robert D. Ray, Governor of Iowa, Before the Subcommittee on Immigration, Refugee and International Law of the Judiciary Committee of the House of Representatives, Washington, D.C., May 24, 1979," General 1: Refugee Act of 1979 (federal), 7, Ray Papers.

40. Donechanh Southammavong, interviewed by author, 2 May 2014.

References

Interviews by the Author

Houng Baccam. 16 February 2014
Nga Baccam. translated by Matsalyn Brown, 6 September 2014
Phuong Baccam. 23 February 2014
Somphong Baccam. 24 April 2014
Thomas Baccam. 23 February 2014
Siang Bachti. 3 February 2014
Bao Lo Cam. 25 May 2014
Wing Cam. 8 August 2014
Richard Freeman. 18 April 2014
Wayne Johnson. 9 March 2014
William Johnson. 8 January 2014
John Judge. 12 March 2011
Thuong Lo. translated by Dinh VanLo, 20 June 2014
Khouang Luong. 22 March 2014
Tomas Muñoz. 19 May 2014
Richard Murphy. 15 February 2014
Heng Ngan. 16 December 2014
Vinh Nguyen. 2 July 2014
David Oman. 13 February 2015
Patricia Palmer. 22 March 2011
Em Quang. translated by Somphong Baccam, 21 June 2014
Kenneth Quinn. 29 November 2011; 11 April 2014
Dara Rasavanh. 15 May 2014
Mike Rasavanh. 15 May 2014
Neth Rasavanh. translated by Matsalyn Brown, 6 September 2014
Donechanh Southammavong. 2 May 2014
Jack Spear. 8 May 2014
Kiet Tran. 15 May 2014
Dau Truong. 12 March 2011
Thuong Truong. 12 March 2011
Dinh VanLo. 10 April 2014
Somkong Vong. 5 May 2014

Archival Sources

Robert D. Ray Papers. Record Group 43. State Historical Society of Iowa, Des Moines, Iowa.
Southeast Asian Images & Texts, University of Wisconsin, Madison, Wisconsin.

Unpublished Sources

Cam, Wing. "ThaiDam Freedom Festival." Presentation for the twenty-fifth anniversary of the Tai Dam in the United States, Iowa, October 21, 2000.
_____. "ThaiDam History." Translated by Dinh VanLo. Unpublished manuscript, Nong Khai Refugee Camp, Thailand, 1975.
Hickey, Gerald. "Social Systems of Northern Vietnam." PhD diss., University Chicago, 1959.
Mukdawijitra, Yukti. "Ethnicity and Multilingualism: The Case of the Ethnic Tai in the Vietnamese State." PhD diss., University of Wisconsin, Madison, 2007.
Our Journey to Freedom: Written by Students of Des Moines Technical School District. Unpublished manuscript, Des Moines, 1980.
Ritz, Marilyn, ed. *Memories of Asian Students.* Unpublished manuscript, Des Moines, 1986.
Soria, Simone, ed. *South East Asia at Hoover High School.* Unpublished manuscript, Des Moines, 1983.

Sources

Adams, Michele, Susan Chuang, and Robert Moreno. *Immigrant Children: Change, Adaptation, and Cultural Transformation.* Lanham, Maryland: Rowman & Littlefield, 2011.
Bachti, Siang. "King Cobra: A Tai History Booklet." *Tai Studies Center* (2000).
Bacthi, Siang, InNgeun Baccam Soulinthavong, and Jack Lufkin. "So We Stayed Together: The Tai Dam Immigrate to Iowa." *Palimpsest* 69:4 (1988): 163–172.
Becker, Elizabeth. *When the War Was Over: The Voices of Cambodia's Revolution and Its People.* New York: Simon & Schuster, 1986.
Bell, Sue, and Michael Whiteford. "Tai Dam Health Care Practices: Asian Refugee Women in Iowa." *Society of Science and Medicine* 24.4 (1987): 317–325.
Bodnar, John. *The Transplanted: A History of Immigrants in Urban Communities.* Bloomington: Indiana University Press, 1989.
Bon Tempo, Carl. *Americans at the Gate: The United States and Refugees During the Cold War.* Princeton: Princeton University Press, 2008.
Bowermaster, Jon. *Governor: An Oral Biography of Robert D. Ray.* Ames: Iowa State University Press, 1987.
Brocheux, Pierre, and Daniel Hemery. *Indochina: An Ambiguous Colonization, 1858–1954.* Berkley: University of California Press, 2011.
Castle, Timothy. *At War in the Shadow of Vietnam: U.S. Military Aid to the Royal Lao Government 1955–1975.* New York: Columbia University Press, 1993.
Chamberlain, James. "The Black Tai Chronicle of Muang Mouay." *Mon-Khmer Studies* 21 (1992): 19–55.
Chan, Sucheng. *Survivors: Cambodian Refugees in the United States.* Champagne: University of Illinois Press, 2004.
_____. *The Vietnamese American 1.5 Generation: Stories of War, Revolution, Flight and New Beginnings.* Philadelphia: Temple University Press, 2006.
Chung, Sanaye, Donechanh Southammavong, and Phonemany Theppanya. "Unburdening Our Mothers' Backs: An Oral History Project." *Monsoon United Asian Women of Iowa,* 2009.
"Congress Approves Indochinese Aid." *CQ Almanac* 31st Edition (1975): 315–320, accessed March 5, 2014, http://library.cqpress.com/cqalmanac/document.php?id=cqal75-1214026.
Cramer, Gail, Nguyen Tri Khiem, Eric Wailes, and Kenneth Young. "Vietnam's Rice Economy: Developments and Prospect." *University of Arkansas Division of Agriculture* 968 (2002): 1–32.
Enemies of the People. DVD. Directed by Thet Sambath. 2010; PBS POV, July 2011.
Dang, Nghiem Van. "Dien Bien Phu: Some Ethnohistorical Data." *Vietnamese Studies* 36 (1973): 7–23.
_____. "The Flood Myth and the Origin of Ethnic Groups in Southeast Asia." *Journal of American Folklore* 106:421 (1993): 304–337.
_____. "An Outline of the Thai in Vietnam." *Vietnamese Studies* 32 (1972): 143–196.
Daniels, Roger. *Guarding the Golden Door: American Immigration Policy and Immigrants Since 1882.* New York: Hill and Wang, 2004.
Demaray, Elyse, and Melody Keim-Shenk. "Always Remembering the Motherland: Tai Dam

Wedding Textiles and Dress." In *Wedding Dress Across Cultures*, edited by Helen Foster and Donald Johnson. New York: Bloomsbury Academic, 2004

Diguet, Eduard Jacques Joseph. *Les Montagnards de Tonkin*. Whitefish, Montana: Kessinger Publishing, 2010.

Evans, Grant. "Apprentice Ethnographers: Vietnam and the Study of Lao Minorities." In *Laos, Culture and Society*, edited by Grant Evans. Thailand: Silkworm Books, 1999.

_____, trans. "The Autobiography of Chao Sai Kham, Governor of Xiang Khoang Province." In *The Last Century of Lao Royalty*. Thailand: Silkworm Books, 2009.

Fall, Bernard. *Hell in a Very Small Place: The Siege of Dien Bien Phu*. Cambridge: Da Capo Press, 1966.

The Farm Crisis. DVD. Directed by Laura Bower Burgmaier. 2013; Johnston, Iowa: Iowa Public Television, 2013.

Finlayson, Andrew. *Marine Advisors with the Vietnamese Provincial Reconnaissance Units, 1966–1970*. Quantico: U.S. Marine Corps, 2009.

Frederickson, Rick. "Best Music of Iowa Archives." *Iowa Public Radio*, 2012. http://iowapublic radio.org/post/best-music-iowa-archives.

Freeman, James, and Nguyen Dinh Huu. *Voices from the Camps: Vietnamese Children Seeking Asylum*. Seattle: University of Washington, 2003.

Freud, Anna, and Sophie Dann. "An Experiment in Group Upbringing." *Psychoanalytic Study of the Child* (1951): 127–168.

Gedney, William. "Review of J. Marvin Brown's From Ancient Thai to Modern Dialects." *Social Science Review Bangkok* 3, no. 2 (1965): 107–112.

Ginio, Ruth. "French Officers, African Officers, and the Violent Image of African Colonial Soldiers." *Historical Reflections* 36 (2010): 59–75.

Grant, Bruce. *The Boat People: An 'Age' Investigation*. New York: Penguin Books, 1979.

Handlin, Oscar. *The Uprooted: The Epic Story of the Great Migrations That Made the American People*. Boston: Little, Brown, 1951.

Hartmann, John. "Computations on a Tai Dam Origin Myth." *Anthropologic Linguistics* 23, no. 5 (1981): 183–202.

Hein, Jeremy. *Ethnic Origins: the Adaptation of Cambodian and Hmong Refugees in Four American Cities*. New York: Russell Sage Foundation, 2006.

_____. *From Vietnam, Laos, and Cambodia: A Refugee Experience in the United States*. Boston: Twayne Publishing, 1995.

_____. *States and International Migrants: the Incorporation of Indochinese Refugees in The United States and France*. Boulder: Westview Press, 1993.

Hixson, Walter. *Parting the Curtain: Propaganda, Culture, and the Cold War 1945–1961*. London: Palgrave Macmillan, 1997.

Karnow, Stanley. *Vietnam: A History*. New York: Viking Press, 1983.

Kashinaga, Masao. "The Transmission of Written Genealogies and Patrilineality Among the Tai Dam." *Senri Ethnological Studies* 74 (2009): 97–115.

Kelly, Gail Paradise. *From Vietnam to America: A Chronicle of Vietnamese Immigration to the United States*. Boulder: Westview Press, 1979.

Kennedy, Edward. "The Refugee Act of 1980." *International Migration Review* 15, no. ½ (Spring-Summer 1981): 141–156.

Keyes, Charles. *The Golden Peninsula: Culture and Adaptation in Mainland Laos*. Honolulu: University of Hawaii Press, 1994.

Kiernan, Ben. *The Pol Pot Regime: Race, Power, and Genocide in Cambodia Under the Khmer Rouge, 1975–1979*. New Haven: Yale University Press, 2008.

LaFont, P.B. "Pratiques medicales des Thai Noirs du Laos de l'ouest." *Anthoropos* 54 (1959): 819–840.

Loescher, Gil, and Jon Scanlan. *Calculated Kindness: Refugees and America's Half-Open Door: 1945–Present*. New York: Free Press, 1998.

Lunde, Mark. *Robert D. Ray: An Iowa Treasure*. Des Moines: The Iowan/Pioneer Communications, 2013.

McAllister, John. "Mountain Minorities and the Viet Minh: A Key to the Indochina War." In *Southeast Asian Tribes, Minorities, and Nations* 2, edited by P. Kunstadter. Princeton: Princeton University Press, 1967.

Miller, Kristelle. Untitled Article *in Iowa Alumni Review* 23 (1969–1970): 8–9.

Mintz, Steven. *Huck's Raft: A History of American Childhood*. Cambridge: Harvard University Press, 2006.

Mondale, Walter. "Speech to the U.N. Conference on Indochinese Refugees." Geneva, Switzerland: Office of the Vice President's Press Secretary, July 1979.

Pitiphat, Sumitr. "The Religion and Beliefs of the Black Tai, and a Note on the Study of Cultural Origins." *Journal of the Siam Society* 68.1 (1980): 29–38.

Pran, Dith, and Kim DePaul, eds. *Children of Cambodia's Killing Fields: Memoirs by Survivors.* New Haven: Yale University Press, 1999.

A Promise Called Iowa. DVD. Directed by Iowa Public Television. 2007; Johnstown, Iowa: IPTV, 2007.

Quinn, Kenneth. "Political Change in Wartime: The Khmer Krahom Revolution in Southern Cambodia, 1970–1974." *Naval War College Review* (Spring 1976): 3–31.

"Refugee Resettlement Hearing before the Committee on Immigration and Refugee Policy of the Committee on the Judiciary." U.S. Senate, 97th Congress, First Session, Des Moines, IA, October 9, 1981.

Rakow, Meg Ragina. *Laos and Laotians.* Honolulu: University of Hawaii, 1992.

Rosenfeld, William. "Please Don't forget the Cambodians." *PACEMAKER: University of Iowa Hospitals and Clinics Newsletter* 7, no. 7, July 1980.

Rummel, R.J. *Statistics in Democide.* Honolulu: University of Hawaii, 1997. Accessed 10 October 2014. https://www.hawaii.edu/powerkills/SOD.CHAP6.HTM.

Schrock, Joann. *Minority Groups in North Vietnam.* Washington, D.C.: Department of the Army, 1972.

Simms, Peter, and Sanda Simms. *The Kingdoms of Laos: Six Hundred Years of History.* London: Routledge, 2001.

Simpson, Alan. *US Refugee Program in Southeast Asia: Subcommittee on Immigration and Refugee Policy.* Washington, D.C.: U.S. Government Printing Office, 1985.

Stuart-Fox, Martin. *A History of Modern Laos.* Cambridge: Cambridge University Press, 1997.

Takaki, Ronald. *Strangers from a Different Shore: A History of Asian Americans.* Boston: Little, Brown, 1989

Tone, Mary Hutchinson. "On the Road to Ioway." *The Iowan* 29 (1980): 37–50.

Tossa, Wajuppa, and Kongdeuane Nettavong. *Lao Folktales,* edited by Margaret Read MacDonald London: Greenwood Publishing Group, 2008.

Turley, William. *The Second Indochinese War: A Concise Political and Military History.* Lanham, Maryland: Rowman and Littlefield, 2009.

The Unfair Burden: Our House Is Full! Displaced Persons from Indochina in Thailand. Thailand: Operation Centre for Displaced Persons Ministry of Interior of Thailand, 1979.

U.S.D.A. "Iowa Farms: Number, Average Size, and Land in Farms." Department of Agriculture National Agricultural Statistics Services, Accessed March 2014. http://nass.usda.gov/Statistics_by_State/Iowa/Publications/Annual_Statistical_Bulletin/2006/06_6.pdf.

West, Elliot. *Growing up with the Country: Childhood on the Far Western Frontier.* Albuquerque: University of New Mexico Press, 1989.

Wu, Frank. *Yellow: Race in America Beyond Black and White.* New York: Basic Books, 2003.

Wuthnow, Robert. *Remaking the Heartland: Middle America Since the 1950s.* Princeton: Princeton University Press, 2013.

Xiong, Vamouachee. "The Little Mouse Girl Who Did Not Want to Marry Her Own Kind." Story told to Karen Harper, 21 February 2005. California State University, Long Beach.

Yale University, "Cambodian Genocide Program 1994–2011." http://www.yale.edu/cgp/ (12 October 2011).

Zahra, Tara. *The Lost Children: Reconstructing Europe's Families after World War II.* Cambridge: Harvard University Press, 2011.

Index

Index   233

Reagan, Ronald 16, 203, 204
Red Tai 19, 21, 22
reeducation camp 13, 55, 109–111, 113, 153
refoulment 196, 197
Refugee Act of 1980 16, 189, 190, 198–203
refugee admission numbers 43, 48, 49, 85, 115, 197; for Iowa 60, 62, 67, 71, 77, 87, 89, 90, 109, 117, 123, 209
refugee children 14, 27–29, 97–99, 142, 181, 182; bullying of 178, 179; English language learning 177- 181; generational tensions 96, 182–186, 188; resiliency 15, 150, 151, 163–169; unaccompanied minors 77, 78, 161
refugee resettlement policy 5, 8–10, 40–42, 46–49, 60, 70, 79–82, 132, 207–209
Republican Party 9, 15, 44, 46, 64, 119
Royal Lao Government 33, 38, 42, 53–55, 86, 91
rural poverty 13, 71, 120, 121

Sa Kaeo, Thailand 14, 135, 137, 167; *see also* Thailand
Sackpraseuth, Kham 175, 179, 180
Sai Kham 52, 53
Saigon, South Vietnam 39, 40, 43, 110–112, 128, 151, 152; *see also* South Vietnam
San Song 23–25, 38, 42
Saythongphet, Somsak 62–64, 68, 76, 82, 92
Senephansiri, Phouvong 177, 180
Senephansiri, Vilayvanh 168, 172, 175
Seng, Chea 159, 160, 168
Shearer, Colleen 9–12, 50, 51, 61–68, 70, 72–77, 79–82, 92, 93, 95, 96, 100–103, 116–118, 123, 124, 191–194, 205–207
Son La, Vietnam 19, 24, 27, 29, 30, 32
Soria, Simone 177
South Vietnam 8, 13, 28, 32, 33, 39, 43, 51, 60, 85, 110, 111, 127, 128, 131, 152, 157, 158; *see also* Saigon, South Vietnam
Southammavong, Donechanh 94, 180, 185, 211, 212
Souvanna Phouma 33, 53, 85
Spear, Jack 61, 62, 65, 66, 96, 101
sponsorship 10–13, 49, 63–72, 74, 78, 80, 81, 83, 87, 92, 102, 106, 131, 132, 141, 207
State Department 5, 8, 11, 16, 49, 81, 110, 114, 145, 192, 198; resettlement of Tai Dam 10, 41–44, 59, 72, 108, 109
Syrians 16, 17

Tai Chronicle 5, 7, 22
Tai Dam 10–12, 40, 50–60, 83, 131, 132; gender roles 12, 27, 32, 33, 57, 93–97, 99, 185; human capital 83–86, 91–92, 107, 108; religion 19–20, 22–25, 38, 42, 103–106; scholarship 6, 7, 25, 35–38, 103
Tai Federation 28, 32, 39, 41, 43, 53, 75, 76, 104, 107

Tai Village, Des Moines, Iowa 210–212
Tate, Debra 140, 141
Thailand 7, 10, 14, 19, 25, 35, 41, 53, 56–60, 99, 114–116, 141, 144, 145, 156–158, 196, 197; *see also* Nong Khai, Thailand; Sa Kaeo, Thailand
Thongchine, Nib 154, 173, 186
Tith, Sovouthy 153, 154, 158, 175, 176
Tith, Viseth 187, 188
Tran, Kiet 13, 111, 112, 114–116
Truong, Dau 39, 110, 111
Truong, Thuong 110, 111
Tu, Ky 152, 160
Twelve Tai Principalities 7, 21, 22, 25–27, 35, 36

Um, Khanny 158–160, 162, 173, 175, 176
United Nations 56, 59, 119, 169, 189, 196–198
United States Catholic Conference 11, 49, 70–72, 74, 78
USAID 10, 39, 40, 64, 84, 86, 107

Vang, Cher 154, 173, 177, 179
VanLo, Dinh 56, 58, 84, 88, 89, 100, 104, 105
Vientiane, Laos 10, 12, 33, 34, 53–55, 85–88, 90, 91, 98–100, 104
Vietminh 28, 29, 31, 32, 35, 52, 113
Vietnam War 13, 45, 46, 126–129; guilt 74, 109, 117, 137, 148, 192, 206, 207; veterans 62, 63, 87, 128, 129, 131, 132
Vietnamese 8, 10, 35–38, 42, 43, 52, 58–60, 85, 86, 109–113, 127, 128, 165, 197; in Iowa 11, 61, 71–76, 118–123, 131, 132, 180–182; *see also* Kinh
voluntary agencies 5, 9, 11, 16, 43, 46, 49, 50, 61, 66, 70–74, 76–81, 124, 209
volunteer tutor program 11, 79, 82, 107, 132
Vong, Somkong 164, 183, 185, 186

welfare 9–11, 16, 43, 50, 66–68, 70–74, 78–81, 85, 91, 93, 101, 106–108, 120–122, 124, 129, 131, 146, 199
White Tai 19, 21, 22, 27, 31
Williams, Arzania 124–127
World War II 8, 28, 47, 102, 113

Xam, Amkha 162, 179
Xayavong, Siamphone 160, 161, 163, 171
Xiang Khoang Province, Laos 10, 32, 33, 35, 52–54, 85, 104, 107

Yang, Fue 156, 157
Yellow Peril 13, 123
Yepsen, David 136, 137

Zeitler, John 73, 74